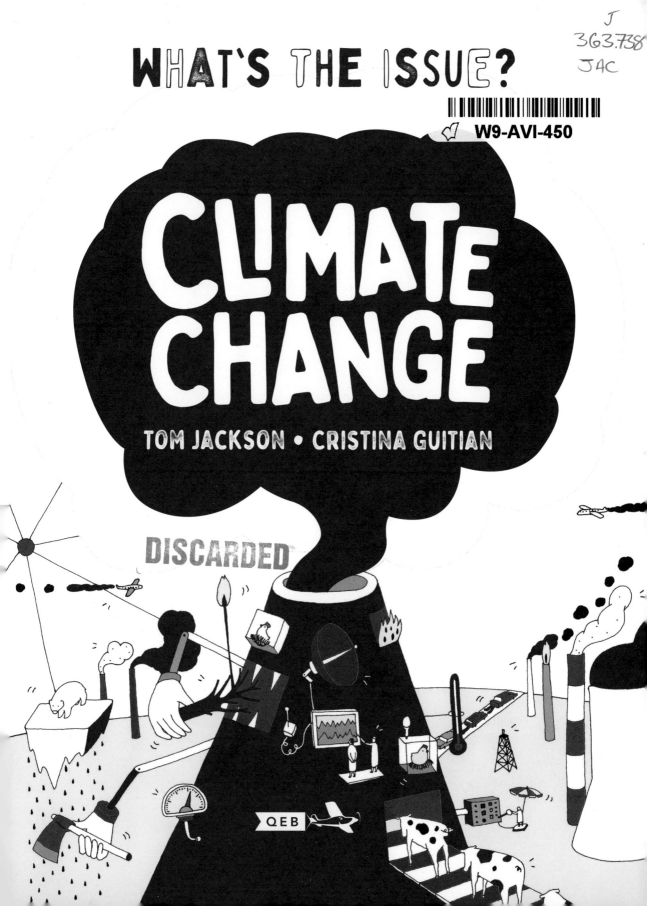

WHAT'S THE ISSUE?

CLIMATE CHANGE

TOM JACKSON • CRISTINA GUITIAN

QEB

Author: Tom Jackson
Illustrator: Cristina Guitian
Designer: Mike Henson
Editors: Claire Watts and Ellie Brough
Creative Director: Malena Stojic
Publisher: Maxime Boucknooghe

This edition first published in 2020 by QEB Publishing,
an imprint of The Quarto Group.
26391 Crown Valley Parkway, Suite 220
Mission Viejo, CA 92691, USA
T: +1 949 380 7510
F: +1 949 380 7575
www.QuartoKnows.com

A CIP record for this book is available from the Library of Congress.

ISBN 978 0 7112 5030 7

Manufactured in Guangdong, China
TT022020

9 8 7 6 5 4 3 2 1

CONTENTS

AUTHOR'S NOTE

WHAT'S THE ISSUE WITH CLIMATE CHANGE?

What is actually happening? Why is it so hard to fix? Do we need to fix it? Climate change raises so many questions and it can be very confusing to understand. You're in the right place to find out more though. This book will help you work out for yourself what you think about climate change. I'll tell you what's what and who's who.

THEN IT'S UP TO YOU TO MAKE AN INFORMED OPINION.

You have to remember that although climate change might not be a new idea for you, it may be new for older people, like your parents and grandparents. We are all going to have to fix it together, and it's a big mission. What do we really know about climate change? It's definitely happening, but, what will happen next? And what's the best way to fix it? Well, that stuff is less clear, and a lot of experts are racing to find out.

SO WHAT DO YOU THINK?
WHAT DO YOUR FRIENDS THINK?
WHAT DO YOUR TEACHERS THINK?
WHAT DO YOUR PARENTS THINK?

What we've discovered so far can sound scary and make it seem like we have no future. But you're wrong there. It'll be hard work but we already know how to fix the climate. It's time to get informed and work out what you think about climate change. Let's start fixing it right here, right now.

OPINIONS MATTER, SO WHAT WILL YOURS BE?

HOT STUFF, NOT COOL

Hot enough for you? We often talk about the weather, don't we? We have always done so because weather is something we all share. Sometimes we like to complain about the weather, sometimes we are pleased by it. But these days we have a new feeling—we are worried, even scared, by the weather. Do we have reasons to be afraid?

HAVING A CRISIS

Have you heard? The **climate** is changing, the globe is warming, Earth will be destroyed, everyone will die. Actually, it's all a bit more complicated than that. Everyone *is* going to die (but not all at the same time); the climate is changing (but it always has done), and the globe is getting warmer (but it has cooled down in the past). Today's climate changes won't destroy Earth, but it could make it much harder for humans and many other **species** to survive here in large numbers.

A WARMING WORLD

The great majority of weather scientists agree that the world is getting warmer very fast. But don't get the sunglasses and sandals out just yet. In the last 140 years, the average temperature of the whole world has gone up 1.44°F. Our perceptions of temperature are barely able to detect such a difference, and it is dwarfed by the rise and fall of air temperatures every day. So what's the big deal?

We will come across all kinds of statistical terms in this book. You might have come across them before, but it's still worth brushing up on them.

Range: This number is the difference between the maximum (highest) and minimum (lowest) values.

Mean: There will be a lot of talk of averages, and in most cases that means the mean. The mean is the number you get when you add a set of numbers together and then divide them by the number of numbers.

Per capita: This means "by head" and it means dividing up a value according to the number of people involved. A very big country might produce more pollution than a very small one, but per capita it might be the smallest nation that is the dirtiest.

Understanding these terms will help you understand the climate statistics in this book.

ALL ABOUT ENERGY

Temperature is a measure of the average amount of heat **energy** inside a substance. Earth's **atmosphere** isn't very hot—on average it's about 57°F—but there's so much air (5.5 million trillion tons of it) that it contains an unimaginably large amount of energy. This energy powers the world's weather, so even a small rise in global temperature indicates a huge increase in energy churning up the atmosphere— and that means more extreme weather among other things.

WHAT DOES CLIMATE CHANGE MEAN FOR YOU?

The world has gotten warmer and looks likely to get hotter still. What will that mean for you and for the rest of the world? What is causing the changes? Can we do anything about it—and if so, what? The questions don't get much bigger than the ones around climate change and global warming.

WHAT'S THE WEATHER DOING?

To understand changes in the climate you need to know what weather is. Climate is the big picture overview of the kinds of weather found at a particular location at a particular time of year. While weather changes every day (or every hour in some places), climate changes take decades.

Water **vapor**, the gas version of water, is not included in the list of gases in the air because its levels go up and down, from more or less zero to four percent of the total. Anything above that and it will soon start to rain!

THE ATMOSPHERE

Earth's atmosphere is never still. The movement of the atmosphere makes air masses of different types collide, and that creates wind, rain, and clouds. Earth's air is a mixture of gases: 78 per cent nitrogen, 21 per cent oxygen, and 0.9 per cent argon. That leaves 0.1 per cent for everything else, including **carbon dioxide** (0.04 per cent) and a whole cocktail of trace gases.

AIR TEMPERATURE

Global warming affects air temperature, among other things, which we will look at later. We now know that heat energy is simply the motion of atoms and molecules in a substance. When the temperature is higher, there is more heat energy and the **particles** move faster. So, at the molecular level, global warming means that the air's atoms are moving just that bit faster.

WHO'S WHO?

BLAISE PASCAL

Pressure is measured in units called "pascals." These are named after a seventeenth-century French scientist named Blaise Pascal who proved that the air around us was supplying a constant pushing force. That force is around the same as the weight of 14 pounds pushing on every square inch of your body.

The atmosphere is hundreds of miles thick, but 75 percent of it is in a lower layer about 7.5 miles high above the surface of the Earth. It is called the "troposphere." This is where all the weather is happening. Above the troposphere is the "stratosphere" (up to 30 miles), the "mesosphere" (50 miles), the "thermosphere," and a very thin exosphere which merges with space around 430 miles up (well above where many spacecraft orbit).

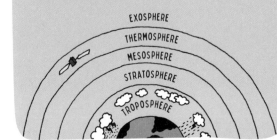

EXOSPHERE
THERMOSPHERE
MESOSPHERE
STRATOSPHERE
TROPOSPHERE

AIR PRESSURE

As well as temperature, the other crucial factor in understanding weather is air pressure. This is a measure of the how hard the air is pushing against an object (or itself). The air pushing down from above creates a constant force, but the exact size of this force can vary. Hot air exerts a higher pressure because its fast-moving particles hit harder and more frequently than the particles in cold air.

GETTING WIND

Wind is caused by differences in air pressure from one place to the next. When air is being warmed by the Sun, its particles move faster and spread out. When a region of cold, low-pressure air forms next to warm, high-pressure air, the warmer air rushes in to fill up the space left by the slow-moving colder particles. The bigger the difference in pressures, the faster the wind.

Weather is all about difference. A weather front is a place where two masses of air meet. When the differences in their temperatures and pressures are great, a more extreme weather system—with stronger winds and heavier rains—will form. There are various kinds of front, and weather forecasters search for them to figure out what the weather is likely to do next. The warming effects of climate change might make extreme weather more frequent.

CLOUDS AND RAIN

As warm air cools, it cannot hold as much water vapor. The vapor turns into droplets of liquid that cling to specks of dust or ice in the air. These specks clump to make a cloud. As the temperature drops, the droplets grow until they are too heavy to hang in the air and they fall as rain. If raindrops fall through freezing air they form snow. Strong winds may blow raindrops high into the sky, where they freeze into hailstones before clattering to the ground.

As well as storms becoming more extreme, climate change could be making the gaps between rainfall grow longer, resulting in droughts. A drought happens whenever a region gets less rain than usual for a prolonged period. That might mean going a month without rain—or several years. The Atacama Desert in Chile does not get rain for 300 years at a time! How would it affect your life if the rain stopped falling?

WHAT'S WHAT?

METEOROLOGY

This is the science of weather. The name comes from ancient Greek and it means the study of things "high in the air." The philosopher Aristotle wrote about meteors, which he called flashes of light "high in the air." Meteors are little rocks from space that burn up in the Earth's atmosphere. Modern meteorologists study the Earth's atmosphere, mainly the climate and weather, in order to forecast weather conditions.

HURRICANE

The most extreme weather phenomenon is the hurricane. These storms form when low-pressure air arrives above the warm ocean near the equator. A vast spiral of clouds forms with winds over 74 miles per hour. It's so big, it can be seen from space. Hurricanes seem to be more damaging in recent years, but we can't say why. Is it because changing climate is causing more hurricanes or because more people live in places threatened by them?

IS DIFFERENT WEATHER A BAD THING?

So, climate change is going to mean we get different weather. Is that always a bad thing? For example, warmer weather could open new trade routes in Greenland's previously frozen waters, but it would cost the loss of the ice sheet and its wilderness and wildlife. Is it worth it? What should we value more?

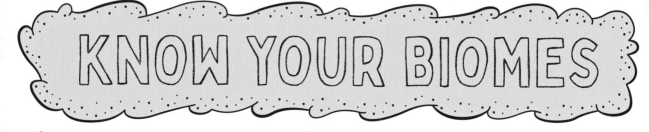

KNOW YOUR BIOMES

Climate is a living part of Earth that divides our planet into a number of large-scale biological communities called "biomes." Biomes include rainforest, desert, and tundra, and their locations are defined by the climate. However, the fossil record shows us that biomes have changed along with the climate in the past. Are they changing again now? And will the plants and wildlife be able to keep up with the rate of climate change?

DESERTS

A desert forms wherever there is under 10 inches of rain every year. Rain may be blocked by a mountain range, as happens in the southwestern United States. Western coastlines in the Americas, with currents bringing cold water and dry air from the poles, also have low rainfall, which is what forms the Atacama Desert in Chile. And land that is far from the sea simply doesn't get much rain, which explains the Taklamakan Desert of western China. The Sahara Desert in North Africa formed for all these reasons.

SAVANNAH

More accurately described as tropical grassland, this biome forms where it is warm but not wet enough for trees to grow in large numbers. However, there is enough rainfall (more than 20 inches a year) for grasses and a few shrubs to thrive.

POLAR REGIONS

The land nearest the poles is covered in thick layers of ice all year round. Liquid water is very rare here, and life cannot survive without water. Strangely Antarctica is the driest place on Earth, and it is this, combined with the winters of perpetual night and deep cold, that make it inhospitable to almost all forms of life.

TROPICAL RAINFOREST

Also known as jungles, these forests grow wherever it is warm and wet all year round. They tend to grow in the **equatorial** region. The heat from the constant sun evaporates water from the oceans which then falls as deluges of rain on the jungle.

TEMPERATE FOREST

This is a mixture of broad-leaved woodlands where most of the trees drop their leaves in autumn to avoid damage by winter frosts. The trees regrow new leaves each spring. These forests grow in milder ("temperate") climate zones, where there is a short, dark winter and a long, warm growing season.

TAIGA

This biome is made up of conifer forests that grow in colder northern areas (another name for it is "boreal"—or northern—forest). In these regions, winters are long and the growing season is short. There is no time to drop leaves and grow new ones, so the conifer trees have frost-resistant, needle-shaped leaves that survive the winter.

STEPPE

This is a temperate grassland where, like in a savannah, it is too dry for forests to grow. The shorter summers make it unsuitable for even small trees, so this biome is characterized by great oceans of grass. These grasslands are known as "steppes," "prairies" and "pampas."

TUNDRA

This treeless frozen land is characterized by permafrost, which is soil that is frozen solid (apart from the very top) all year round. No tree can put down roots to grow here. When the short summer thaws, the surface turns into a marshland. Only the fastest growing plants, like moss and sedge, can grow and reproduce in the short time before winter returns.

THE SAME BUT DIFFERENT

Each biome makes a patchwork of territory across the globe, often appearing on every continent. For example, there are grasslands in South America, Africa, and Australia. They grow in each place because the climate is suitable, but their wildlife communities are very different. In Africa, the grass is eaten by antelopes and bison; in Australia, it is eaten by kangaroos; and in South America, it is eaten by guanacos (a relative of the llama) and guinea pigs!

Biomes are closely associated with latitude—the location on the globe, north or south of the equator. This is because the climate is impacted by day length. Earth rotates on its axis once every 24 hours, but the axis is at an angle to the Sun. That means that in the northern summer, the northern hemisphere is tilting toward the Sun. The Sun does not set for many weeks in the far north near the poles, and elsewhere the summer days are much longer than the nights. Meanwhile in the southern hemisphere, it is winter and the nights are longer than the days. At higher latitudes, the range of temperatures between winter and summer is very large. In the tropics, the weather conditions stay broadly similar all year round.

Altitude, or how high the land is, can have an effect on climate. Air thins out as you go higher and thin air is colder, because it has fewer gas particles in it. So it cannot hold as much heat energy as the air at sea level. In some parts of the world, the slope of a tall mountain range can be divided into a series of mini biomes. The tops are like the poles—very cold. Climbing down, we would pass through alpine tundra, then conifer forest growing above the snow line. Temperate woodlands grow on the foothills, which turn into jungles in the steamy lowlands.

WHAT'S WHAT?

TROPICS

The warmer regions of Earth are described as "tropical" because they sit within two imaginary lines that encircle the globe, the Tropic of Cancer, north of the equator, and the Tropic of Capricorn, to the south. In spring and autumn, the Sun is positioned directly above the equator. In midsummer, it shifts to be above a Tropic—remember the summers are six months apart in the north and south. So the tropics are a warmer area because the Sun is shining down from more or less overhead all year round.

BIODIVERSITY

There are an estimated 8.7 million species of living things on Earth. Only one species of animal lives in the southern polar biome (the emperor penguin), while half of all animal species live in rainforests! The diversity of life on Earth is a product of evolution which shaped species as natural climate changes altered habitats. That process takes millions of years, and the concern is that climate change is happening too fast for evolution to keep up.

SHOULD WE SAVE THE WILDLIFE?

A warming globe could rewrite the biome map. Dry climate zones, like deserts, might grow in size while other biomes might shrink. If that happened, then most wildlife would lose their habitats, driving them to extinction. Should we focus on saving wildlife? Or to what extent is it okay to lose **biodiversity** if we can save people?

THE GREENHOUSE EFFECT

A greenhouse lets light in from outside but keeps the heat inside. Earth's atmosphere works in a similar way in a process called the "Greenhouse Effect." This natural phenomenon is largely responsible for climate change. However, without it, there would be no life on Earth.

ENERGY IN

Earth gets its energy from the Sun in the form of light and heat. Other kinds of solar ray, like **ultraviolet**, are filtered out by the atmosphere (more on that later). Light bounces around between the gas molecules in the atmosphere, with blue light being scattered farthest. That's why the air looks blue when you look up, but it is transparent when you look around. When the light and heat in sunshine hit the surface of the Earth, the land and ocean warm up.

ENERGY OUT

Earth's surface does not glow with light like a star. It does reflect some of the sunlight, which is why astronauts can see it as a beautiful coloured ball from space. However, the planet converts most of the energy it receives as visible light into invisible heat, and this is what radiates back out into space.

The amount of carbon dioxide in the air has risen by a third in 250 years, and that is trapping extra heat. If we look at Venus, we can see what happens when a planet has a large amount of carbon dioxide in the air. Venus's air is almost pure carbon dioxide, and its average temperature is 864°F! The air pressure is 90 times higher than on Earth—enough to crush your body flat—oh yes, and it rains pure acid!

GOOD GREENHOUSE

A greenhouse stays nice and warm for exotic plants that would die in the cold. And the Greenhouse Effect does a similar job for us on Earth. Without the warming effects of carbon dioxide trapping heat in the atmosphere, the average temperature on Earth would be −0.4°F, and most of our world would be covered in a crust of ice.

WHAT'S WHAT?

GREENHOUSE GAS

It is harder for heat to radiate through the atmosphere than it is for light. Small amounts of gases we call "**greenhouse gases**" block its path. The most significant of these is carbon dioxide. Its molecules absorb heat coming up from the Earth's surface, preventing it from leaving the atmosphere. As a result, more energy reaches Earth than escapes it, and that makes the planet warmer. The glass of a greenhouse does the same thing: light shines right through it, but much of the heat cannot escape.

WHO'S WHO?

EUNICE NEWTON FOOTE

The term "Greenhouse Effect" was invented in 1902, but the idea for it came from the work of the American Eunice Newton Foote in 1856. She showed that the different gases that made up the air warmed up at different rates in sunshine—and carbon dioxide got much hotter than the rest.

IS ALL CLIMATE CHANGE NATURAL?

If the Greenhouse Effect is a natural process, why do we regard the changes humans make to it as unnatural? Surely our civilization is a natural phenomenon of Earth just like volcanoes and earthquakes? How does looking at the problem this way change how we might choose to fix it?

THE CARBON CYCLE

You breathe out four cups of carbon dioxide every couple of minutes. Gasp! However, the gas is an entirely natural substance which is fundamental to life. Living things on Earth constantly remove carbon dioxide from the air but at the same time they release it. This is a small part of a greater circulation of carbon-based materials called the "carbon cycle." The root cause of global climate change is the way humans are upsetting the balance of this natural process.

FOOD WEBS

Plants use the Sun's energy to manufacture complex chemicals such as proteins, oils, and carbohydrates as part of their life cycle. These chemicals contain carbon that originated in the atmosphere. Animals eat plants to get at the energy and other nutrients these chemicals contain. Plant-eating animals are eaten by meat-eaters, and the carbon chemicals, known as "biomass," spread through a network called a "food web." At any one time, the global food web contains 600 million tons of carbon, all locked away inside the bodies of living things.

PHOTOSYNTHESIS

Plants do not eat food to fuel their bodies (just imagine if they did). Instead they use a process called "photosynthesis," where chlorophyll, the green chemical in leaves, traps the energy from sunlight. That energy forces water and carbon dioxide molecules to combine into sugar, which is used as a fuel source. The water the plant needs comes up through the roots, while carbon dioxide is taken directly out of the air.

Food webs are not all about plants, plant-eaters, and meat-eaters. There are also waste-eaters, or "detritivores." They do the job of eating waste—basically poop and dead bodies. Detritivores include vultures and other scavengers, plus the fungi and bacteria that rot away the remains of the dead. These organisms eventually convert this food source back into carbon dioxide gas. And the cycle continues...

WHAT'S WHAT?

CARBON PUMP

Sometimes biomass is not rotted down by the food chain and converted back into carbon dioxide. In a process called the "carbon pump," these carbon-rich chemicals sink to the ocean bed and form sediments, which eventually become carbon-rich rocks. Chalk, limestone, and marble are all rocks largely made from once-living bodies. Measuring the power of the carbon pump to take carbon dioxide from the atmosphere is a valuable part of understanding climate change.

RESPIRATION

Oxygen is a waste product of photosynthesis. Oxygen is used by animals to burn sugars in food in order to release a supply of energy. This process, called "respiration," is the opposite of photosynthesis—it turns sugar into water and carbon dioxide. So you (like all animals) are breathing in oxygen for use in respiration and breathing out the carbon dioxide produced. Carbon dioxide is of no use to you, but the plants are glad to have it.

CAN WE FIND HARMONY WITH NATURE?

Some argue that humans should live in harmony with nature, perhaps especially with the carbon cycle. Therefore we should focus our efforts on rebalancing the carbon cycle with the aim of ending global warming. Is that the future we should aim for? Or should we always expect to cause some pollution and environmental damage?

FOSSIL FUELS

A fossil is familiar enough. It is the remains of a once-living thing that has left its mark in ancient rocks. Generally, we think of a fossil as a stone dinosaur bone or crystal-encrusted seashell, but most of the fuels we use are also the remains of long-dead life and therefore are fossils too—and that is a big problem.

Scientists have been wrongly predicting when the world's oil wells will run dry throughout the last century. Once gone, we would have to use cleaner forms of energy. However, fracking and other new extraction systems continue to reach fuel reserves that were previously beyond reach, meaning the world can continue burning fossil fuels for many more years. But should we?

WHAT ARE FOSSIL FUELS?

Fossil fuels are made from the remains of living things which have been squeezed and heated underground for millions of years. There are three types:

Coal is a solid fuel composed of soot-like carbon mixed with impurities. It is made from the remains of tree trunks, and mostly dates back to the Carboniferous Period about 300 million years ago. This was when the first wood plants evolved, and the detritivores that rot wood down today didn't exist. So, great blankets of dead wood ended up buried underground.

Petroleum means "rock oil." This thick, black liquid contains several thousand types of hydrocarbons, made from carbon and hydrogen. They include flammable liquids, like gasoline, and sticky fluids, like wax and tar. Petroleum forms from the sludge of dead material that gathers on the seabed and is eventually buried.

Natural gas is a mixture of the smallest hydrocarbon chemicals, including methane and propane. They form in the same way as petroleum, but the same gases are also formed by some decay processes at the surface.

FOSSIL CARBON

All fossil fuels are rich in carbon. This carbon was once taken out of the air by photosynthesis—and turned into biomass. The biomass was then siphoned off by the carbon pump and ended up underground locked out from completing the carbon cycle. Digging up and burning fossil fuels releases that carbon back into the air. We have been burning fossil fuels in increasing amounts for the last 250 years.

WHAT'S WHAT?

FRACKING

Gas and oil are generally extracted from reservoirs deep underground where the fuel fills tiny holes in porous, sponge-like rocks. As these sources begin to run out, however, a new system called "hydraulic fracturing" or "fracking," is being used to extract gas locked away inside rocks called "shales." A hole is drilled through the rock and a thick liquid is pumped down it at great pressure to make the shale crack and release its gas.

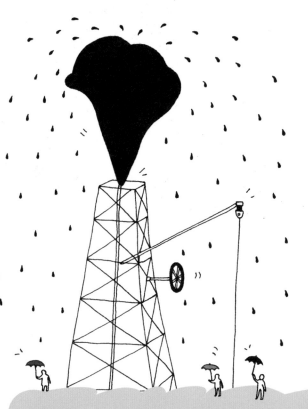

HEAT OUTPUT

Coal is the dirtiest fossil fuel because it contains impurities, such as sulfur, that create pollution as it burns. It also releases twice as much carbon dioxide for the same amount of heat produced as natural gas. Natural gas is the most efficient fossil fuel because it is made from the smallest molecules, which burn more efficiently. Liquid fuels, like gasoline and diesel, are halfway between the two. They are used as car fuels because they are easier to pump and store than gas fuels.

WHY NOT BURN ALL FOSSIL FUELS?

There could be enough natural gas and other fossil fuels to power our needs to the year 2300 and beyond. If we do so, there will be five times the amount of carbon dioxide in the air as there is now, and the average global temperature will be 71°F. It won't affect us now, so should we carry on as we are?

GLOBAL WARMING

About 250 years ago, for every million molecules of gas in the air, 280 of them were carbon dioxide. Today, carbon dioxide levels are at more than 400 parts per million. All that extra carbon dioxide has been released by burning ancient fossil fuels. Over a similar span of time, the average global temperature seems to have increased—although data from the early phases is a bit sketchy. The question is, how are these two facts connected?

INDUSTRIAL REVOLUTION

The rise in carbon dioxide levels in the air began with the Industrial Revolution in the eighteenth century. Coal was being burned to smelt iron and as a fuel for the new steam engines that powered factories and soon transport. History has progressed in a similar direction ever since. In the last century alone, the amount of fossil fuel consumed each year has increased by a factor of 12. We have, of course, plenty to show for our use of energy, with a larger, healthier, and happier human population than ever before. However, all that progress appears to have come at the cost of dangerous climate change.

THE HOCKEY STICK GRAPH

When climate scientists plotted a graph of climate data over the last 1,000 years, it looked like an ice-hockey stick, with a sharp rise at the end. For 900 years, the climate stayed more or less the same, forming the long handle of the hockey stick. In the twentieth century, global temperatures increased rapidly—creating the "blade" of the hockey stick—and temperatures have been climbing ever since. Scientists argue that the climate is warming too fast for it to be a natural change, and it must be caused by humans. Some people still don't believe it though—why don't they trust the scientists? We'll look at that later.

WHO'S WHO?

MATTHEW FONTAINE MAURY

This American sailor devoted his life to plotting the routes of the ocean currents. He enlisted the help of the world's naval navigators, giving any ship willing to take part a set of charts to help them use the currents to cross the oceans faster. In return, he asked the crew to keep a daily record of air and water temperatures and other weather observations. These records starting from the 1850s are where our information about global temperature data begins.

SOURCE OF THE PROBLEM

Fossil fuels are burned for the energy they contain. Here are the main reasons people around the world burn fuels and how much greenhouse gas they each contribute.

- Producing electricity and heating buildings (25 percent)
- Producing food, paper, and wood, and managing land (24 percent)
- Manufacturing and industry (21 percent)
- Transport (14 percent)
- Building (6 percent)
- Other (10 percent)

This list shows that a lot of the fuels burned are burned in our own homes, so we can start there to begin to solve the problem.

Global concrete production releases more than three times the greenhouse gases as travel by air, if you consider all the energy produced during its production. This is called "embodied energy." Concrete is made by mixing sand and gravel with a glue-like cement to make a thick slurry which is molded and then sets into hard rock. The cement is made by roasting limestone (calcium carbonate) which drives out carbon dioxide.

DEFORESTATION

The amount of carbon dioxide in the air is not just affected by burning fossil fuels. Cutting down forests, especially dense tropical rainforests, reduces the amount of photosynthesis taking place, so that less carbon dioxide is removed from the air. In 2017, the area of one football field of forest was cleared to make way for farms every second. This rate is rapidly accelerating.

SLASH AND BURN

Forests are not simply cut down. They are cleared using the slash and burn technique, where the trees are felled and cut up before being set on fire. The ash left behind helps to make the soil more fertile for crops (for a short time at least), but the burning converts most of the jungle biomass into greenhouse gas. Every year, deforestation adds nearly 5.5 billion tons of carbon dioxide to the air, which makes it the third biggest contributor of greenhouse gas after China and the United States.

Rainforest trees pull water from the soil, through the roots, and up through the trunk to the leaves, where some of it leaks out as steamy clouds of water vapor in a process called "transpiration." The water vapor hanging over the forest adds to the next downpour of rain. Cutting down forest removes this local water supply, and so rainfall across the region drops, and the climate changes from a jungle biome to a grassland or desert.

The soil contains around 2,700 billion tons of carbon in the form of **minerals** like limestone, and the oily, waxy, and gunky leftovers of once living things. That total is five times the biomass of living organisms and four times as much as the amount of carbon in the air. However, intensive farming techniques which overwork the soil reduce its carbon supply, inevitably releasing it into the air as a greenhouse gas.

WHAT'S WHAT?

SPACESHIP EARTH

The American Richard Buckminster Fuller was an architect, mapmaker, and inventor. In 1968, he wrote a book called Operating Manual for Spaceship Earth, in which he suggested that humans turn the raw materials of Earth into knowledge, and the more knowledge we accrue, the better we get at using Earth's resources. We have certainly used a lot of Earth's raw materials, and we do know a lot, but do we use our resources for the right things?

CARBON FOOTPRINTS

Every country is responsible for how much greenhouse gas it releases, which can be called its "**carbon footprint**." The largest emitter of greenhouse gas is China, which releases 27 percent, just under a third of the global total. The United States gives out 13 percent. However, the average Chinese person gives out 7.7 tons of carbon dioxide, half as much as the average American, who gives out 19.8 tons, but a hundred times more than the residents of many African countries.

IS IT WORTH IT?

The development of technologies such as flight, electronics, and better healthcare seem to have caused an accidental climate **crisis**. These technologies make our lives more comfortable, but the repercussion of that could be that people in the future will have harder lives because of the climate fallout. Is that a price worth paying for giving billions of people a good life?

OTHER GREENHOUSE GASES

Carbon dioxide gets a lot of attention when we're talking about climate change, and quite rightly too! This is the greenhouse gas that we produce in the largest amounts and it is directly linked to the fuels we burn and the energy we consume. However, there are other gases to take into account. Although we may churn them out in smaller amounts, they are often more powerful greenhouse gases.

METHANE

This is the simplest hydrocarbon compound. Methane is released from swamps and bogs as bacteria break down tough plant materials. It's also in the farts and burps of large herbivores as gut bacteria break up their plant foods. The number of domestic cows in the world is likely to breach 1 billion soon, and each one toots out around 2,200 pounds of methane a year. We emit five times as much carbon dioxide, but just one methane molecule traps 23 times as much heat as one molecule of carbon dioxide!

FLUORINATED GAS

Better known as "CFCs" or F gases, these entirely artificial gases are used in fridges and spray cans. CFCs were designed to never break down, so they would be harmless to humans. However, we release 11,000 tons of fluorinated gases a year. That's 40 times less than carbon dioxide, but F gas traps more than 10,000 times as much heat as carbon dioxide. By law, F gas must not be released into the air, but collected and made safe.

CFCs have been banned since the 1980s because they were destroying the ozone layer. The ozone layer is a natural barrier made from a special kind of oxygen—called ozone—that filters out harmful high-energy rays from sunlight. Those same rays were smashing up the CFC molecules, which destroyed huge quantities of ozone. This removed the natural filter, increasing the risk of sunburn and skin cancers. CFCs have now been replaced by other F gases that do not hurt the ozone layer. The layer is now recovering but the new F gases still impact climate change.

THOMAS MIDGLEY

When this American chemist invented CFCs in the 1920s as a safer gas for use in fridges, he didn't realize the environmental damage CFCs would cause. The same isn't true of Midgley's other invention—leaded gasoline. Adding lead helped gasoline burn better in car engines, but made the exhaust more poisonous, impacting air and soil quality. Midgley knew this but went ahead anyway. Leaded gasoline was not phased out until the twenty-first century.

NITROUS OXIDE

About 5 percent of all greenhouse gas is nitrous oxide. This is also called laughing gas, and dentists sometimes use it to numb pain. However, the gas is no laughing matter, because it is 300 times more powerful than carbon dioxide as a climate changer. It's not dentists causing the problem. Most of the nitrous oxide comes from the fertilizers used on farms and from car exhausts.

WHAT'S THE PRIORITY?

These other greenhouse gases are all associated with food: methane is released by the production of milk, cheese, and meat; nitrous oxide is from growing plant crops; F gas is used to keep it all fresh and healthy. How will managing carbon emissions affect the food industry?

CLIMATE DENIAL

Some people do not accept that climate change is happening, or say if it is then it's all entirely natural. We've seen worse weather in the past, they say, and we'll see better in future. This kind of thinking is called "climate denial." That's a strong term meant to brand climate-change naysayers as having a hidden reason to argue against the evidence of climate scientists. However, some climate deniers are just scared and confused.

CONSPIRACY

Sometimes opposition to climate change comes in the form of a conspiracy theory, which suggests that climate change is a **hoax**. The dangers of climate change are presented as phony threats meant to weaken the more powerful (and worst polluting) nations. The people behind the hoax are believed to be either foreign powers wanting to take over the world or international revolutionaries who hate personal freedom and want to enforce some extreme form of government.

THE HUMAN REACTION

As we get older, we will all remember years that were very snowy or when rainfall caused serious flooding or a summer of heatwaves. "What's this climate change rubbish then?" we'll say. "We remember when the rain/wind/snow/heat was worse than this." It's a mistake to judge climate change on these extreme events. We are good at remembering such things, but we are oblivious to the small, steady increase in global temperature, which is the indication of climate change.

TOO MUCH INFORMATION

Gas and oil companies sometimes **sponsor** climate science research. They say they need to know the truth because if we stop using fossil fuels, they will go out of business. So, they had better be ready for whatever happens next. However, climate science is hard for non-scientists to follow and we rely on climatologists for information. When research teams paid for by oil companies produce reports that climate change is not caused by humans, can we trust them not to be **biased**?

Climate science is built on agreement, or consensus. Nearly all climatologists agree that climate change is happening and that it is being driven by human activities. There may be disagreement over what exactly will happen next, but scientists all argue that we should try to solve the climate problem.

Climate denial has become a part of nationalism—a way of thinking that puts your own country above all others. The solutions to climate change are global—every nation needs to help. However, that goes against nationalism, which acts in the best interests of the nation, not the world. As a result, some people will argue that to believe in climate change is unpatriotic. Another common argument is that other countries should act first, to avoid putting your own nation at a disadvantage.

MEDIA BIAS

News providers try to offer a balanced view of complex subjects. They do this by allowing people with opposing views on a subject an equal say. This approach can work for politics, which is based on opinion, but is not suited to science, which is built on evidence. A climate change story will include comments from one scientist who argues that it is a problem, and from another who denies that it is. Both sides are presented to the viewer as being equal. But are they?

TRUE OR FALSE?

There are many stories of a genius scientist going against the thinking of all the others to reveal a new way of understanding nature. Could it be true that the tiny group of scientists who argue against climate change are right all along? How would you go about finding out?

NATURAL CLIMATE CHANGES

Earth has changed a lot over the years. There are seashells in the rocks near the top of Mount Everest showing us that this land was once under the ocean. And the same is true of climate. Six million years ago, the world was warmer and wetter. Then it began to cool down and dry out, reducing the area of Africa's jungle as grasslands grew in size—and that is where our ancestors started to live. Thanks, climate change! So what creates these natural climate shifts?

SOLAR HEATING

All of Earth's heat comes from the Sun, and there are three ways that the supply of warmth can fluctuate and create changes in climate. Together these mechanisms create a long-term, although still erratic, system of warming and cooling called the "Milankovitch Cycle," which results in ice ages, or glacial periods, and warmer interglacial periods (like now).

Tilt of Earth's axis: This creates the change between summer and winter, due to the way the planet tilts toward and then away from the Sun each year. The angle of the tilt varies slightly every 40,000 years. When the tilt is more pronounced, the difference between summer and winter weather is also more pronounced. Bigger climate changes are caused when the tilt is reduced. There is less difference between summer and winter, and winter snows don't thaw, building up over centuries into **glacier**. Today, Earth's orbit is about halfway through this cycle, with the tilt reducing.

ICE AGE

Earth has witnessed many ice ages, when the world was much colder than now. The last one ended about 11,000 years ago. The polar ice caps covered much more of the Earth, especially in the northern hemisphere where ice covered most of Europe and the United States all year round. The ice age came and went due to the Milankovitch Cycle. We are now in a warmer period, an interglacial period called the Holocene. The whole of human history has taken place in this single phase of Earth's climate.

Eccentricity: Earth orbits the Sun in an ellipse, or oval, which means that the Sun is 3 million miles farther away in July than in January, and Earth gets 6 percent less solar energy. The orbit slowly morphs from a near-perfect circle to a slightly squashed oval and back again every 100,000 years. These differences are small but the distance from star to planet changes significantly. When the orbit is circular, the differences in solar heating barely change throughout the year. However, during the most elliptical phase, the amount of heat can vary by 30 percent. Now, Earth's orbit is quite elliptical but is becoming more circular.

Precession: This is the hardest part to visualize. Earth's entire orbital path moves around the Sun—like a hula hoop swinging around your waist—only it takes 26,000 years. This has the effect of changing the time of year when Earth is closest to the Sun. At the moment, it is in January, which means the southern winter is considerably warmer than the northern winter. When precession moves Earth's closest approach to the spring or autumn (in around 7,000 years), the difference between summer and winter, north and south, will be reduced.

LITTLE ICE AGE

There is no strong evidence that the 11-year sunspot cycle has any impact on how much sunlight hits Earth. However, sunspots follow a longer cycle over many centuries. There have been periods of almost no sunspot activity, which appear to match up with cold periods on Earth, such as the Little Ice Age of the seventeenth and eighteenth centuries, when winters in Europe were considerably colder than they are now. If a link exists between sunspots, solar activity, and these low temperatures on Earth, no one can explain it.

Volcanic eruptions do not always make the globe colder. They also release large amounts of greenhouse gases. It's estimated that volcanoes release somewhere between 0.17 and 0.5 billion tons of carbon dioxide each year. That's a big number, but we should be clear: the carbon dioxide released by human activity annually is 80 to 270 times as much as volcanoes.

GLOBAL DIMMING

The Little Ice Age may have had an altogether different cause. A series of enormous volcanic eruptions between the thirteenth and nineteenth centuries could have cooled the planet. Volcanoes release vast quantities of sulfur dioxide gas—sometimes more than 110,000 tons of it. This gas floats above the troposphere and forms a haze of sulfuric acid droplets which block out sunlight and reduce surface temperatures. The haze slowly spreads and contributes to a worldwide cooling process called "global dimming."

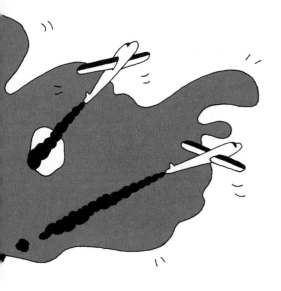

SUN SPOTS

Our star, the Sun, has a direct impact on our climate by varying how much heat it throws out. The Sun is always very hot (10,000°F on the surface), but every so often, a dark patch appears on the Sun's surface. This is a sunspot and it is only a chilly 5,400°F or so! Sunspots are an effect of the Sun's tangled magnetic field. They last a few months and each one is generally bigger than Earth. The number of sunspots rises and falls over an 11-year period. At the height of the cycle, there can be 200 spots.

The aftermath of the 9/11 attacks in the United States in 2001 revealed that human activity contributes to global dimming. All aircraft in North America were grounded for three days after the attack. Climate scientists noticed the air temperature rose very fast in that time. Ordinarily thousands of jet engines would be blasting soot into the stratosphere, which would block out sunlight. Ironically, as well as contributing to global warming, air travel also reduces global temperatures!

WHAT'S WHAT?

THE YEAR WITHOUT A SUMMER

The 1815 eruption of Mount Tambora in Indonesia spewed 11 billion tons of ash, dust, and gas into the atmosphere. The cloud reduced sunlight worldwide and the following year became known as "the Year Without a Summer." Rivers in the United States were still frozen in June, and harsh frosts killed crops across Europe leading to famine. India and China's summer rainfall came late and led to devastating flooding.

WHERE'S THE EVIDENCE?

So the world's climate has undergone major changes in the past, and many people prefer to think that the current changes are completely natural and the worries for the future are overblown. What evidence would you use to try to change their minds?

EL NIÑO

The world's most powerful natural climate phenomenon is called "El Niño." It's the result of a vast mass of warm water, often 9°F above the seasonal average, that wells up in the western Pacific, and spreads out until it hits the coast of Peru at the end of the year. The warm water brings with it rains that help make bumper crops. Over the next few months, the warm water disappears, to return again in four or five years.

CHRISTMAS GIFT

In 1892, a retired sea captain gave a talk to a geographical society in Lima, Peru. He revealed how the fishermen and other seafarers along the western coast of South America sometimes reported a strange phenomenon. Where normally cold water flowed up the coast from the south, occasionally warm water flowed down from the north. Because this happened around Christmas time, the Spanish-speaking sailors called the phenomenon "El Niño," meaning "the boy," referring to the baby Jesus.

El Niño is just one half of the ENSO (El Niño-Southern Oscillation), which sees the entire tropical Pacific climate swing between two extremes. If the winds over the ocean strengthen instead of fade, then the warm water concentrates in the west, and the east is distinctly colder and drier than usual. This opposite state to El Niño is called "La Niña," meaning "the girl"—obviously.

The global climate depends on how much warmer than the average El Niño is and how long it persists. Additionally, the Pacific is thought to be a heat sink for the planet, and some of the stored heat gets out through the ENSO. The start of an El Niño phase sees food prices rising in some countries, because the ensuing droughts dwindle the food supply. If climate change makes El Niño stronger, then we can predict what will happen and where.

WHAT'S WHAT?

NORTH ATLANTIC OSCILLATION

Europe's weather is influenced by North Atlantic Oscillation (NAO). This is the difference in pressure between the northern ocean and the waters nearer the tropics. Normally there is a big difference in air pressure that sucks in strong winds from the Atlantic producing mild and wet weather in Europe. When the NAO has only a small pressure difference, the wind comes from the east, bringing cold, snowy weather.

WIND DIRECTION

In normal conditions in the tropical Pacific, winds blow from east to west. That blows the warm surface waters heated by the Sun toward the west, eventually reaching Indonesia and eastern Australia. During El Niño, the winds fade away, and the warm water drifts east, creating warm, wet conditions along the coast of South America. However, for the western Pacific, El Niño means weather that is cooler and drier than normal.

GLOBAL IMPACT

The changes caused by El Niño can be felt far beyond the Pacific. East Africa gets a stronger wet season while there is often a drought in southern Africa. The drought in the western Pacific spreads to Southeast Asia, which is normally well fed with rainstorms from the ocean. Rainfall increases in the southern parts of North America, while the northern region enjoys a milder than usual winter. Only Europe is largely untouched by the climate swings.

PREPARE OR PREVENT?

Understanding oscillations like ENSO and NAO better will help us to predict and plan for extreme weather events, such as storms and droughts. How much time and energy should people spend on adapting to climate change, rather than preventing it?

DAISYWORLD

Understanding the way climate works is hard enough, and figuring out how it is changing is even tougher. So let's look at how climates change in a simpler way, make it more black and white—literally. We'll imagine a planet that is populated only by black and white flowers. Welcome to Daisyworld. This hypothetical globe will help us understand a process called "climate feedback."

ALBEDO

Daisyworld's climate system is driven by "albedo," which is a measure of the reflection of the Sun's radiation. A totally black planet reflects nothing and has an albedo of zero; a planet covered in a mirror would reflect everything, giving it an albedo of 1. Earth's oceans score about 0.2 and dry land reflects less than that. The most reflective parts of Earth are the clouds and ice caps with an albedo of 0.8 or more. Just like the flowers on Daisyworld, the ratio of ice, cloud, sea, and land has marked effects on how hot the planet gets.

HOW DO FLOWERS GROW?

When the temperature of the Daisyworld is average, there are an equal number of flowers of either color. The black flowers on Daisyworld thrive when temperatures are low, and the white ones grow best when it is warmer. So the ratio of flowers swings from one extreme to the other. A higher proportion of white flowers reflect the Sun's heat and cool the planet, reducing the whites and boosting the blacks. Black flowers absorb the Sun's heat, leading to global warming, and more white flowers and fewer black ones.

WHAT'S WHAT?

FEEDBACK LOOPS

Daisyworld is an example of a negative feedback loop, where an increase in one thing causes its own reduction. An increase in black flowers on Daisyworld leads to a reduction in black flowers. On Earth, clouds are controlled by a negative feedback system. Hot weather evaporates the oceans making more clouds. The clouds reflect the Sun's heat, cooling the planet, cutting the rate of ocean evaporation, and reducing cloud cover.

EXTREME LOOPS

Climate changes can also involve positive feedback loops, which, instead of balancing a system, send it into an extreme state. The ice cover on Earth is controlled by positive feedback. Ice forms when it is cold and reflects heat, making it colder still. As the temperature falls, the ice increases and the temperature falls further. This is one of the drivers for Earth's ice ages. The opposite happens when Earth warms up. The ice cover reduces and so does Earth's albedo, which leads to warming. And as you can guess: warming equals less ice, equals more warming.

Feedback loops are also at work with greenhouse gases. Water vapor is subject to positive feedback. When the atmosphere is warmer it can hold more moisture, which increases warming. Carbon dioxide is controlled by negative feedback: a rise in atmospheric carbon boosts temperatures. That increases the growth rate of plants, which then take more carbon out of the atmosphere. Think about that loop. It's going to be important.

WILL EVERYTHING BE ALRIGHT IN THE END?

Daisyworld is meant to show that Earth may fluctuate between wild extremes of climate but there is a natural pull toward average conditions. No matter what we do or do not do about the climate, Earth should handle the changes just fine, with or without us. Are we happy for it to manage without us?

MODELING CLIMATE

So now we are getting somewhere. We understand more about weather and how climate zones form, and we see how human activities can change the factors that control both of them. But what next? How do we know things are going to get worse in the future? Those answers come from inside a supercomputer that models today's climate and fast forwards it to the future. Let's take a look at what happens next.

Modern climate models give each sector dozens of variables. The models account for things like humidity, surface temperature, time of day, and cloud cover, as well as altitude, latitude, soil types, vegetation, and ocean currents. And we must not forget the levels of those all-important greenhouse gases. Each sector is now a cube, allowing air to rise and fall as a swirling current. And the GCM has layers of grids that create a 3D atmosphere.

SUPER MODEL

The usefulness of a model is judged on how closely it reflects the real thing. Climate models, or GCMs ("general circulation models") divide the world into a grid and give every square, or sector, a set of variables, such as air pressure and temperature. Each sector is left to interact with its neighbors, which changes its "weather." The first GCM from 1956 was very crude and couldn't tell the difference between ocean and land. Models have got better since, but how can we tell if they are useful?

FUTURE PREDICTIONS

The first useful climate models were developed around the start of the 1980s. They were designed to model single aspects of the climate, such as the link between carbon dioxide in the air and air temperatures. These models predicted that by 2100 the average global temperature will rise by 2.7 to 8.1°F. Models since then have shown other things that might change on the planet, like sea level, storm frequency, and droughts, but they also predict around the same temperature rise over the coming century.

A modern GCM divides the surface of the planet into tens of thousands of grid sectors, each made up of 20 layers. Each sector contains 1.5 million variables that affect each other and the variables of sectors around them. This is the culmination of decades of work in using math to predict the weather. In 1922, the first mathematical weather forecast was made, but it took six weeks to calculate by hand, long after the weather it predicted had been and gone.

WHAT'S WHAT?

HINDCASTING

The purpose of the first GCMs was simply to make a mathematical model of the atmosphere. The next step was to use it to study the future climate, but could we trust what the model told us? The trick was to wind back the clock and make the model do some "hindcasting," using weather conditions from the past to predict the conditions today and see if the model got them right.

DATA SOURCES

A model is only as good as the data used to set it up. The earliest reliable global weather observations date back to 1880, and this information was used to prove the worth of the first GCMs. Today's models rely on a vast wealth of data collected by a global network of weather stations on land and at sea and in space. This data is used to fine tune new models so they match the actual climate as closely as possible.

For the last 20 years, a fleet of sensors called "Argo floats" have been bobbing around the oceans collecting data about water temperatures, saltiness, and the flow of currents. So far 4,000 have been dropped into the sea and left to drift. Most are programmed to sink to a depth of 0.6 miles, and every ten days plunge to 1.2 miles before surfacing to broadcast their findings to a satellite.

POSSIBLE FUTURES

Climate models are not only used to show how a changing climate may cause problems in the future (don't worry, we will get to those soon enough), they also help us understand how effective our efforts to solve those problems will be. The model runs backward just as well as forward, so you can model what we need to do now to ensure global temperatures rise only a small amount—it's already too late to keep things as they are.

WHAT'S WHAT?

IPCC

The Intergovernmental Panel on Climate Change (IPCC) is a group of scientists who have been asked by the United Nations to advise the world on what to do about climate change. They've said if we do nothing the climate models say it will be at least 5.4°F warmer by the middle of the century. If we cut our greenhouse gas emissions in half by 2030 and then to zero by 2050, we can keep the long-term rise to about 2.7°F. Although other scientists say we'll need to cut emissions sooner.

THE BUTTERFLY EFFECT

It is said that when a butterfly flaps its wings in Africa it can cause a hurricane in the Caribbean. This "butterfly effect" describes how a tiny change in the starting variables can result in enormously different end points. If the butterfly is still, there is no storm, but the addition of a single wing beat is enough to change that completely. This idea belongs to a field of mathematics called "chaos theory," but it was discovered by a weatherman called Edward Lorenz in 1961 as he developed a simple climate model.

The models do not just predict temperature rise, they paint a picture of a world with more flooding, more droughts, and shifts in climate zones. Places that are prime farmland today may be deserts or swamps one day. Places that have a mild but wet climate will not be transformed into sunny and dry places. Instead they'll just get wetter. Areas that enjoy warm and pleasant weather now will become hot and unpleasant.

TOO SOON TO WORRY?

All the trouble stored up by climate change won't really cause trouble for another 30 years or so. Based on the evidence, how soon will we need to take drastic action?

ANCIENT CLIMATES

Another powerful weapon in the fight to understand how climates work and prove that our situation is not just a natural one is to look back at the way climate changed in ancient times. The study of ancient climates is called "paleoclimatology," and it offers a stark warning about the rate of climate change. There is evidence of what the weather was like many years ago locked away in ice, fossils, and rocks—even inside trees.

ICE CORES

The ice covering Antarctica and Greenland is more than 6,500 feet thick in places. A thin layer of ice is added each year, so it took hundreds of thousands of years to grow that thick. Paleoclimatologists extract long cores bored from the ice. Tiny air bubbles in the ice reveal the proportions of gases in the air when the ice formed, holding a record of the atmosphere going back almost a million years. The ice core records form a link between greenhouse gas levels and the ancient temperatures that are revealed by other climate clues.

Oxygen exists in two isotopes, O-16 and O-18. Oxygen 18 is rarer but slightly heavier than oxygen 16. When an ice sample contains a larger proportion of oxygen 18 than average, this is a signal that Earth was much warmer. The extra energy in the weather systems was enough to lift the heavier oxygen 18 atoms from the ocean and add them to the air.

LOUIS AGASSIZ

In the 1840s, this Swiss botanist went public with evidence that much of the world was once covered in glaciers and so it must have been much colder in the past. In other words, he discovered ice ages. He did this by searching for the boulders and ridges of gravel, or "**moraines**," that are dumped by retreating glaciers, and found them in places thousands of miles from any ice.

MICROFOSSILS

As well as rings in wood, plants leave another indicator of climate. Plants produce vast quantities of pollen, which builds up in soils, deep sediments in lakes, and eventually in rocks. These grains appear as intricate and identifiable structures under the microscope, and botanists can link them to habitats and climate types. For example, the presence of cactus pollen in Arctic mud is a signal that this area was once a desert.

TREE RINGS

The rings in a tree's trunk record the climate in the past. Trees grow slowly in winter, adding a thin layer of dark, hard wood. In summer, faster growth results in a broader band of pale, soft wood. Together, the light and dark make one year and so locations in the trunk can be dated precisely. The width of the pale band reveals the nature of the growing season; a thick band shows it was warm and wet, a thinner one indicates a colder than normal summer.

The exact structure of the calcium minerals in the shells of sea creatures gives a clue to the prevailing conditions. During ice age conditions, the seashells form mostly from calcite, but during warmer "greenhouse" phases, the shells are mostly aragonite.

SNOWBALL EARTH

Around 2.4 billion years ago, it's likely that the whole surface of the planet froze solid. This "Snowball Earth" had a surprising cause: oxygen. The first photosynthesizing organisms, cyanobacteria, evolved a few million years before and had been pumping out oxygen into the air. Back then there was much more carbon dioxide and methane in the air. The cyanobacteria used up carbon dioxide and added oxygen to the air, which burned away all the methane. As a result, the amount of greenhouse gas in the air plunged and so did the temperature. It is likely that the world was iced up for 300,000 years!

THERMAL MAXIMUM

We are currently living in an ice age, or at least a warmish gap between ice ages. This is a cool period of Earth's history. The last hot period was the Paleocene–Eocene Thermal Maximum (PETM) around 55 million years ago. Global temperature was 14.4°F higher than now, sea levels were higher, and the weather was far wetter. There was no ice anywhere, and there were jungles filled with giant reptiles at the poles. The cause of the PETM is unknown. Fires, volcanoes, and comet impacts might be to blame, but the leading theory is a sudden release of methane from the seabed.

Around 750 million years ago, it looks like another huge ice age froze Earth for about 150 million years. Climatologists have found moraines from a glacier in what was then a tropical region of the planet. The world got so cold that almost all of the oxygen in the air was removed. Once the world warmed up again and oxygen returned, the world became filled with life, with every kind of animal life we see today evolving in the warming oceans in what is called the "Cambrian Explosion."

ANOTHER HUMAN CLIMATE CHANGE

The invention of agriculture around 8,000 years ago led to farmers clearing forests to make way for fields. That would have boosted carbon gases in the air but not enough to warm the climate. However our behavior may have cooled it. The colonization of the Americas by Europeans in the 1500s led to the deaths of more than 50 million Native Americans—mostly through disease—over about 100 years. Their unused farmland returned to forest resulting in a rapid decrease in carbon in the air.

The first trees evolved around 350 million years ago, and vast forests pulled out gargantuan amounts of carbon dioxide from the atmosphere to turn into wood. As we've seen, the carbon cycle was not fully formed by then, and the carbon stayed in the wood long after the tree had died. However, new living trees continued to gush out oxygen. The dwindling atmospheric carbon led to a rapid cooling and drying of the planet, and the lush forests died out.

EVIDENCE FROM THE PAST OR THE FUTURE?

There are no absolute answers in the study of climate change. Climate models make hazy predictions of the future, and paleoclimatology pieces together patchy pictures of climate change in the past. Which approach gives the best explanation of what is going on?

45

RISING SEA LEVELS

So far we've focused a lot on the rise in air temperature, but climate changes in the past have also made the sea levels rise and fall. This time they are predicted to go up, but by how much? Almost half of us live within 60 miles of the ocean, and most of the world's biggest megacities—Tokyo, Mumbai, Lagos and New York—are ports right on the coast. Oh, we do like to be beside the seaside, but will that be true in the future?

It is estimated almost 90 percent of the extra heat added to Earth's climate by human activities over the last couple of centuries has warmed the oceans. The measured increase adds up to a rise of 0.2°F. This seems tiny but the ocean is a vast system and predicting the effects of even small changes is difficult. The upper part of the ocean rarely mixes with the deeper parts, but understanding how heat spreads through the oceans is crucial for figuring out sea level rise.

HEAT SINK

Earth is a water planet, with oceans covering more than 70 percent of the surface. All that water is a vast reservoir of heat. The top 10 feet of ocean (on average 63°F) contain as much heat energy as the whole of the atmosphere. Below that depth, the oceans get very cold, very quickly—all the way to the bottom, on average 2.2 miles down. The deep ocean is between 32 and 37.5°F and because of the saltiness, seawater does not freeze until at least 28.4°F.

MIXING IT UP

Seawater warmed at the equator gets saltier due to evaporation, and it is blown toward the poles by strong winds. The extra salt makes the surface water dense, and nearer the poles it cools down and becomes denser still, enough to sink to the bottom—taking heat energy down with it. The cold deep water moves away from the poles along the seabed, and the force of this subsea flow pushes up water from the deep equatorial oceans to replace the warm stuff being blown away at the surface. The result is a global loop of currents called the Ocean Conveyor Belt (of which currents like the Gulf Stream are a small part). The Conveyor mixes surface waters from every ocean with the cold stuff deeper down.

WHAT'S WHAT?

HEAT CAPACITY

Water and air do not increase in temperature at the same speeds. To make water rise by one degree requires 1,000 times more heat than is needed to increase air temperature by the same amount. This feature is the heat capacity of a substance. Water's high heat capacity has a wider effect on climate, meaning coastal areas stay cool in summer, but the water holds on to its heat and becomes a warming influence on coastal climates in winter.

THERMAL EXPANSION

You may have heard that ice melting in the Arctic will make the sea levels rise. We'll talk about that later, but the bigger cause of sea level rise is the water expanding as it gets warmer. Water molecules move around faster and take up more room as they get hotter. So far the oceans have warmed only a fraction of a degree, but we must take into account just how much water there is out there. Earth's oceans fill 0.32 billion cubic miles of space. Mount Everest takes up just 14 cubic miles. If all of that water expanded just a tiny bit, sea levels would rise noticeably. To predict how much it will expand we need to figure out how ocean mixing is spreading extra heat to the deepest water.

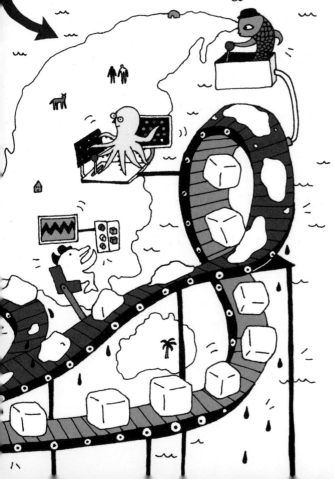

WHAT IS SEA LEVEL ANYWAY?

To see if sea level is rising we should first work out what sea level is. That is not easy. Firstly, the sea is never level, it rises up to shore and falls away again twice a day with the tides. Nevertheless, there is an average location that is identified as mean sea level, and from which the height or altitude of hills and mountains on land are measured. (The altitude of sea level is 0 feet.) Secondly, the mean sea level in one place does not always match the sea level somewhere else. The surface of the ocean bulges in all kinds of places for all kinds of reasons. So mostly we work with a sea level measured at one place. That works fine for measuring land but makes tracking sea level changes very tricky.

ICE COVER

If the world's remaining ice melted what would happen to the sea level? The answer depends on where the ice is. Ice shelves float on the surface of the sea, a bit like the ice cubes in a drink. The ice (or any object) floats because it pushes away its weight in liquid water. When it melts, it has not added any extra material, so the sea level stays the same. (However, losing ice cover will have other serious climate effects, see page 36).

The last ice age began around 130,000 years ago. The average temperature plunged by about 21.6 degrees, and much more of the world's water became glaciers, or thick sheets of solid ice that covered the land and oceans. That left less liquid water to fill the oceans, so the sea level dropped by 427 feet. So what goes down, must come up. We are still technically in an ice age, because there are ice caps covering the poles, but around 15,000 years ago the ice began to melt and refill the oceans.

48

FUTURE SEA LEVELS

Predicting sea level rise is tough. Since 1900 the best data suggests it has risen almost 8 inches. Since 1993, sea level has been monitored much more accurately by satellite. This shorter span of research suggests that we will get another 12 inches of rise this century. That doesn't seem too bad, depending on where you live, but this is just the mean sea level. High water marks will go up by a greater proportion (again, quite how much depends on location). Rich coastal cities will have to build defenses against **storm surges**, and poor ones will be flooded more often—and perhaps abandoned. We'll look at that in more detail on page 62.

We'll look at that in more detail on page 62.

WHAT'S WHAT?

ICE SHEETS

An ice sheet covers dry land. When it melts it adds new water to the ocean making sea levels rise. By far the largest sheet covers Antarctica. It contains 60 percent of all the freshwater on Earth's surface. If it melted, the ocean would rise by 190 feet! However, no one thinks this will happen. However, more serious is the smaller Greenland ice sheet. If that went, the sea would rise by more than 23 feet. The rate of melting in Greenland seems to be going up fast, but the models suggest that it will be around for many centuries yet.

SHOULD WE RISK IT?

Out of all predictions, those made about the ocean have the widest range of possibilities. Sea level has the potential to devastate entire cities, drive many millions from their homes, and destroy important farmland. But it might not. Should we take a cautious approach or be optimistic?

ACID IN THE SEA

It is easy to forget that seawater contains a lot more than salt and water. Okay, it is mainly water, but it also contains oxygen, lithium, and even traces of gold. One of its most important ingredients is carbon dioxide, which dissolves in it to make a substance called carbonic acid. This is the harmless stuff that releases the bubbles in a fizzy drink. As the oceans get warmer, they absorb more carbon dioxide, and are becoming gradually more acidic. The acidic sea is not quite fizzy yet but there are many other damaging effects.

CORAL BLEACHING

Corals are tiny jellyfish-like creatures that create rocky reefs on the seabed. The reef is home for hundreds of types of sea creatures, making it as crowded and productive as a rainforest on land. The corals even provide homes inside their own bodies. A coral's color comes from microscopic algae that live in its tissues, supplying the coral with sugars made by photosynthesis. In return, the corals protect the algae and supply them with carbon dioxide from the water. In the 1980s, coral started going white, or bleaching. The reasons are complex but the extra acid in the water stressed the corals causing them to expel the colorful algae. Without the algae, the corals die, and so does the rich habitat around it.

An acid is a chemical containing hydrogen atoms that pop off easily and attack other chemicals. Acidity is measured in pH, with numbers under 7 being acids. However, the natural pH of seawater is 8.25, which makes it alkali, the opposite of an acid. Since 1750, the pH of seawater has reduced to about 8.15 due to the addition of dissolved carbon dioxide. It might not sound like a big change but that pH change means there is now 30 percent more hydrogen in the water looking for chemicals to attack.

THINNER SHELLS

Corals take calcium carbonate from the seawater to make shells. Many other sea creatures from shrimp to sea snails also do this. However, the acid waters are eating up the carbonate chemicals so the shellfish have less to use. Fewer shellfish survive in acidic waters, and those that do have thinner shells. Think back to the idea of the carbon pump (on page 19), where the shells of dead sea creatures sink to the seabed and become rock, thus removing carbon dioxide from the air and water. Ocean acidification caused by extra carbon dioxide reduces the power of the carbon pump to do that.

ACID RAIN

Extra carbon dioxide is not all bad for the oceans because on land it has the opposite effect. Some of the carbon dioxide in the atmosphere dissolves in rainwater, and this time it makes the water actually acidic—about pH 5.6. That is powerful enough to gradually eat away at rocks, washing minerals into rivers and then the sea in a process called weathering. High concentrations of carbon dioxide result in more weathering, and the extra rock chemicals it dumps in the ocean work to reduce the water's acidity.

WHAT'S WHAT?

ANOXIA

As well as taking in more carbon dioxide, warm water holds less oxygen. While the oxygen level is still high near the surface, in deeper waters the oxygen levels are getting too low for large animals to live. **Marine** biologists are finding that animals like big squids, and fish that normally hunt in the dark waters a few hundred feet down, are being forced to live up nearer the surface, where there is enough oxygen. This kind of forced migration could be upsetting the oceans' food webs.

CAN WE SAVE THE CORAL?

Coral reefs are very precious and bleaching is caused by more than high ocean temperatures and acidity. It also happens because of the sunscreen chemicals used by the divers and other tourists who come to look at the reefs. Should we stop people from visiting the remaining corals to give them a good chance of survival?

Climate models look for averages among the billions of variables that ricochet in all directions, increasing and contracting in range. The averages cancel out the extreme events of beastly winters and sodden summers to create a steady indication of change, a gradual trend toward a warmer world. However, when certain future conditions are reached, the model's gradual trend can veer off suddenly heading at speed toward an extreme future. This is called a climate tipping point. Are we heading for one?

SATURATED SEAS

About 40 percent of the extra carbon dioxide that has been released by human activity over the last 200 years has been absorbed by the ocean. This proportion of the gas has not been involved in global warming directly. However, the oceans are getting full, and appear to be absorbing less carbon dioxide today. More of our emissions end up in the air, and climate models predict that the additional carbon dioxide is accumulating around the North Pole. So in the future we might expect more of the global heating to be focused on the colder, icier parts of Earth.

POLAR COLLAPSE

Glaciologists who study ice sheets and shelves say it is possible that a sudden rise in global temperature might make the melting of Greenland's ice sheet rapidly accelerate. So instead of taking **millennia** to thaw out, it dumps its water into the oceans in a century or two, swamping the coasts with much higher seas. Similarly, ice shelves around Antarctica might suddenly break up and drift away, leading to a reduction in Earth's albedo and a surge in global warming.

Ice sheets disappearing all of a sudden is probably unlikely, but just by slowly getting smaller they will impact the climate. The differences in the saltiness of seawater is very significant. A lot of salt makes water dense so it sinks, and that process helps to drive the Ocean Conveyor Belt (see page 47) and other marine currents. Melting Arctic ice will reduce the saltiness of the water, so it won't sink so much. That will slow, and perhaps stop, the Conveyor that brings warm waters (and air) to the North Atlantic. That in turn could tip the climate of North America and Europe into having much colder winters. Ironic isn't it? Global warming might make some places colder.

(see page 47)

CLATHRATES

Methane is also found on the sea floor in strange substances called clathrates. A clathrate looks like a piece of ice, and most of it is water, but you can set it on fire because methane is trapped among the molecules. It has long been thought that melting clathrates may have caused sudden warming in the past.

GAS LEAK

A major threat of a sudden climate tipping point comes from methane, a more powerful greenhouse gas than carbon dioxide. Large amounts are locked away in permafrost, which is the mud beneath the Arctic tundra that is permanently frozen solid. The permafrost is melting and its methane is leaking into the air. The Earth holds about 2,000 times as much methane as is released every year by humans. Just 5 percent of that gas suddenly bubbling into the air would more than double warming from the Greenhouse Effect.

IF IT'S TOO LATE, WHAT NOW?

When the climate reaches a tipping point it means it swings into a new normal (and not a nice normal). There is nothing we can do to return the climate to how it is now. So do we let it happen and adjust to the new normal? Or do we try everything we can to limit the effect? What can we do to slow down the melting?

ANOTHER MASS EXTINCTION?

There are an estimated 8.7 million species living on Earth. Habitat destruction, hunting, and pollution make survival tough for many species, but the biggest killer could be climate change. In the past, large swathes of life have died out rapidly. The biggest instances are mass extinctions of which there are five on record. Some experts say we are currently living through the sixth.

MASS EXTINCTIONS

The most famous mass extinction was the last one, 66 million years ago. A meteorite is thought to have smashed into what is now Mexico, wiping out the dinosaurs and 76 percent of all species. That was actually a small one. The other four killed more. In the Great Dying 251 million years ago, 96 percent of species were lost. The causes of mass extinctions are hard to verify. Suggestions include vast volcanic eruptions and effects from nearby exploding stars. These cataclysms led to rapid climate changes, which reduce growth, eliminate habitats, and shatter food webs. It is this that causes the extinctions.

The number of species living today is probably the highest it has ever been in the history of the world and the extinction rate is also at an all-time high. In normal conditions, somewhere between 0.1 and 0.01 percent of species become extinct every year. The rate today is thought to be near 1 percent. On top of that, 10 percent of species are at risk of extinction in the near future.

SPEED OF CHANGE

Evolution can handle climate change if it is slow enough. Already we see changes in the boundaries of the world's biomes, with plants and insects normally associated with warm regions setting up home in places that were once too cold or too dry for them. Shifts like this do occur naturally, and wildlife communities gradually evolve to match the changes. Evolution needs hundreds of generations to have an effect, but as with other mass extinctions, human-made climate change may be too fast for it. While many species lose the struggle for survival, others will do very well, but overall diversity appears to be plummeting.

WHAT'S WHAT?

NATURAL SELECTION

This system is often summed up as "survival of the fittest." This means that the individuals that fit the environment best will survive longer (and have more offspring) than those that do not fit so well. As the environment changes, what accounts for a "good fit" changes too. So gradually, over the generations, the general features of a species evolve, and eventually new species form.

Extinction is part of evolution by natural selection. More than 99 percent of all species are extinct. Some, like the pterosaurs, are gone completely. No relatives survive today. However, the dinosaurs are only pseudoextinct, because their relatives are still thriving today—many people eat dinosaurs at Christmas. Birds, including turkeys, are the dinosaurs that survived the mass extinction.

WHAT'S IN IT FOR US?

So as climate changes threaten biodiversity, how should we approach that problem? Do we work to ensure that land and sea continue working for us, making the food we need, for example? Or should we try to save as many species as possible? Can we do both?

DISEASE IN A WARMING WORLD

Not more bad news! What's this about diseases? People are suffering from diseases all over the world already, so how can that get any worse? True enough, there is no evidence that diseases are getting more common due to climate change, but experts in public health are considering what might happen in the future. Here's what they have come up with.

SPREADING VECTORS

At the moment, tropical diseases, such as malaria, are limited to warm places around the equator. These diseases are spread by "vectors"—animals that carry the disease from person to person. The most familar vectors are mosquitoes, which spread malaria along with zika virus, West Nile virus, dengue fever, and yellow fever. However, ticks (lyme disease), flies (sleeping sickness), and even snails (bilharzia) can also make you sick.

SANITATION

Dirty water is the source of serious diseases like dysentery, cholera, hepatitis, and typhoid. Climate change could give these killers a double boost. It's predicted that the impact of climate change will force people to move into overcrowded cities and camps, where sewage systems will not be able to efficiently remove human waste (and the bugs it contains). In addition, the warmer conditions will be ideal for the bugs so they will grow faster in the dirty water.

In a warming world, these critters will be able to set up home in more parts of the planet. Disease-spreading mosquitoes thrive wherever it is warm and damp. Today their extreme northern limit is southern Spain, China, and the Midwest of America. They only survive here for a few weeks a year and are easy to control. If we do nothing, by 2080, malaria, yellow fever, and the rest may well have spread to Alaska, Scandinavia, and the Arctic, putting an extra 1 billion people at risk.

RESISTANCE

At the moment, we can cure these illnesses if sufferers get the right treatment and drugs. However, evolution isn't on our side. Already the bugs are evolving resistance to medical treatments, and if there are more of the germs in the future infecting more people, that process of becoming resistant will speed up. On the flip side, when diseases start to affect wealthier northern countries, perhaps more money will be spent on finding vaccines.

WHAT'S WHAT?

PATHOGENS

Something that causes disease is called a "pathogen." Pathogens may be microscopic worms (river blindness) or single-celled bugs like protozoa (malaria) or amoebas (dysentery). However, mostly pathogens are bacteria (cholera) or viruses (yellow fever). Bacteria are living germs that set up home inside the body. Viruses are not really alive. Instead they are packets of DNA that invade a body cell.

WHEN DO WE ACT?

The spread of disease is scary. However, even in a warming world, the world's medical experts could save many lives. It will cost a lot of money to research cures and deliver it to those in need. Should wealthy countries be doing more to prevent diseases now before the problems spread and get worse?

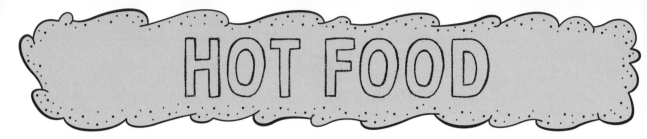

HOT FOOD

The biggest land habitat of all is an artificial one: farmland. About a third of all land is used for agriculture. Another third—covered by ice sheets, mountains, and deserts—is too inhospitable to produce food. The last third includes all the wild places: the forests, swamps, and savannas. As we've seen, climate change could shift the locations where wild habitats can exist. But what's going to happen to all the farmland?

FERTILITY BELTS

Most of the world's staple crops are grown in highly productive areas, which have climates just right for the crops. Wheat likes dry and warm grasslands, but is killed by drought. Rice needs a good supply of warm rain, but too much washes the plants from the soil. Climate change may cause these growing zones to move or shrink. To harvest the same quantities of crops in the future, farmers may have to use more land or develop new technologies to feed the world.

Growing food in a warming world is one problem, but storing it will be another. Changing weather patterns, such as longer dry spells followed by short but heavy rains, leads to more pest insects and fungal blights. That has a domino effect on stored food, which will be more prone to rotting or drying out.

WATER CONTENT

In a warming world, the amount of rainfall across the globe is likely to rise, but it will fall harder and for longer on fewer places and become much more scarce in others. This is how much water is needed to make just 2 pounds of different food:

Chocolate: 4,500 gallons
Beef: 4,000 gallons
Cheese: 800 gallons
Bread: 420 gallons
Cabbage: 63 gallons

We will have to make some tough choices about what to use water for.

ENERGY CONSUMPTION

The modern farming industry uses a lot of energy to get food from field to plate—about a quarter of greenhouse gases come from this process. Only a fifth of the energy is actually used to grow the food. The rest goes into processing it into products and transporting them across the world. One answer is to buy more raw ingredients instead of processed products and to eat food grown near to where we live.

WHAT'S WHAT?

FOOD MILES

This is a way of understanding how far different ingredients have traveled to reach you. Rice, coffee, sugar, tea, and many fruits may have traveled halfway around the world, while potatoes, carrots, and green vegetables may have been grown a few miles away. It often makes sense to reduce the food miles of your meals by eating food grown locally.

The proportion of farmland on Earth is still going up, and mostly that is being achieved by cutting down forests, often in the tropics. Some of the cleared land is used to grow palm trees that produce oil which is used in everything from shampoos to ice cream. Some forest is being replaced by pastures for cattle. Beef fetches high prices for the farmer, but rainforest soils can only grow enough grass for the herds for a few years. After that the land may become a useless **dust bowl**.

NEW FOODS

Is changing what we eat going to help with climate change? Changing the way we source ingredients is one way to help, but the biggest benefit to the climate and environment would come if we changed what we regard as food. For example, eating insects could solve many problems—think crunchy locust kebabs or succulent grub stews. We'd catch fewer fish and need fewer livestock, freeing up land for planting more forests. Do you want fries with your beetle burger?

Another way to make use of bugs would be to use maggots to recycle the nutrients in food waste (and even human poop) into food. Don't reach for the sick bag just yet. We wouldn't eat the maggots, but we could feed them to farmed fish or pigs—and then eat those. It sounds yucky, but maggot meals might solve a lot of our problems.

FEEDING THE MOST

Putting aside all ethical arguments, how do we use our farmland to feed the most people? Raising animals for food uses more than 70 percent of available farmland but provides only about a third of the nutrients we need. Land devoted to producing a vegan diet can feed almost twice as many people as land that supplies the meat-rich diet many eat today. However, land producing a diet that also includes dairy can feed even more, and producing a little meat (20 percent of today's levels) is a more efficient way to use land than a wholly vegan system.

BIOFUELS

Gasoline is a liquid mixture of small hydrocarbon chemicals. It is possible to make similar chemicals from sugar to create a liquid biofuel which can be mixed with gasoline. When we burn fuel that is 15 percent biofuel, we cut the carbon emissions by 15 percent, because the sugar took carbon dioxide from the atmosphere as it grew. However, if fields are growing biofuel crops, where will we grow food?

Not all farms grow food. For example, 3 percent of the world's fields are used to grow cotton. It takes 1,200 gallons of water to make 1 pound of cotton, and the crop emits almost twice as much greenhouse gas as wheat. So make sure you use your cotton clothing for a long time to make those high energy and water costs worthwhile!

WHAT'S WHAT?

GMOS

Some people think the climate challenges facing agriculture should be fixed using genetically modified organisms (GMOs). These crop plants have had new genes added to make them immune to diseases or tough enough to withstand drier conditions. GMOs are banned in many places, due to concerns over how they might mix with wild plants and create "superweeds." Is that a risk we'll have to take? What do you think?

WHAT'S FOR DINNER?

It can be argued that industrial societies have made food cheaper and given us more choices than ever before. Now you know the cost of all that choice, do you think it's worth it? Before you decide, though, consider an alternative: less treats and few sweets, just the same simple food, day in, day out. Food for thought.

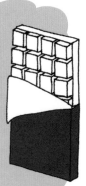

HUMAN DISASTERS

There is no way to get around this, I'll admit. This book might seem no fun—full of predictions of doom and gloom—but it will get better, I promise. Before we get to that, though, it's going to get a bit worse. Let's look at how climate changes in the coming decades may lead to problems so serious that they will take away people's jobs, homes, and even lives.

FIRE!

Wildfires regularly spread through forests in California, Siberia, or southern Europe, and each one seems to be bigger, more devastating than the last. The hot summers and dry winters predicted by climate models create the conditions for fires to start. But climate change isn't the whole cause. Fire is a normal part of many forest habitats. It clears out dead wood and some trees' seeds need the heat from fires to sprout.

FLOODING RISKS

River flooding is caused by heavy rain or winter snows that thaw in spring. Rivers generally break their banks in the same places, but sometimes they spill over in a new way, flooding a town or city that has previously avoided the problem. This may be because the rainfall is heavier, but flooding can be made worse when new buildings along the banks or changes to land use upstream change the way the water drains.

Forest communities are growing as people move there, attracted by the space and natural beauty, but still connected to the modern world via tech. Because there are more people, more homes are in danger when forest fires start. Of course, people will suppress fires to protect their homes. However, eventually nature takes over and sets the forest alight. These postponed fires are bigger and hotter than more frequent fires, and cause more devastation.

THE MALDIVES

The lowest nation on Earth is the Maldives, a country made up of hundreds of small coral islands, or "atolls," in the Indian Ocean. The highest point in the Maldives is 6 feet above sea level, so by the most conservative estimates of sea level rise, the entire nation will be under water in 600 years, and most of the smaller atolls will be gone by 2100.

STORM SURGES

Strong winds and storms out at sea—not least hurricanes—can make a bulge of seawater called a "storm surge" big enough to flood any coastal city. Sea level rise may mean that coastal cities like London, Shanghai, and Miami will suffer damaging and dangerous floods more often. The clean-up costs will be huge, and before long people will decide that life in a city inland will be easier, safer—and cheaper.

As storm surges increase, high seas may steadily wash away towns along the shore. The coasts will be left to become wild muddy marshes and sand dunes. This kind of land takes the power out of storm surges and protects people farther inland. Wealthy cities may choose to build elaborate flood defenses. London's famous Thames Barrier is designed to block a storm surge coming up the River Thames from the sea. It is already being used twice as often as initially planned.

63

DRYING OUT

Climate models suggest that most of the populous parts of the world—China, India, the east of North America—will become much rainier in the future. The opposite is true in western North America, southern Europe, and southern Asia, which are predicted to dry out, become more prone to wildfire, and eventually become deserts. Today's desert areas, such as the Middle East and North Africa, will expand, destroying the farmlands there.

GO NORTH!

Migration north from the arid regions of Central America, Africa, and the Middle East is already at record levels, as people search for a better life. Climate change may be a major factor, but the other reason for moving is security—people want a job in a safe place and to make a better life for their children. The hardship caused by war or economic troubles can sometimes be traced back to local, perhaps short-term, climate changes.

Large sections of the human population rely on water from melting glaciers high up in cold mountains. In Asia's Himalayas range, vast glaciers feed the rivers of India, Pakistan, and Bangladesh, providing water for 800 million people. These glaciers are melting fast, and a third of the ice will be gone by 2100, meaning less water for people. India is one of the few regions where climate change will raise rainfall but create bigger deserts at the same time.

HEAT INDEX

Temperature is not always the best way to measure how hot it is. When it is too hot, our bodies sweat to get rid of unwanted heat. In dry air, sweat evaporates taking extra heat with it. However, when the air is humid, sweat does not escape, and you feel hotter in the same temperature. A "heat index" system takes this into account by expressing what the conditions feel like. Increased humidity from climate change could make certain places almost unbearable to live in. For example, it might become normal for summer days in the Persian Gulf to have a heat index of 170°F.

LACK OF FOOD

Climate models are able to pinpoint regions around the world where problems in agriculture will put the food supply at risk. They include North America's "wheat belt," the soy plantations of Brazil and the cattle stations of Argentina and Australia. The food problem extends to the sea, where changes will reduce the fish and seafood available in the South China Sea, eastern Pacific, North Sea, and Gulf of Mexico.

WHERE DOES EVERYONE GO?

It is estimated that by 2050, more than 400 million people will be looking for new homes because of climate change and the war and poverty it might produce. Some migrants will move within countries—away from flooded coasts or droughts—while others will hope to settle in a new country. How should the needs of internal and external climate migrants be met?

RESOURCE WARS

Cheer up, what's the worst that can happen? Oh, yes—climate change might cause wars. In fact, it already has, many times over. Human beings have focused a lot of time and money on getting better at warfare over the centuries. The history books tell us that wars have many causes, but at their heart all wars are about the space and resources a society needs to prosper—usually at the expense of another. In a warming world, good territory will be more in demand.

LAND AND WATER

Chinese chronicles show that warring periods over more than 1,000 years generally followed a period of cold, dry weather, which would have reduced the food supply. Today, something similar is happening along the borders of Chad, Nigeria, and neighboring countries in West Africa. The world's sixth largest lake used to fill this region. The lake has now shrunk to less than half its size, and hunger and hardship have driven people to join rebel armies fighting for control of the remaining fertile land.

SEA ROUTES

The Northwest Passage is a route connecting the Atlantic Ocean to the Pacific via the Arctic Ocean. It has foiled even the smartest sailors because it is often blocked by ice. However, if global warming melts away the Arctic ice, then this region will become busy with cargo ships. Whoever controls these waters will also have the right to look for oil and gas in the seabed there. Countries are already sending ships and submarines into the Arctic to make a claim for the new territory—and the arguments over ownership are starting.

VIKING CONQUESTS

The Viking conquests may have been due to climate change. Viking expansion out of Denmark and Sweden occurred during the Medieval Warm Period, which hit its peak 1,000 years ago (and when temperatures—in Europe at least—were similar to today). Frozen territory in the north was thawing into farmlands and the Norse population boomed, making people go "viking"—journeying—to the east and west, fighting when needed, to find new places to live.

Vikings settled in Iceland in the ninth century. The story goes that the name for their new home was meant to discourage too many other people coming. The following century, the Vikings found Greenland, and this time gave it a name to attract more settlers. However, the temperatures there began to drop, and by about 1450 Greenland got too cold even for Vikings. Today's Inuit people moved in around the same time.

FINGERS CROSSED?

It is hard to judge predictions, especially when they only warn of bad things. Is it better to just wait and see what happens? There are more risks to doing nothing compared to the costs of doing something even if it turns out to be unnecessary. What would happen if we were to take action on climate change, and it proved to be unnecessary? Could some of our actions have other benefits?

WHO'S RESPONSIBLE?

So we get it—climate change is a huge problem. The whole world will have to agree on a way to fix it, and it'll take a lot of time and money to fix. We'll take look at how we might go about saving the planet next. But that's the easy bit. A tougher question is who's going to pay for it all?

PER CAPITA

Perhaps we should assign responsibility "per capita," or per person. India accounts for 17 percent of the global population but produces only 6.5 percent of the greenhouse gases. That's 1.9 tons per capita. Compare this to the United States where 5 percent of the world's people produce 13 percent of the emissions, or 17.6 tons per capita. The worst offender is Qatar, where the per capita carbon footprint, or personal carbon emission, is 49.6 tons.

PRODUCERS BY COUNTRY

The simplest way of allotting responsibility for climate change is to add up how much greenhouse gas a country produces. At the moment, the world releases the equivalent of 49.6 gigatons of carbon dioxide each year. This figure scales up the quantities of other, less common but more potent gases to account for their effects as if they were carbon dioxide. China produces 29 percent of the total. Add in the United States, European Union, India, Russia, Japan, and Brazil and we reach 50 percent. These are rich places—they can pay for it all.

There is a strong argument that today's richest countries grew rich from decades, even centuries, of polluting that has created climate change. The problems of climate change may make some of these same countries poorer, but other countries will get richer. The divide is roughly north-south with rich countries like the United States, Australia, and China becoming slightly poorer by 2100. India and most of Africa may get considerably poorer, while northern Europe, Canada, and Russia may get much richer. Where do you live?

HISTORICAL CONTRIBUTIONS

The problem of climate change began around 1750 with the dawn of the Industrial Revolution. The countries that began to burn fuels first (and benefited from them for the longest) have contributed most to the problem. Of the 1.44°F of warming measured to date, the average contribution is 0.0072°F per country. However, a handful of countries caused much more. For example, the United States created 0.27°F of warming, the United Kingdom 0.058°F and Brazil 0.088°F. These countries along with France, Germany, India, China, Russia, Indonesia, and Japan have created 60 percent of the warming.

WHAT'S WHAT?

CARBON EMISSIONS TRADING

The international agreement to reduce greenhouse gases issues permits that allow countries to emit a certain amount of carbon dioxide (reducing the amount each year). However, if one country wants to avoid having to cut back, it can buy the carbon permits from other countries that do not use them. The system is complex, but one of the ideas behind it is that rich but polluting countries end up paying poor but clean ones.

WHO IS RESPONSIBLE?

There are many places to lay blame for global warming and ways to slice up the responsibility for reducing greenhouse gases and fixing climate change. But is that the only way to get things sorted out? Will insisting on justice create a global agreement that works?

RENEWABLE ENERGY

Now for some good news. You know this climate change thing? We can fix it. However, it will mean some big changes to the way we live, travel, and eat. The biggest change will be in replacing fossil fuels with new forms of clean energy. There are already many options to choose from, but, as ever, we still need to solve a few problems before we can rely on 100 percent carbon-free power.

GOING WITH THE FLOW

To make electricity the normal way you need to make a generator spin. Thermal power stations use fuel to boil water and make a flow of hot steam. That flow runs through a turbine, making it spin, and that spins the generator. Hydroelectric power plants make use of a natural flow—the current of a river. Damming the river ensures the flow of water is always powerful enough to drive the turbines—and once the plant is built it makes carbon-free power day and night!

Damming rivers makes clean electricity, but the construction carries a significant cost. Dams are the biggest pieces of concrete on the planet, and, remember, making concrete releases a lot of carbon dioxide. Also, a dam works by creating a deep reservoir that floods the river valley upstream and upsets the whole freshwater habitat.

WIND POWER

The wind is another natural source of flow, this time caught by a windmill or a wind turbine. A wind turbine looks like an immense propeller, but, while an airplane propeller's blades spin in order to push back the air, the wind pushes on the wind turbine and makes it spin. Each turbine has its own generator sitting on top of it, connected directly to the blades. About 4 percent of the world's electricity is made by wind, and that number is set to rise.

TIDAL POWER

The tides contain a vast amount of energy, about a sixth of the power used by the world. But it isn't easy to build in the sea and structures only last a few years. Also most places have tides with a small rise and fall of about 3 feet. However, where the tidal difference is much higher, the energy can harnessed with a "barrage"— a dam that crosses a river mouth. Only a few barrages are in use because of the ecological damage they create.

Wind turbines are quick and cheap to build without causing a lot of emissions. The best place to put wind turbines is out at sea where winds blow almost continuously, uninterrupted by hills and valleys as happens on land. The largest are 850 feet high (like a 75-story building) and their blades sweep out an area seven times bigger than a football field. Around 60 of these turbines can make enough carbon-free power for a million homes.

WHAT'S WHAT?

TIDAL LAGOON

A new design of power plant could revolutionize tidal power. An area of seabed is enclosed with a high wall. The incoming tide fills the lagoon by passing through the wall via turbines, which then drive generators. The water goes out through the turbines when the tide falls. Tidal lagoons would be very expensive to build, but adding houses and recreational facilities might help to fund them.

Solar power can work on a small scale too—you can put the panels on your roof. These panels may be used to heat water for use in the home, but increasingly people are adding solar panels for generating their own supply of electricity. In some countries, when a private solar system is making more power than needed, it sends its current into the public supply grid—and the homeowner gets paid for the power that it provides.

SOLAR POWER

The energy in the sunlight that hits the Earth is enough to supply all of our energy needs more than 10,000 times over, but less than two percent of our electricity is made using this energy source. There are two obvious flaws: first, the Sun does not shine at night (doh!), and second, the solar panels need to be kept clean to allow the sunshine to do its work. Rain washes them clean, but where there is plenty of rain there is seldom much sunshine.

PHOTOVOLTAIC OR SOLAR THERMAL?

There are two ways to generate electricity using solar energy. Solar thermal power plants have arrays of curved mirrors which concentrate the sunlight into hot beams. Usually the sunlight is used to boil water inside a pipe that runs in front of each mirror. The flow of steam created drives a turbine. The second kind of solar power is photovoltaic (PV), where sunlight hitting a solar cell (made from silicon, germanium, and other chemicals) makes an electric current flow through the material.

GEOTHERMAL

Earth's deep interior is very hot and, in volcanic areas, this heat creeps up to the surface, creating hot springs. A geothermal power plant creates an artificial hot spring by sinking a deep pipe into the hot ground. Cold water going underground is heated, and returns to the surface super-hot and at very high pressure—perfect for making turbines spin. Geothermal power plants can't be built everywhere though. Where's your nearest volcano?

WHO'S WHO?

RICHARD SWANSON

This American engineer was an early advocate of solar power. He proposed that the cost of solar panels (which his company made) would reduce in price by 20 percent every time the number of solar power plants doubled. This is Swanson's Law and it has largely held true. In 1977 in America, it cost $76.67 to make 1 watt of electricity with a solar cell. Now the cost is $0.36—and falling.

WHAT'S WHAT?

GRID PARITY

When will it be just as cheap (or cheaper) to build a **renewable** plant than a fossil-fuel plant? Renewables are quite cheap and quick to set up but they only produce small amounts of power and need replacing sooner. A full-scale coal plant costs a a great deal of money to build, but will produce large amounts of energy for decades. So the two are compared using a "levelized cost," which accounts for these differences. China will achieve solar parity in 2023, and the UK and Germany will hit wind parity in 2024. By 2030, probably before, most countries will have reached grid parity for renewables.

USING BIOMASS

Biomass energy makes use of the remains of plants and animals. This can mean using wood as a fuel or burning waste like straw, bark, or nutshells that are left over from harvests. As we've seen, food crops can be also converted into liquid fuels to replace gasoline. Finally, food waste and sewage can be digested to create "biogas," a mixture of methane and other flammable gas fuels. Biomass energy releases carbon dioxide as it burns, but it is renewable because its source material is always being replaced with fresh growth.

This is the mix of energy sources used by the world today for generating electricity, fueling transport, and providing heating:
Fossil fuels: 79 percent
Nuclear: 2 percent
Firewood: 9 percent
Hydroelectricity: 4 percent
Other renewables: 6 percent
Reducing climate change to safe levels requires that carbon emissions be reduced to net zero by the year 2050, so all our energy will come from renewables.

OTHER ENERGY SOURCES 21%

FOSSIL FUELS 79%

NUCLEAR ENERGY

Although it isn't renewable, a nuclear power plant is often described as low-carbon. It works like other thermal power stations but instead of burning a fuel, it uses highly controlled nuclear reactions in uranium to give out heat. The production of electricity itself releases no carbon, but some experts argue that the construction of the plant and the preparation of the nuclear fuel result in more carbon dioxide being emitted by a nuclear plant overall than a gas-fueled one.

Building a nuclear power plant is far more expensive than the equivalent in wind and solar. Additionally, after their 60-year life span, nuclear plants cannot be simply turned off and demolished. The plant's reactors are highly radioactive and need to be made safe, which takes another 50 years. The most dangerous radioactive waste has to be sealed and stored away for many thousands of years before it is no longer a danger.

WHAT'S WHAT?

FUEL CELLS

A fuel cell uses a chemical reaction to create an electric current. It does this using a supply of fuel—most often hydrogen and oxygen. Oxygen can be taken from the air, but hydrogen has to be purified using a source of energy. As part of the energy storage problem, excess energy could be deployed to create a supply of pure hydrogen for use in power generation whenever and wherever it was needed.

STORING POWER

We are yet to find a good way to store the extra energy that's produced on sunny and windy days so it can be used on still, cloudy days. In the future, we might use large rechargeable batteries for storing power—we'll look at that on page 81. Today, the best storage system is PSH (pumped-storage hydroelectricity), although it is not suited to all environments. This uses the excess power in the system to pump water up to a high reservoir. When power is needed, this water is used to generate electricity.

WHO SHOULD PAY?

Phew, we can replace all the old dirty power stations with cleaner alternatives. No need to worry about climate change now! But the transition will cost money. Should governments pay to build wind and solar systems, or should power consumers (you and me) be asked to pay more for current dirty power to fund new cleaner systems?

REDUCE, REUSE, RECYCLE

The big changes required to control climate change—cleaner power sources, new ways of making food, and carbon-free transport—will only happen if you and I choose to reduce our carbon footprints. The carbon footprint of the entire human population is 1.75 times what the world's climate can sustain. By August each year, we are using more resources than we should, and every year that we do it, the problem gets worse. What can we do individually to help?

THE KYOTO PROTOCOL

Governments have been trying to figure out a way to solve climate change since 1992, when the first Earth Summit of leaders was held in Rio, Brazil. In 1996, an agreement called the Kyoto Protocol was made in Japan for rich countries to reduce greenhouse gas emissions. This was applied to all countries in the Paris Agreement of 2012, which aimed to keep global warming to less than 3.6°F.

CONSUMPTION AND EMISSION

The average human alive today has an annual carbon footprint of 3.86 tons of carbon dioxide. This will have to drop to 2.2 tons per person to reduce our total carbon footprint to the level required by the Paris Agreement. Based on today's energy mix, this is how much carbon some everyday items and activities use:

- 4 cups of milk = 0.9 pounds of carbon (7 hours out of a year's carbon)
- Cheeseburger = 10.7 pounds (3 days, 5 hours)
- Flight from New York to London = 2.5 tons (4 years, 43 days, 39 hours)
- Train journey from London to York = 22 pounds (9 days 17 hours)
- Car journey from York to London = 282 pounds (85 days)
- Using a computer for 8 hours = 1.3 pounds (10 hours)
- Cardboard box (100g) = 0.73 pounds (6 hours)
- Plastic food wrap (100 g) = 1.54 pounds (11 hours)

That's quite shocking, isn't it? These figures will improve when renewable energy sources become more common, but we will need to cut down on what we consume, and choose to use (and reuse) products that last and can be recycled.

The Paris agreement balances the needs of different countries to ensure every country has to work together. If one country were to opt out, then it could benefit while letting everyone else work to solve the problems. Soon other countries would opt out too—and the problems are not solved. In 2017, the United States, one of the most significant polluters, opted out of the Paris Agreement.

IMPORTING EMISSIONS

The carbon footprint of a product is allotted to the country where it is made, not where it is used. So, a country that makes nothing and buys everything from abroad is given a low carbon footprint. China is the largest manufacturing country, and it exports more than 660 million tons of carbon dioxide every year. The United States imports half of that, with wealthy countries like Japan, France, Germany, and the UK taking much of the rest.

It is often said that the pressure on natural resources is due to the huge—and growing—human population. However, the number of children in the world hasn't got any bigger for more than 20 years. Birth rates are highest in poorer countries (with low carbon footprints) where the healthcare system is poor and not every baby survives. The rise in human population does not come from an increase in birth, but a reduction in death rates. That's good, right?

WHAT WILL YOU DO?

While the majority of the action will need to come from governments and organizations, we can all play our individual part. How can you reduce your personal carbon footprint? And how should we make sure that others do not cheat and emit too much?

TECHNOLOGICAL SOLUTIONS

So let's take stock: we need to convert to renewable energy and we need to cut back on wasteful consumption and unnecessary travel. However, a helping hand from new technology will make life a lot more comfortable. Here are some suggestions of new ways of doing things—some more likely than others—that will help to save the world.

REWILDING

Planting more trees and allowing land to simply go wild could suck out the problematic carbon dioxide. A recent study found that 1.2 trillion trees (around 150 per person) would be enough to reduce the amount of human-produced carbon dioxide in the air by nearly 70 percent. Even when you set aside land used for fields and cities, 11 percent of Earth's land surface could be covered in forest. Let's go!

While reforesting the treeless areas of wealthy industrial countries seems like an easy fix, the pressure of farmland will continue to grow in tropical countries that have rising populations and more forests than fields. Here, people can use agroforestry, a method of growing crops among the trees or in small clearings in the forest. Agroforestry is ideal for growing nuts, fruit, and oil plants, three products we will need plenty of if we reduce meat consumption in the future.

HYPERLOOP

This proposed transport system sends pods through long tubes with most of the air removed. Because there is no air resistance in front of the pod, a blast of air behind it pushes it forward at great speed. Hyperloop transport will rival air travel for speed, although there are many technological hurdles to overcome to make the system safe for humans.

CARBON CAPTURE

Imagine a factory that didn't emit carbon dioxide but removed it instead. Carbon capture technology can clean smoke from burning fuels before it emits carbon into the atmosphere. However, if the technology is to make a dent in the climate change problem it needs to remove carbon from the air. Prototype systems are all far more expensive than planting a tree but could work much faster. Once captured, the carbon dioxide could be pumped back underground into oil and gas fields where it came from, or turned into solid minerals like calcium carbonate.

TRAVELING WITHOUT MOVING

In the future, flying will become a very costly form of travel. Instead we might use a system called "telepresence," which combines video-messaging technology with robotics. Instead of traveling in person to a location—for a family event or business meeting—you could be there "in robot." Enhanced by virtual reality technology and more agile robotics, telepresence could be as good as being physically present and so end intercontinental travel for good.

THERMOPHOTOVOLTAICS

About 40 percent of the energy coming from the Sun is visible light, which is picked up by photovoltaic (PV) cells. Thermophotovoltaic (TPV) cells would be able to make use of 90 percent of the Sun's energy. They would even make electricity at night from the heat in the atmosphere! TPVs also collect heat energy from non-solar sources. Adding TPVs to clothing means your own body heat could be used to charge your phone—or whatever we will call personal devices in the future!

ENHANCED PHOTOSYNTHESIS

Leaves are like natural solar panels. They use photosynthesis to turn light into useful energy in the form of sugars. However, a third of the light (and its energy) is reflected by the leaf. This is why they look green—that light is not harnessed by the process. More efficient leaves would use all the light and so appear black. Engineers are looking at ways of upgrading the natural photosynthesis process (using genetically modified algae) and diverting the energy captured by it to make electricity.

There are advances in solar thermal technology as well. So-called "power towers" use curved mirrors to focus all the sunlight into one location at the top of a central tower. The temperatures up there are immense and the heat is used to melt salt— not quite the stuff you put on food, but something similar. These molten liquids hold their heat very well and so can be used to generate electricity 24 hours a day.

A SMART GRID

The fossil fuels we currently use to power our homes and cars will mostly be replaced by electrical systems. Instead of a boiler or furnace, your house will have a big battery which will recharge when power is cheap, and sell electricity back to the grid when you have too much. That means that as well as supplying power, the smart electrical grid connected to millions of home batteries will also be a power storage system.

ELON MUSK

This South African billionaire inventor wants to use technology to save the world. He had the idea for the hyperloop transport, he owns an electric car company, and he has a plan to set up a permanent colony on Mars. Another Musk venture is the Gigafactory in Nevada, the largest lithium battery manufacturing site in the world. Gigafactory 1 began working in 2017 in Nevada but is still being built, and there are plans to build three more around the world.

High-power rechargeable batteries are based on lithium ion technology. Although this is highly efficient, it has a high carbon footprint to manufacture. Recycling batteries will help to reduce that. But as we shift to a battery-based power system, the demand for raw materials may damage the environment—causing more climate change! Lithium mining needs vast amounts of water, which is a problem because most of it is in desert areas. Even more problematic is the cobalt in batteries, which comes from Central Africa, where wars have been waged for decades over who controls this and other minerals.

CAN SCIENCE SAVE THE DAY?

The future sounds kind of fun with all these new climate-saving inventions. Isn't it tempting to leave it to the geeks to solve the climate crisis? But is that going to work? Is it not up to all of us to work out what the future will be like? And shouldn't we all be doing our part in some way?

CLIMATE ENGINEERING

We know that our activities are changing the atmosphere and that has domino effects on the oceans and climate. So far we have looked at how we can make our activities less damaging to the planet. But why stop there? Why don't we re-engineer the atmosphere and oceans to stop the climate problem from happening? It'll be a big job— the biggest in history.

The most out-of-this-world climate engineering proposal is to launch vast sunshades into space. Made from reflective mirrored plastic, these lightweight spacecraft would unfold in orbit. To reduce the intensity of sunlight by 1 percent would require a space mirror (or fleet of mirrors) to cover 0.62 million square miles (three times the area of Spain).

DIM AND DIMMER

If climate engineers could make the atmosphere reflect more sunlight back into space, the rate of climate change would be slowed. There are two possible approaches to "global dimming." We could mimic a volcanic eruption and spray tiny specks of dust into the stratosphere, which would block out sunlight. Alternatively, we could make clouds that form at low altitudes over the oceans much more reflective by adding minute particles of salt. This could be done using robot ships to spray seawater into the sky.

SEEDING THE OCEANS

Climate engineers are considering ways of making algae grow faster in the oceans. That would remove carbon dioxide from the air, and it would stay in the oceans as the algae died and sank to the seabed. It's believed that the Paleocene–Eocene Thermal Maximum (the last time the world got really hot) ended because this happened naturally. Most ocean fertilization plans involve dumping millions of tons of iron-rich chemicals into the water to boost biological activity.

WHAT'S WHAT?

BIOCHAR

The ancient people of the Amazon had trouble growing crops in the poor soil of the rainforest. They boosted its fertility by mixing in charcoal, creating what is now called "terra preta" (black soil). The process adds nutrients to the soil, but it also takes carbon from the air and buries it in the ground. Fast-growing wood could be converted to charcoal or "biochar" on industrial scales and added to soils where its carbon would stay locked away for thousands of years.

The albedo of the oceans can be increased by simply blowing bubbles. The wake of a speed boat appears white because tiny bubbles of air are mixing with the water. Robot ships could form plumes of bubbles by pumping air into the surface layer of water, which would help reflect heat.

BRIGHTEN UP

People in hot countries often paint their homes white to reflect the Sun. We could do that on a vast scale and increase the planet's albedo. A "cool roof" uses reflective paints to bounce back heat and light. Another plan is to genetically modify crops to be paler and create a real-life Daisyworld where fields reflect heat at the same time as growing food. The final step (a very big one) would be to cover deserts in shiny plastic sheeting.

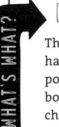

IS CLIMATE ENGINEERING THE ANSWER?

Let's be honest, we cannot stop climate change completely. A proportion of it is almost certainly natural, but the human element has led to the threat of a very fast change in the conditions on Earth—too fast for nature to adapt. Climate engineering sounds risky, but it might give us more time to meet other challenges. What do you think?

IS PLAN B PLANET B?

So what are our chances? We know the problems, we've got a good idea of how to fix them. However, perhaps we need an insurance policy, or a backup plan. It won't be cheap and it might make us complacent. Insurance takes the worry out of things, but you only make a claim when things go very badly wrong. Plan A is to save the world, but Plan B could be to move to another planet. All aboard?

WHERE IS PLANET B?

Venus is our nearest planet but has global warming problems far beyond our own. The nearest Earth-like planet (or at least our best guess at one) would take 6,300 years to get to. That leaves one possible candidate for our backup planet: Mars.

LIFE ON MARS

Before you get a fitting for your spacesuit, you should know what it will be like on your new home. You might choose not to go. The atmosphere is mostly carbon dioxide, but it is much thinner than on Earth, with a pressure that's around 200 times weaker. That means Mars is always very cold. Midsummer temperatures never go above 68°F, and in winter (which lasts 180 days) it is −193°F!

If you go outside on Mars without a spacesuit, before the cold kills you, the lack of air will suck all the oxygen out of your body and you'll collapse in 15 seconds. The air is bone dry so it never rains. When a windstorm starts, it can last for weeks, whipping up a dust cloud that covers the whole planet. And when it's sunny, the ultraviolet radiation, unfiltered by the planet's atmosphere, would give you a serious sunburn.

GETTING THERE, BUT NOT BACK

Elon Musk's SpaceX company is designing a spacecraft that could carry 100 people to Mars. The ticket price—about $250,000—would buy you a one-way trip. On landing, the new arrivals would build a base using components from their spacecraft and with supplies sent by automated landers from Earth. The idea that Mars is a solution to climate change on Earth isn't a very serious one. Only a few hundred people could go there every year. The rest of us are stuck here.

EUGENE CERNAN

Only 21 people have left Earth's orbit. These were the Apollo crews who visited the Moon 50 years ago. The last man on the Moon (so far) was Eugene Cernan. He summed up the Apollo mission this way: "We went to explore the Moon, and in fact discovered the Earth." The pictures of Earth taken by the Apollo astronauts changed the way people saw our planet. We realized that it is a speck of life among the vast nothingness of space, and it needs looking after.

SpaceX plans to have a colony that makes all its own food and energy by 2050. The colony will grow plants in airtight greenhouses. Mars has two of the essential components for that: carbon dioxide and sunlight. It's hoped that the missing component—water—exists as ice in Martian rocks. As well as feeding plants, water can be split into oxygen (for breathing) and hydrogen (which can be mixed with oxygen as a fuel source). If there's no water, the Mars colony is over before it begins.

IS MARS EVEN OURS?

Rovers are on Mars searching for signs of life. If it's there, it will be rock-eating bacteria (we have those here, too). However, human settlers will bring germs with them—which might kill the Martian life. We could make Martian life extinct. Does that mean we shouldn't go?

HAPPY 2050?

The year 2050 is going to be a big year. This is when the human population is predicted to hit its peak, at somewhere between 10 and 11 billion. This is also the year when the world will need to have succeeded in cutting its greenhouse gas emissions to small and manageable amounts—perhaps to zero. We'll have a much better idea of what climate change has in store by then. What will life be like in the year 2050?

CIRCULAR ECONOMY

In 2050, it's likely that we will have a circular economy, focused on keeping waste and emissions to a minimum. Every product will be designed to be reused many times, with components that can be separated without damaging them so they can be remade into something else. For example, a tall office block could be reassembled as a series of houses—as you could do with modeling bricks. Finally, the original materials will all be recyclable so they can be used as raw ingredients for something new.

Today the goal of companies is to sell more and make more money. This is part of a system called "economic growth." But as we run out of resources, we need to change to a circular economy where companies focus on making the most of raw materials rather than increasing profits. An economy with no growth—will that even work?

The raising of livestock for meat may well still be a very small part of farming and perhaps dairy and poultry farming will continue in some places. But artificial meat will be grown in factories from genetically modified cells. The cells could even be printed into the shape of a steak.

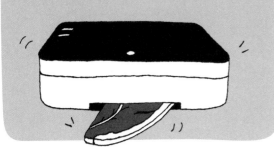

WHAT'S WHAT?

EMANCIPATED VEHICLES

In 2050, it may be that no one owns a car, and in fact all cars are emancipated from ownership— that is, they own themselves. Controlled by AI, the self-driving electric vehicles will work as taxis, and the money they earn will be used to pay for power and maintenance. The onboard AI will decide for itself what to do. It might move to a remote place where it is the only taxi, or upgrade itself into a luxury ride charging a high price.

DISPLACED PEOPLE

Let's say that renewable energy and clever new tech allow us to cut greenhouse emissions. Nevertheless, there will be regions where it becomes impossible for people to live. By 2050, at least 400 million will have been displaced. Climate change will open up large areas of northern lands that were once too cold for habitation. It is likely that entire new cities will be built in Russia, Scandinavia, and Canada, and these places will probably grow in importance.

MANUFACTURING ON DEMAND

In today's manufacturing system, everyday items such as clothes are made in large amounts in one place—often China—and then exported all over the world. That is very costly in terms of resources. In 2050, 3D printing technology will be used to make anything you need—either from a pre-set blueprint or following your own design— in your locality so there will be no need for long-distance cargo journeys.

HAVE YOU MADE UP YOUR MIND?

I told you, the story of climate change is long and complicated. There is a lot to consider. Individually and as a society, we have some hard choices to make. What do you think? Can we fix the planet and secure the future?

PROS AND CONS

How do you feel about climate change? Terrified? Energized? The world can't stay as it is right now. Something has to give, and deciding what we want to keep and what we can do without will take some careful thinking. What we've learned so far will help, I hope, but it might also be useful to think about the different ways we can divide good from bad to help us form an opinon.

THE PRECAUTIONARY PRINCIPLE

This approach says that if something is uncertain you should plan for the worst-case result. The precautionary principle is at the heart of the debate between people who want do something about climate change and those who don't. The latter group argue that we aren't really sure whether our actions are leading to problems. It would be a waste of money to plan for something that might never happen. Climate change campaigners opt for the opposite approach. Doing nothing is too risky for the wellbeing of the planet and human race.

The precautionary principle sounds like an easy system to apply. If in doubt, be cautious. However, already in the battle for a cleaner planet, the precautionary principle has resulted in more climate change. After a tsunami in Japan damaged nuclear power plants, nuclear power was banned in Germany. However, to meet the country's power demand, it made more electricity using coal, which arguably was more damaging than using nuclear.

FINDING CONSENSUS

It is all very well having a clear personal idea about what should be done about climate change, but for anything to actually happen a plan that has the backing of a large group of people is needed. Only then will there be enough political power to force those who don't agree with the plan—who might want to prosper by going against it—to comply with it.

ETHICAL SYSTEMS

Ethics is a way of thinking that shows you what is bad and what is good. There is more than one way of making that distinction.

Utilitarianism: This system thinks about positive and negative consequences, treating them like a sum. It says that the idea of morality is to increase the positives (happiness) and minimize the negatives (suffering). Dividing the Earth's carbon budget equally among all people is a clearly utilitarian decision, but by itself it may not lead to a resolution of the problem.

Virtue: A good person is driven by virtuous qualities, such as generosity, kindness, and patience. So behaving well shows others that you are virtuous. Striking or protesting for more action on climate change is a virtuous act. However, displaying virtues will not in itself solve the climate problem, but will bring awareness to the issue.

Duty: In this system, being moral is doing the right thing even if you suffer as a result. Good behaviors come from duties, which are things that are self-evidently good, such as helping people in pain. But is saving wildlife a duty? Or cutting down on waste? What happens when duties conflict with each other?

MIND MAP

You've reached the end of the book and now know a lot more about climate change, but what do you think about it? It's pretty scary, isn't it? But the main thing to remember is that we can work together to solve this problem. After learning about different moral theories, what do you think is the best approach to solving climate change? Is there one correct way or are there many? Who should lead us toward a solution—our leaders, scientists, or maybe you? I can't tell you the answer, because there isn't one! You have to make your own informed opinion, but now you have the tools to do just that. This mind map is a starting point to build the big picture of climate change. There's a lot to get your head around, isn't there? Every subject leads to another, and every question answered ends up with more things to ask. I always think that's what makes this stuff so interesting: the way a wide array of subjects all seem to link together. Makes you think, doesn't it? So, now you have the information, what will you do with it?

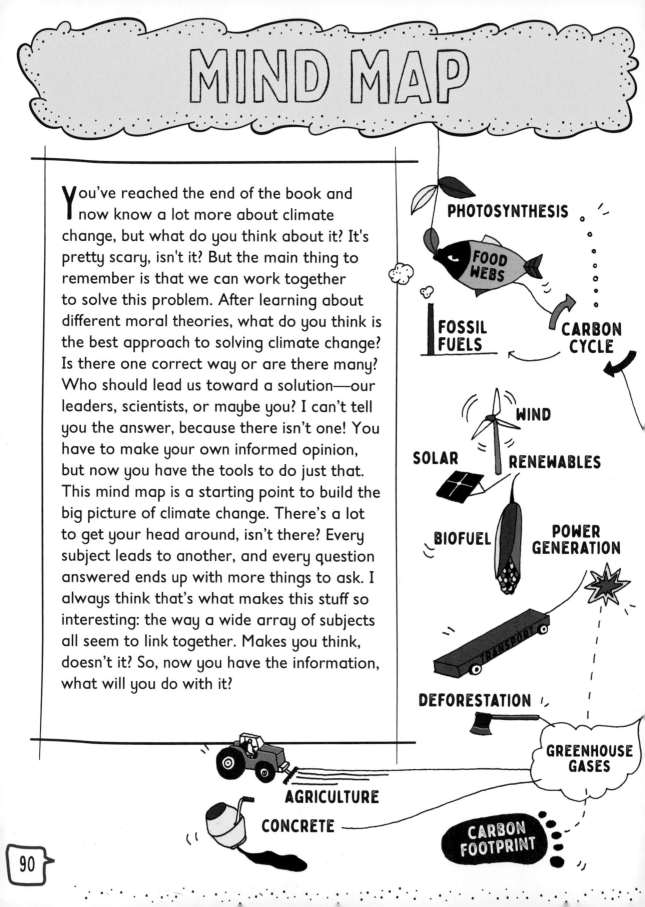

PHOTOSYNTHESIS

FOOD WEBS

FOSSIL FUELS

CARBON CYCLE

WIND

SOLAR

RENEWABLES

BIOFUEL

POWER GENERATION

TRANSPORT

DEFORESTATION

GREENHOUSE GASES

AGRICULTURE

CONCRETE

CARBON FOOTPRINT

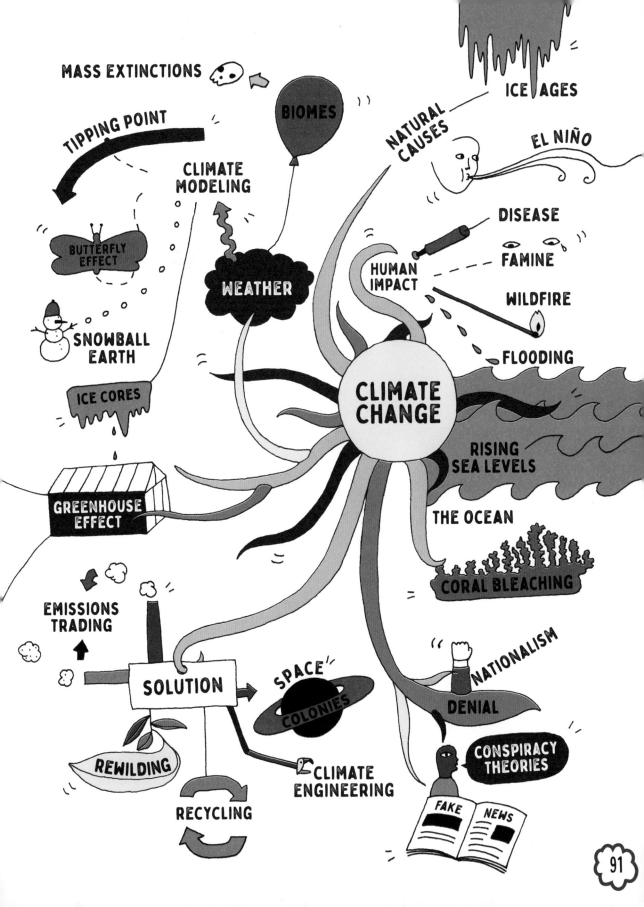

MASS EXTINCTIONS

TIPPING POINT

BIOMES

CLIMATE MODELING

BUTTERFLY EFFECT

SNOWBALL EARTH

ICE CORES

WEATHER

NATURAL CAUSES

ICE AGES

EL NIÑO

DISEASE

FAMINE

HUMAN IMPACT

WILDFIRE

FLOODING

CLIMATE CHANGE

RISING SEA LEVELS

GREENHOUSE EFFECT

THE OCEAN

CORAL BLEACHING

EMISSIONS TRADING

SOLUTION

SPACE COLONIES

NATIONALISM

DENIAL

REWILDING

CLIMATE ENGINEERING

CONSPIRACY THEORIES

RECYCLING

FAKE NEWS

atmosphere a mixture of gases that surrounds a planet or moon.

bias an unbalanced view of something, where one idea is promoted over alternative or opposing ideas

biodiversity the variety of living things on Earth

biomass a measure of the amount—calculated as the total weight—of a particular kind of living thing, or materials made by living things.

blight a fungal disease that attacks plants

carbon dioxide a gas made by combining carbon and oxygen, as happens when fuels are burned. Carbon dioxide is the main greenhouse gas causing climate change.

carbon footprint a measure of how much greenhouse gas is released by a person or an activity. A high carbon footprint contributes to climate change.

CFC short for chlorofluorocarbon, an artificial gas developed for use in industry.

climate a description of the weather experienced in a certain region over a normal year

crisis a period of intense difficulty that has many complex problems to solve

dust bowl farmland that is no longer fertile as it has been stripped to dust

energy an ability to make a change in a natural process. Everything in the universe is giving out and receiving energy all the time.

equatorial to do with the region around the equator, the imaginary line that divides Earth into a northern and southern half

fossil fuels substances that are formed from the remains of dead animals and plants that release a large amount of heat and light when burned.

glacier a slow-moving flow of ice that forms in cold areas, such as mountain ranges and polar regions

greenhouse gas a gas that contributes to the greenhouse effect that traps heat in the atmosphere

hoax a complex trick designed to deceive a large group of people

marine to do with the oceans

millennium a period of 1,000 years

mineral a naturally occurring solid substance. Common minerals include limestone and calcite.

moraine a strip of gravel and rock that forms at the bottom end of a glacier where the ice melts into a stream or river

oscillation a rhythmic or regular process that moves back and forth between two extremes.

ozone the normal form of oxygen has a molecule made from two oxygen atoms (O2). Ozone is a more unstable from where the molecule contains three atoms (O3).

particle a small unit. All substances are made from particles arranged in a particular way.

renewable meaning that supplies never run out because their source is constantly renewed

species a unique kind of plant or animal that has a particular set of characteristics.

sponsor to pay for someone to do something that is not your normal set of activities

storm surge a big wave that is formed by powerful storms out at sea and is blown onto land causing flooding

ultraviolet invisible light waves that carry more energy than visible light, which can damage the skin if the energy is not absorbed by dark pigments

vapor another word for a gas, often used to describe the gas form of water that is below 212°F. When water boils at 212°F that gas formed is called steam.

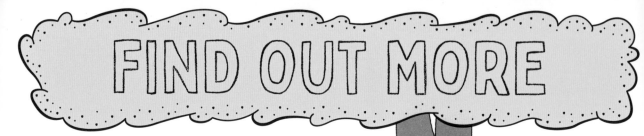

FIND OUT MORE

Now over to you. Use these resources to continue your exploration of climate change. You can find out more in books and on websites. Every good science museum will have exhibits about climate and the way it is changing, and there are apps that will help guide you through a low-carbon lifestyle. The story of climate change is still being written—and you should be part of it. Good luck!

BOOKS

There are many books written about climate change from all points of view. These ones are a good place to start.

No One Is Too Small to Make a Difference, by Greta Thunberg, Penguin, 2019

There Is No Planet B: A Handbook for the Make or Break Years, by Mike Berners-Lee, Cambridge University Press, 2019

How Bad are Bananas?: The Carbon Footprint of Everything, by Mike Berners-Lee, Green Profile Books, 2020

WEBSITES AND ONLINE ARTICLES

All the evidence for climate change is made available to the public on the Web.

Carbon footprint calculator
www.carbonfootprint.com/calculator.aspx

NASA: Climate Kids
www.climatekids.nasa.gov

Time for Geography: Climate change evidence
www.timeforgeography.co.uk/videos_list/climate-change/evidence-climate-change

All web addresses were correct at the time of printing. The Publishers and author cannot be held responsible for the content of the websites, podcasts, and apps referred to in this book.

MUSEUMS

Museums are great places to visit and discover more about the process of climate change in an interactive way.

The Climate Museum, New York City, New York

Museum of Science, Boston, Massachusetts

Wonderlab, Bloomington, Indiana

PODCASTS

Listen to people discuss the big questions while on your way to and from school, or at home, with these podcasts.

Flash Forward: EARTH season
A show that discusses possible future scenarios with scientists and experts.

Costing the Earth (BBC)
A podcast that looks at human impacts on the environment and how the environment reacts.

GAMES

You can learn more about how things might change in the future and how society might deal with these changes by playing these games.

A selection of online mini games on the theme of climate change.
www.climatekids.nasa.gov/menu/play

CO2 (board game)

APPS

Learn more on the go with apps which you can download to your smartphone.

Earth Now, NASA (iOS and Android)

Together, WWF (iOS)

A FEW FINAL QUESTIONS...

What is the best way to tackle climate change? Should governments make people reduce their carbon footprints? Or is it up to each individual to change their own lifestyle?

The full effect of climate change won't be clear for several generations. Should younger people have more of a say about what to do about the problem than older people, who likely won't be around? Is that fair?

Does this book make you want to change the way you live, what you eat, and how you shop? If so, how can you convince others to do the same?

INDEX

PAY FOR RESULTS

A PRACTICAL GUIDE TO EFFECTIVE EMPLOYEE COMPENSATION

KAREN JORGENSEN

MERRITT PUBLISHING, A DIVISION OF THE MERRITT COMPANY
SANTA MONICA, CALIFORNIA

Pay for Results

First edition
Copyright © 1996 by Karen Jorgensen

Merritt Publishing
A Division of The Merritt Company
1661 Ninth Street
Santa Monica, California 90406

For a list of other publications or for more information, please call (800) 638-7597. In Alaska and Hawaii, please call (310) 450-7234.

Library of Congress Catalogue Number: 96-075085

Jorgensen, Karen
Pay for Results—Taking Control
Includes index.
Pages: 334

ISBN: 1-56343-136-X
Printed in the United States of America.

Acknowledgments

I want to thank the business leaders who contributed to this book and allowed me to use their businesses as examples. Also, the stalwart staff at Jorgensen: Susan Barlow and especially Keith and Brian Dowling. Without them, this book would be only a dream. I also would like to acknowledge Jim Walsh and Jan King at Merritt Publishing for their superb guidance.

I will acknowledge that we all are constantly learning and growing. Each unique individual has a real purpose in supporting our lifestyles as Americans. Paying for results helps us all to understand and respect each other for our contributions.

I have always wanted to share my experiences and ideas with CEOs and business leaders. I remember—as a personnel manager—thinking: "If they would only let me run the company for a month, I could really show them."

I used to believe I knew all the answers. Now I'm not so naive.

Each company's rewards and incentives are unique and tailored to specific business needs. They do have common elements and processes. Compensation and rewards are always changing with our evolving business structures. This book is a small step toward "telling it like it is"—to provide a guide to the business owner in identifying result areas, measuring communications and rewarding staff for their unique contributions to a business's success.

Pay for Results isn't just about incentives, it's about changing behavior to improve your company's strategic advantage. CEOs cannot change behavior, but they can provide employees with incentives that focus on required results—to encourage group, team and individual behavior changes and support the growth of American businesses.

Karen Jorgensen
La Crescenta, California
June 1996

This book is designed to be used as a tool to help business owners and managers build effective employee compensation programs. It is not a legal reference. If any reader has questions about the legal status of a pay plan he or she is considering, he or she should consult a labor attorney or human resources expert.

Pay for Results is the seventh title in Merritt Publishing's "Taking Control" series, which seeks to help business owners deal with the host of extraordinary risks facing the modern business enterprise. Upcoming titles will cover customer service, making presentations to bankers or investors and other topics. To keep these projects—and the series as a whole—well focused, the editors at Merritt Publishing welcome feedback from readers.

PAY FOR RESULTS

TABLE OF CONTENTS

Introduction:
The Rules for
Paying People Are
Changing

Rewards and recognition are becoming more and more important in the workplace. The nature of employment and the benefits that people look for in their jobs are changing on what seems like a daily basis. Traditional methods of motivation and compensation—slow, steady advancement over a long career—no longer work.

In our rapidly changing business environment, keeping employees focused and efficient is more and more difficult. Keeping them content is almost impossible.

Businesses are caught in the squeeze between customer expectations of increased service and lower cost and employee expectations of continued salary increases.

Too many businesses underestimate the contribution and synergy attainable by giving employees a partnership stake in improving business results.

In the age of management gurus, such as Deming, Juran and Peters, many companies talk about quality, continuous improvement and empowering employees—but they don't follow through by allowing employees to contribute, understand and affect the bottom line.

This book is written to help the enlightened businessperson empower employees and pay them more for better results. It will give that person the tools for finding, compensating and—most importantly—keeping good people.

In today's competitive markets, paying more can

Motivating and empowering employees

occur only if your results are better than your competition's. Understanding how to communicate, measure and reward results will add strategic value to any business.

This book has been written to help you solve this dilemma. Incentives can provide the key to success in motivating employees to support your business goals and improve your bottom line. I know how to do this because I've been in your position.

For 10 years, I was a personnel manager. I had great jobs, first in banking, then in T.V. and radio at Golden West broadcasting with Gene Autry. I struggled to grow and learn as much as possible in a profession that was relatively new and uncharted. As I learned from peers, experience and business coaches, I grew aware of the communication gap between rank-and-file employees and the hard-driving leaders who ran American business.

With the introduction of such issues as workplace diversity, generation-specific management and global competition, the gap has widened.

On the other hand, I've observed managers and whole businesses that were successful in motivating and empowering their staffs. Those businesses flourished, and their staffs became important resources for growing and expanding the business. You can build this kind of resource.

Having learned by observing, I went back to school, read, researched and practiced improving working environments for managers and individuals. Paying for results came up over and over again as an important ingredient in creating a successful environment.

After spending several years as a consultant to private business, I became a lecturer for The Executive Committee (TEC). I spoke to MBA students at UCLA and groups of CEOs all over the United States. I was able to respond to success and failure factors with numerous clients through my consulting practice.

This book is a culmination of those many years of experiences, observations and research. This book is dedicated to improving our work lives, improving an owner's sales and profits and improving the employee's commitment and success.

As goals and desired results become clear, employees become empowered—they stretch and grow to achieve those goals. Personnel problems are more likely to resolve themselves. Slackers in the staff are weeded out by their peers; people tend to leave an environment where their contribution clearly is measured as substandard.

Clear results linked to fair measurement allow discipline to be a function of teaching and coaching—not of punishing. In business, as in sports, poor performers sit on the sidelines. If possible, you should encourage them to sit on your competition's bench.

Using this book to develop new pay practices will support your goals and strategies. Varying compensation as your business fluctuates provides a cushion of protection against rising costs and pricing.

Paying for results is the key to success in today's volatile business environment. Providing measurements of results that are objective and clear will focus your employee's energy on your sales and profit.

CHAPTER 1:
THE CASE FOR
INCENTIVE-BASED PAY
PLANS

Introduction

Most companies are caught between the need to keep costs down for their customers and the expectations of more money for their employees. Clearly, the traditional practice of setting salaries and raising them annually is being challenged. That kind of system, which places primary emphasis on an employee's seniority, usually doesn't allow the level of flexibility that progressive companies need.

A well-known employee-compensation success story occurred when Springfield Re-Manufacturing Company (SRC) was purchased by its management from International Harvester. SRC rebuilt transmissions and re-manufactured engines. In the transition, Jack Stack became an owner/president. Jack had always believed in incentivizing his staff and finally had an opportunity to use incentives to motivate his employees effectively.

When the new owners took over SRC, the company was strapped for cash. It was not in a financial position to pay employees more base salary or provide the benefits that had been available before in the bigger firm. There was quite a bit more risk involved in staying with the newly formed company. To offset the risk and lack of benefits, Jack used incentives to retain top employees.

The incentive plan paid everyone a reward if the company made a profit. The company, along with all employees, reviewed its financial position weekly. In order to make the incentive understandable to

Using incentives to create "ownership"

the employees, Jack spent a great deal of time communicating and championing the incentive plan. The incentive plan was built around increasing sales and improving efficiencies to gain more profit to repay debt. It also encouraged continued growth and quality.

Although the books of the company were open, some employees didn't understand how their jobs fit into the profit picture, so the company began an extensive training program to teach employees how their behavior could improve the company's results.

Employees were encouraged to be responsible, to make suggestions and to monitor their progress. Departments reported regularly on their performance, and employees were held responsible if results were not achieved.

Bonuses were paid out quarterly to all employees if the company met its financial goals.

Within a few years, the company repaid the debt associated with the sale and grew its internal systems.

SRC's rewards were the incentive. The incentive was both a communicator and a motivator. Jack has been very vocal both in print and in the media in encouraging incentives to improve company results by rewarding employees who contribute directly to the company's success.[1]

With the incentive plan in place, Jack wrote, "Everyone starts thinking and acting as owners, not as traditional employees who are just doing the job."

Springfield Re-Manufacturing grew from $16 million in the 1980s to more than $80 million in sales today. The stock, worth 10 cents in the early 1980s is now worth more than $20. It has gone from 100 to more than 600 employees, while continuing to use incentive plans.

Faced with hard choices, many companies manage the prices of their goods or services by freezing their biggest cost factor—labor. To maintain market share, they look at layoffs, salary freezes and outsourcing.

Incentives offer an alternative to seniority-based pay systems. Incentives pay for results. They provide

---

[1] For more details on SRC's story, see *The Great Game of Business* by Jack Stack (Currency/Doubleday 1992).

pay based on measurable achievement and accomplishment of company, team or individual goals.

Although *gain share*—a complex method of rewarding bonuses based on improvements in productivity—has been around a long time, most progressive employers look for concrete, practical guidelines to develop *incentive pay*.

Unlike base pay, incentives are not entitlements. Employees can earn additional money based on achieving strategic goals set by the company. But there are no guarantees. The money isn't earned if the goals aren't achieved.

That said, not everything should be in a state of flux. Steady **base pay** is still necessary, because it establishes a person's standard of living. Base pay is normally determined by market standards or averages. It's tied to time—hourly pay, monthly wages or an annual salary.

Progressive employers usually try to complement market-driven base pay with incentives such as at-risk pay that will provide additional compensation when agreed-upon goals are reached.

This chapter will introduce some basic concepts of progressive compensation plans. It will define incentive rewards, explain why incentive systems are important and provide an overview of characteristics of successful plans. It also will explain why companies need to pay for results, rather than time, to succeed in today's global economy.

An Economic Perspective

In the late 1980s and 1990s, American business has experienced a lengthy economic stagnation. In the late 1980s, this wasn't surprising—companies had to deal with a recession. Technically, that came to an end in late 1992. However, by 1996—four years into an economic recovery—employers remained cautious about increasing operating costs by spending a lot of money on new hires.

Faced with this data, economists explain that the United States is experiencing changes that are bigger than the short-term cycles of recession and expansion. Anyone working on the front lines of employment issues could have told them that.

An alternative to seniority-based pay

Jobs are paying less today

Jobs are paying less than they have in the past. In economic terms, this means inflation-adjusted wages have not kept up with economic growth. A Bureau of Labor Statistics (BLS) Employment Cost Index showed that the wages and benefits average is about 2 percent lower than five years ago and 5.5 percent lower than 10 years ago. Even the pay for a new college graduate has fallen and remains below 1989 levels. According to a national survey by Robert Half and Associates, nearly 80 percent of jobs in accounting, information systems and banking received below-inflation raises.

There are a host of reasons why real wages have fallen for the American worker.

- There is a trend by U.S. employers to control raises and curb salary growth. In the 1980s, average increases for all wage earners averaged between 7 and 10 percent each year. In the 1990s, businesses have cut annual increases back to 3 or 4 percent. (In 1994, the total average salary increase across the U.S. was 4 percent—this includes all promotions and raises.) Many companies do not give automatic increases at all—maintaining salary levels from 1990 or earlier.

- A global economy and recently changed import and export tariffs have contributed to a leveling of wages throughout the world. This has lowered wages in developed countries—such as the U.S.—and raised wages in poor nations. Foreign competition keeps U.S. prices down—and companies are more mobile, able to move manufacturing facilities to new locations where labor is cheaper.

- Technology changes have a dampening effect on wages. Computer automation increases efficiency and decreases the need for many workers, especially traditional clerical and support positions. The workers that are needed at the entry level must possess strong technical skills. More tenured workers need to continue learning new skills. Some workers simply become obsolete because they do not keep up with technology.

8

- Old business measures that focused on revenue growth and gross margins have been replaced by measures that evaluate more industry-specific standards of *efficiency*. Progressive employers put money into training and technology. They keep their workforces familiar with technology and marketplace developments. Spending resources on training limits the dollars available to increase wages. Employees who have trouble maintaining efficiency are less valuable—those who can't keep up are, frankly, expendable.

- Employers hold down payroll costs by using part-time, temporary and outsourced[2] workers. This is partly due to the impact of technology on clerical and support positions—but it's partly a result of lifestyle changes. Employees at all levels want flexibility and alternatives to the traditional work environment. At their simplest, these desires mean casual dress and more flexible schedules. At their most complex, they mean employees who work at home or *project teams* made up of freelance contractors rather than full-time employees. In this sense, the advent of telecommuting —which is largely over-hyped—has actually changed the way Americans work.

- Employers are using incentives to supplement earnings. In a recent survey of Fortune 1000 companies, more than 50 percent were using some type of lump sum payout to reward workers.

  When you give cash as an incentive or bonus to an employee, it does not increase base pay or compound wages. This is important, because salary increases have a compounding effect on wages over time.

  For example, if a company increases wages 5 percent annually, after the first year each $100 of salary becomes $105. After the second year, it becomes $110.25; after the third, $115.76—and so on. By the tenth year (when the adjusted salary is $162.89

---

[2] This term, which has become common in the 1990s, includes consultants, professional or executive-level temps and leased employees.

A shift in investment priorities

per original $100), that company is paying an additional $12.89 per original $100 in cumulative raises—*each year.*

By paying a cash lump sum, there is no compounding and original wages stay the same each year.

The Reascendency of Capital

For most of the twentieth century, the United States has led the rest of the world in economic output and efficiency. As you know, the last two decades have seen the European common market and such Asian economies as Japan and Korea catch up to American technology, quality and management efficiency standards.

American companies are hard pressed to pay employees more when product and service pricing must be kept low to compete.

What you are seeing—and probably feeling—is a reascendency of capital investment in the American economy.

For the first half of this century, if an American company put money into capital improvements, it could count on a substantial return. So companies did just that. Factories, railroads and mills were built with little attention paid to cost control. American businesses flourished by expanding infrastructure—building offices, enlarging factories and increasing output.

After the Second World War, labor became a bigger issue than capital investment. The plants and infrastructure had been built; they needed to be run efficiently. Businesses put money into labor and labor-related issues; many adapted a military approach to hiring and developing workers.

There were lifestyle changes, too. Non-cash benefits—like life or health insurance and pension plans—became popular. Cost of living raises became institutionalized and averaged 10 percent or more. If a company had a problem, it threw more people at it. Big companies added employees daily.

By the late 1980s, the investment return on labor came to a screeching halt. Businesses stopped increasing pay and staff size. The economy flattened, and we began an era of massive corporate consolidation.

This era of consolidation has already begun to give way to another era in which capital investment becomes primary.

With the reascendency of capital investment, companies must invest cash into improving technology—not employees. Employees feel the squeeze of a tight economy and flatter pocketbooks. They feel disenfranchised because of what they perceive as radical changes.

You begin to hear employees—and organizations representing labor—complain that loyalty has been replaced with heartless efficiency. Or greed.

Daily, companies are announcing that they are "re-engineering," or downsizing. They are transferring their need for people to a need for technology, equipment and efficiency.

In this environment, the employees you keep need to feel empowered to act decisively amidst chaos. Incentives are a good vehicle for accomplishing positive results.

By using variable pay plans, you can make capital investments without having to shrink labor costs. You can use variable pay to reward results, while you direct fixed dollars toward business improvements.

Variable pay helps you channel labor costs to their most efficient application. It encourages profitability. Used well, it can even press for revenue growth.

Incentive Pay

Incentive pay is not a new management tool; it has been around since the 1930s. It also goes by various names including *new pay, variable pay* or *alternative rewards.*

Whatever it's called, it hasn't been hugely popular. According to U.S. Chamber of Commerce statistics, incentive pay constitutes less than 1 percent of the total payroll for employees in all industries.

But, as we've noted before, recent changes in the economy have led some employers to look to incentives as a solution to otherwise stagnant pay levels.

Characteristics of effective incentive plans

And that's a good thing.

Basically, incentive pay is additional pay earned beyond normal weekly, monthly or annual salary. It's paid in the form of additional current cash to the recipient. Companies that pay incentives usually tie the payout to individual or team achievement of a goal. The goal often relates to profit, sales growth or customer service improvement.

Effective incentive plans usually share several key characteristics:

- Objective goals are set based on growth, profit or service plans.

- The plan helps you communicate with staff, allocate resources and evaluate performance.

- The plan helps your employees participate in meeting objectives and watching measured results unfold.

- Most importantly, the plan provides measurement—for both you and your employees—in a neutral manner that's not subjective or susceptible to personality conflicts among staff members. When goals are achieved, employees are rewarded.

A well-administered incentive plan allows you to concentrate on the cycle of *management by setting objectives* (MBO). In fact, it encourages you to follow this kind of management model.

The management by objective system

EFFECTIVE MBO SYSTEM

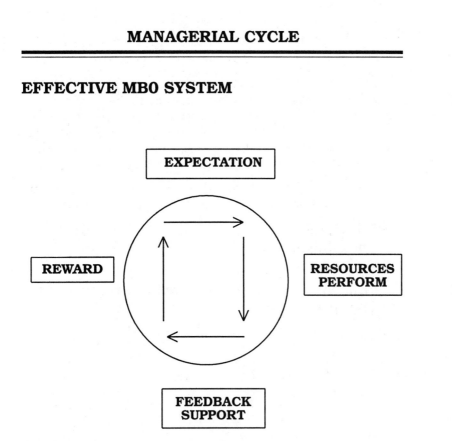

An effective management by objective system starts with clear expectations. A manager sets specific goals, guidelines and standards for an employee. Secondly, the manager is responsible for providing resources for the staff member to meet the goals and to perform the work assigned. Feedback and ongoing support are important so that the relationship between the manager and the employee continues to focus on goals and expectations during the MBO cycle.

The final step in the process is evaluating the employee's success in meeting those goals and expectations—then providing a reward based on the level of success. Here's where the incentives come in.

Then the cycle starts again, as the manager and employee set new expectations.

An incentive pay plan can also solve one of the toughest dilemmas you face: Employees—especially strong performers—want more money...and they want it all the time. You need to make sure you're

Using incentives to retain top performers

getting a return on your biggest personnel investments.

Unskilled or semi-skilled workers are a ready commodity in most industries and regions. Skilled workers with solid experience and proven ability can command premium pay. And these top performers are usually the ones with the best connections to the marketplace. If they feel their only route to advancement and a bigger paycheck is to change employers, they're in the best position to do so.

Incentives protect your operation without bankrupting you. They prevent key employees from leaving by involving them in your company's success.

With incentive pay, you can provide a base pay for employees that is at market—and, so, control fixed costs. You can also provide total compensation that is over market by adding an incentive paid only under certain circumstances—such as when your company has earned a predetermined profit.

Traditionally, fixed labor costs for profit-driven, private-sector organizations have increased at the same pace—or faster than—labor costs in the economy at large. Through the 1970s and 1980s, cost of living adjustments (COLAs), explicitly designed to keep fixed labor costs ahead of inflation, pushed numerous big for-profit employers toward insolvency.

With incentives, the same profit-driven organizations can dramatically flatten the increases in fixed labor costs, while still providing additional pay.

By shifting labor costs to incentive-based variable pay, you can continue to price products and services competitively. You also can retain and reward the skilled workers who contribute to your organization's success.

There appears to be a direct correlation between business success and incentive rewards. One survey of privately owned businesses[3] indicated that incentive pay was used to improve business results, encourage teamwork and motivate employees.

Companies recognized the effectiveness of their incentive plans in delivering positive bottom line results. More than 63 percent of the presidents or CEOs surveyed felt their businesses improved with the use of incentives. Among the most commonly cited benefits: better intra-company communication and sharper industry competitiveness.

Incentives improve communication and competitiveness

THE BENEFITS OF MOVING TO VARIABLE PAY	
Improved Communication	70 percent
Improved Results	67 percent
Improved Pay-For Performance Link	62 percent
Improved Morale	53 percent
Faster Teamwork	50 percent

UNITED STATES — Comparison of Salary Budget Trends to Salary Structure Trends

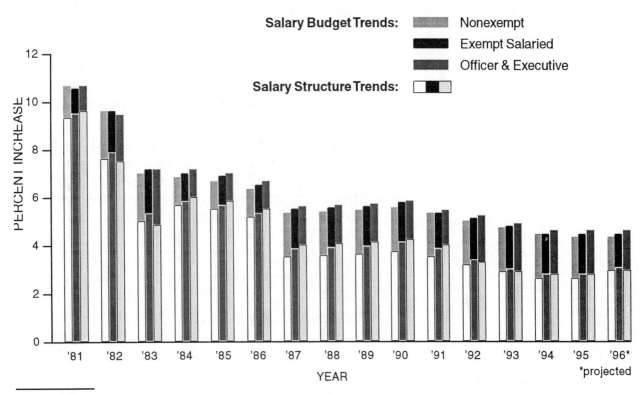

[3] *The Impact of Incentives and Bonuses on the Bottom Line*, The Executive Committtee.

Profit sharing plans pay a percent of the profit

Variations on the Theme

The term *incentive pay* can apply to all kinds of compensation programs—but some common variations on the theme occur. In fact, there are, typically, seven types of incentive pay or variable pay plans that make up the majority of the total:

- **Management By Objective (MBO) Plans**. As we've mentioned before, these are among the most progressive plans. They incorporate incentives not only into compensation, but also into the management structure. They tie managers' bonuses to specific company, team and/or individual goals.

- **Profit Sharing Plans**. These awards are based on company profits. Some percent of profit is used to fund the plan. Money is distributed based on a predetermined formula linked to the size of the profit margin.

- **Group or Team Incentives**. These awards are based on predetermined team performance measures. They are usually awarded to the team as a group, with members taking either equal shares or weighed shares based on position or seniority.

- **Gain Sharing Plans**. In these plans, awards are based on cost control or productivity improvements. Financial gains are shared with employees using a predetermined formula that reflects the percentage gain achieved.

- **Incentive Plans**. These are simple cash awards tied to sales, profit, customer service or quality goals of a company, and paid to groups or all employees based on a mathematical formula. Achieving business results triggers a cash payout.

- **Sales Incentives**. These are paid to salespeople based on commissions or other sales criteria.

- **Discretionary Awards**. These plans use cash awards based on overall company performance—but they are not awarded uniformly. They are normally given, personally, by a CEO at year end. Judgment rather than measurement is used to determine amount.

Discretionary awards are the most common form of incentive pay—prevalent in many successful companies. They're easy for management to implement; they also can be dangerous.

When incentives are awarded at a manager's discretion, employees do not know how their behavior influences their compensation on an ongoing basis. Many plans of this nature are perceived as unfair. When employees don't know the evaluation criteria used to make bonus decisions, they often assume favoritism is involved.

No matter how much you try to discourage the practice, employees tend to compare the bonuses they receive either directly or indirectly. In most cases, amounts awarded become known—if only approximately or inexactly—and discussed. There are usually hard feelings when bonus amounts are not equal. And there is a big margin for error in the information that spreads.

By relying on personal judgment rather than objective measurement, you also minimize the impact of your awards. Discretionary bonuses diminish the bang you get for each compensation buck.

Still, many business owners like the simplicity and spontaneity that discretionary bonus plans allow. If you're sold on this method, you should try to establish some basic parameters for how bonuses are awarded[4].

The goal of most variable pay plans—whatever specific form they take—is to change behavior. Successful plans are designed to improve performance. Efficiency is boosted, and improvements are made by communicating clear goals to employees and rewarding behavior that leads to achievement.

Incentive plans work best when they're designed in sync with a company's strategic objectives. And these objectives are pretty easy to identify. One reliable survey concluded that 77 percent of all incentive pay plans use financial goals (sales, profit or budget objectives), 33 percent use productivity

---

[4] Later in this book, we will consider how to change a discretionary *thank you* at the end of the year to a more reliable incentive.

Employees' varying levels of understanding

goals and 25 percent use quality goals. (The total adds up to more than 100 percent because most companies have more than one goal.)

Successful plans use the increased performance to fund costs. If you can't link the bonuses you pay to specific improvements, you probably need to reconsider how you award people. (And the odds are you're relying too much on discretionary judgment.)

Self Interest and Bounded Rationality

Academics who study human resources issues and even general business management often look for the common characteristics that all employees share. Chief among these are *self interest* and *bounded rationality*.

All employees have self interest. At some level—and it may be right near the surface—people watch out for themselves. Workers evaluate their behavior, job, salary and benefits based on self interest. They think about what work does for them.

Of course, different employees will have different levels of self interest. Some consider the long-term prospects of the company—and of themselves—when they evaluate their jobs. But even in these cases, self interest is a motivator.

If people are motivated by self interest, rewarding them for achieving results will reinforce a link between personal and company interests. This link will encourage behavior that supports company efficiency.

When it comes to their jobs, people focus their self interest primarily on money. So, money is the easiest way to establish the efficiency link. Other forms of compensation may be useful—but none works as clearly, across all levels of a workforce.

Bounded rationality is a phrase that refers to an employee's level of understanding. All employees have the ability to understand what their company does and what their roles are within that system—but this ability is limited to their level of comprehension.

Some employees need little explanation of a new concept or task. Others need repeated explanations, and some employees may never understand a new process.

For example, when new competitors enter a market in which your company does business, some employees will thrive on the challenge. They'll study the competition and the market and look for new ways to do business.

Other employees will respond more slowly. They may complain that the new competition means trouble for your company. They may adapt as time goes on—but they may not, becoming obsolete because they can't or won't change.

Each kind of employee has a level of understanding, or bounded rationality, when it comes to competitor input.

Part of your challenge in motivating employees is understanding how to present information as goals—and how to explain how all employees can help achieve these goals.

An individual may be motivated by a need for recognition, activity or the integrity of work—but these issues tend to prevail in more senior, professional positions (and not always even there). Once you move beyond one individual, abstract values become more difficult to use as motivators.

If your business requires performance at the team or division level, you will need to return to the common denominator of employment: money. Once an employee understands how his or her behavior leads to increased pay, he or she will repeat the behavior that leads to the reward.

The basis for incentive plans lies in the belief that rewards motivate behavior. Money is one of the strongest motivators—it both satisfies the impulse for self interest and overcomes bounded rationality by reinforcing efficiency links.

A successfully designed plan is simple enough to be understood by all employees. You know you've succeeded when your most recent front-line hire can explain what your company does, how it defines achievement and what role he or she plays—however small—in that process.

Present information as a goal

The characteristics of successful plans

The Four Properties of an Effective Incentive Plan

Incentive pay plans come with many different designs, goals and objectives. Each company is unique in the way it measures success and what contributes to excellence. Although these plans are unique to each company, successful reward systems do have four common characteristics:

1) **Measurement** plays a key role in determining reward. Good plan results are announced and quantifiable. Measurements are trusted and communicated often.

2) **Avoiding judgment** is part of the design. They are not subjective, and always provide a reward if a goal is achieved. There is no allowance for a manager or CEO to change the rules of the reward. The goals are preannounced and rewards depend on achieving results—not the discretion of managers or their opinions.

3) **Links** between rewards and efficiency are apparent. Good plans link the reward to the strategic business plan of the company. The reward is given based on results that will ensure the future success of the organization. This means the business planning process is very critical to the success of an effective incentive plan.

4) **Timeliness** is essential. Incentives are paid in a timely manner, as soon as possible after a goal is achieved. There is also a timely window of completion—and an end to all plan periods. (Normally, incentive plans are redeveloped at least once a year.)

You can remember these four properties by the acronym MALT. All good incentive plans include the four properties. But, beyond these properties, three broader prerequisites support a successful plan.

1) **Vision**. In order to set goals and anticipate results, a business needs to be able to forecast future direction. Strategic planning can clarify vision and design tactics to achieve results. The planning process establishes company objectives, and goals can

be set based on those objectives. Vision is necessary to foresee upcoming direction and connect business strategy to results.

2) **Communication**. A well-designed incentive is a key communication device. It communicates direction, expectation and company objectives to all participants. With the communication comes focus on results. Employees can anticipate and function more efficiently if they are all focused in the same direction.

3) **Simplicity**. Designs need to be simple and able to be easily understood by every employee. Simple goals, simple explanations and simple examples work best. Designs should be tailored to ensure all employees comprehend goals and how they contribute to goal achievement. Complex plans are suspect; employees don't trust complex design. Once everyone understands the plan, then complexity can be added little by little. But, in general, plans that become too complex don't succeed.

Extending our MALT metaphor from above, you can remember these three requirements as Vanilla, Chocolate and Strawberry. (The ice cream parlor imagery will stop here, I promise.)

These prerequisites are really just the fundamentals of good management.

In order to truly be effective, a plan must be backed up by a strong vision of the future and what results will help a firm achieve success. CEOs and executives need to prepare a strategic plan for the company that identifies market, sales, profit, costs and efficiencies needed to improve operating methods. Some firms include all employees in strategic planning; in other firms, the owner or president plans alone. There's no single best way to do this—but it does need to be done.

Once the plan is established it needs to be communicated to everyone. In this way, many companies are like horse-drawn wagons: The staff are the horses, harnessed up and ready to go—but the wagon won't go forward unless the horses are all pulling in the same direction. The strategic plan,

Everyone needs to understand the priorities

results needed and the incentive plan communicate direction to all staff.

Communication is both a prerequisite to and a product of a good incentive plan. The plan pulls people together to combine energy, talent and effort toward a common goal. Incentive plans communicate continuously to all staff how the results are occurring and what behavior, effort or achievement can influence ongoing results in a positive way.

When employees understand the goals of a reward system, they are better able to identify how their daily tasks affect the whole. Consider the receptionist—often a good example of how vision is communicated. Your receptionist may get several calls at once. Which one has priority? Existing customers or potential new business can call at the same time. If goals are communicated, the receptionist knows which call to put through first.

The communication of the plan and how it relates to each employee links the business together as an undivided team.

Competition Versus Coordination

The structure and style of business efficiency is constantly changing. New products, new markets and new customer demands drive constant improvement, updating methods and upgrading technology.

The military hierarchy that supports top-down compensation reviews no longer fits every business situation. It doesn't even fit most business situations. Likewise, the patriarchal style of the father-figure employer taking care of child-like employees is breaking down. It's being replaced by performance management and incentives.

In short, business is becoming more decentralized. Because people and products move more independently than ever, you need to identify business goals strategically, communicate them clearly and share the financial rewards when goals are achieved. These things will coordinate far-flung personnel and operations—even if they're doing business in the same building.

A system of goals and reward creates a partnership

among workers and functions. This demands an ongoing process to drive productivity, quality and customer satisfaction.

You don't reinforce teamwork if you espouse team communication and decision-making but leave compensation decisions to a single manager (even if that single manager is you). By centralizing pay decisions, you encourage subjectivity and discourage input from all sides.

Traditional compensation plans did a few things right. They were easy to administer, and they fostered competition. But both of these virtues often turned into vices. The ease of administration often led to lazy administration. The competition often focused on favoritism rather than performance.

Competition is useful in many situations—but team efforts can be derailed by intense personal competition. You will usually do better if the competition exists among groups. Groups foster coordination on at least a modest level.

This is yet another reason that progressive companies are adopting market pay systems and incentive pay plans.

Conclusion

Progressive companies continue to maintain salaries at the market level, and compensate with variable pay for better than average results. Variable pay or incentive pay continues to supplement wages as the company meets its goals. If the company does not meet goals, there is no incentive payoff, so labor costs remain at market.

It's become a cliche that employees are the most valuable assets of most modern businesses. But it's true. Their knowledge, service and information are critical to any level of sustained success.

You're caught between the need to stay competitive by holding down costs of goods and services to customers and the need to pay employees more for their contributions. Incentive plans provide a flexible pay process that is not tied to time, but tied to results.

Properly designed incentive plans improve business results, foster teamwork and improve communication. Properly designed plans pay for themselves in

Tying pay to results supports teamwork

23

the form of increased sales, efficiency and profit-ability. Incentives empower employees and create a true partnership of the staff and the organization. And they do it cost effectively.

Chapter 2:
Determining Pay Philosophy and Policy

Introduction

Before you can begin to implement any kind of pay plan, you have to determine some basic parameters. Chief among these: your company's basic pay philosophy and a compensation policy that covers the fundamental matters of how you pay employees.

Many employers bring in outside consultants to help customize a pay plan for their company. If you do this, it makes even more sense to define some basic terms first, so the expert you bring in doesn't spend a lot of time early on doing what you can—and should—do yourself. (This is a good rule to follow whenever you hire consultants, no matter what their specialty.)

Like so much else about running a business, these basics may develop and refine themselves over time and with experience. That's fine. No philosophy or policy should be so rigid that it can't reflect the lessons of experience.

However, you need a place to start—a framework within which you set specific plans. These basics make up that framework.

Pay Philosophy

As part of your business plan, you need to develop a pricing philosophy for goods or services based on the quality, content, customer service standards and marketing strategies you choose. Likewise, in order to make consistent hiring and promotion decisions, you need to develop a pay philosophy.

Your pay structures reflect your values

Your pay philosophy should reflect the hard economic realities of your pricing structure and market share—as well as softer issues, like corporate culture, industry standards and growth strategy.[1]

A company's beliefs and values are reflected in its pay philosophy. The pay philosophy you choose is neither good nor bad on an abstract level. The defining question is whether it suits the needs of your company and the business you do.

Conservative companies avoid variable pay, while entrepreneurial ones put a major portion of pay at risk. Cash-rich companies can afford to be expansive with pay, while cash-strapped ones pay tightly with the market (or even below it). The type of industry, profit margins and operating philosophy will all be considered in developing a pay philosophy.

Some companies—fast-food restaurant chains are a good example—pay low salaries and face constant turnover. This might sound like some horrible Dickensian approach, but it may be a legitimate reflection of the people who take the jobs—and how seriously they take them.

Other companies—professional groups such as law firms or accountant firms are good examples—pay over market and expect employees to rise to their level of pay. This draws in top-notch prospects. But it also encourages managerial disappointment and employee burnout. (Of course, many lawyers and accountants will argue that this is an acceptable approach to developing talent.)

Most companies fall somewhere in between the extremes of McDonald's and Gibson, Dunn & Crutcher.

Pay Philosophy Check List

This is a check list to evaluate your company's philosophy. Answers to these questions will give you a sense of your company's pay philosophy.

1) Do you believe your company pay is at, above or below the market?

2) Do employees in general feel their pay is at market, above or below market?

---

[1] Throughout this book, you'll read about *hard issues* and *soft issues*. This distinction isn't a glib judgment of what's important and what's not. It refers, instead, to the simple matter of how directly issues affect your profitability. Hard issues impact it directly; soft issues impact it—but indirectly.

3) How do you know what the market is? How often is market researched?

4) Are medical benefits, vacation and sick pay for your organization, at market level above or below market?

5) Do you have any long-term benefits, such as 401(k) or retirement plans, and do you feel they reflect the marketplace?

6) Do you have salary problems recruiting new employees?

7) When new employees are hired, are their starting salaries sometimes greater than the salaries of existing employees doing similar jobs?

8) Is there a consistent process for providing pay increases, or does the employee who complains loudest get the raise?

9) Do people quit over salary issues or leave for more money more often than expected?

10) Do people feel the pay process is fair?

11) Does the company disclose compensation information and general grades and ranges to employees?

12) Do employees know why they got a raise?

13) Does the company share its financial success with all the employees?

14) Are bonuses or incentives tied clearly to expected and achieved results? Are the goals of the company clear to all staff?

By answering these questions, you get a sense of your company's historic pay philosophy. Some companies spend time planning their compensation strategy. In others, the pay practices evolve from the owner's belief and value system. The pay philosophy is a good indication of how people are treated in an organization. If it's hard to get a raise, regardless of how the company is doing, you can usually be assured recognition is also difficult to obtain, and employees probably are treated as if they are not valued.

Pay philosophy differs for different businesses. Some companies adopt a pay philosophy that pays

Explicit pay philosophies justify tough decisions

programmers more than the market, but every other job at market. Some pay office workers more than factory workers—others, vice versa. Pay differs for businesses with different types of emphasis.

The most useful general observation: Progressive companies usually provide base pay at market and offer incentives to increase total compensation to above market levels when company performance meets predetermined goals.

Some companies define their pay philosophies explicitly in employee handbooks or other material. This can be a useful tool when you need to support a tough pay decision—not awarding a raise is a common one—that an employee doesn't like.

An example of an explicitly stated pay philosophy is:

PAY PHILOSOPHY

The objective of our total compensation package is to pay above the market when individual performance, team and company performance goals are achieved. The company will compensate all of its staff based on the individual's job performance level, type of position, internal equity and market salary basis. Salaries will be at or near the market base for similar-size companies, duties and skill levels. Additional compensation will be variable based on business, team or individual performance.

This company is an equal opportunity employer, and this policy is administered and based on job performance, market data and job responsibilities only.

Hutchinson and Bloodgood is a CPA firm that has been very effective in growing its business and has three large offices. It is an old firm, and it is very important for it to retain good CPAs. Its product and service to clients is high quality with value added, and only the top professionals can meet the company's high standards. Its pay philosophy is to pay employees and CPAs above the market, and in order to maximize this philosophy, the company actually has made a policy of paying overtime to all employees that are working more than 7½ hours in a day.

Most other CPA firms don't pay professionals for overtime. Bright CPAs who have recently been certified know they have to put in long hours to prove themselves. They know they will be paid a better total wage at Hutchinson and Bloodgood.

This philosophy has helped the company hire and maintain an excellent workforce. When an ad is placed for an employee, they have hundreds of candidates to select from because of this compensation philosophy. This is one company that does not need professional recruiters to obtain good talent. It saves thousands of dollars each year in turnover and recruiting costs by paying above-market wages through its overtime policies.

How Information Is Gathered

Some companies include regular surveys of salaries paid by competitors or comparable companies as part of their pay philosophy. This is an important and valuable consideration. It's a good idea.

To evaluate internal pay, external research of salary information is critical. There are numerous published research findings that provide salary information on U.S. jobs. Commercial surveys can be purchased at a discounted cost by members of industry groups or companies that have contributed salary information to the survey.

Survey data is broken down by size of company, geographical location and industry. To obtain the most accurate market information, the closest match must be made to the actual business conditions of the company reviewing survey data.

This information also is usually categorized by job content, not salary titles. Titles can be misleading, since the same title may have different job duties in two different companies. Valid salary information is always shared with a brief explanation of job content and duties.

Surveys can be purchased from industry vendors or local employment-related services. CPA firms, recruitment services and government agencies conduct market surveys and provide research data as part of their services. Large public libraries have survey data as part of their research material.

Overtime as a recruiting tool

Survey your marketplace's salaries

Annually, most trade magazines conduct surveys of major industry players. Survey data is incorporated into industry articles and reference material. The Chamber of Commerce, Labor Department and other non-profits also provide local salary information.

You can customize surveys, too. You might develop your own questionnaires and send them to specific competitors, local firms that compete for employment talent and/or other businesses that might provide useful information.

Customized surveys should maintain confidentiality of data. When responses are tabulated, you can present them in a format that protects the identity of the reporting companies. This will increase the likelihood that other companies will cooperate.

To encourage participation in a survey, results are shared with the participants. By sharing results, all the participants also receive useful market information. When information is shared, the companies reporting the salaries are unidentified. The information is presented on a general basis only.

When using survey data, care should be taken to make sure jobs are really comparable. Information on size of company, actual responsibilities and demographics should be taken into account.

When comparing salary survey information, the weighted average salary should be used. The weighted average represents the mean, or the middle of the market. This means half of the salaries surveyed actually will be from below the market average and half will be found above. The average rate will give the mid-point of the marketplace base salaries.

The timing of a survey is critical. At the beginning of the compensation process, standards should be developed and surveys conducted. Market data needs to be current. Only recently surveyed data is relevant. Generally, the market moves slightly behind the cost of living changes. Companies should evaluate the market at least annually to ensure accuracy of data. Once the market data is collected, evaluation of internal equity can be accomplished.

American City Bank was an independent whole-sale bank with 200 employees and 15 branches that was growing in Los Angeles. It hired tellers, loan officers and administrative staff. At $150 million in assets, it was an important contender for financial talent. Its turnover of experienced bank personnel seemed to be too high. The company discovered that its turnover was close to 30 percent per year. The executives felt this was far too high to provide the quality service necessary in their market area.

As part of the turnover investigation, they discovered that salary was one of the contributing factors to the turnover problem. Once that was discovered, the executives decided to do an extensive market survey to evaluate all salary levels.

They selected 25 key jobs in the bank that could be compared easily to their competitors. Once those jobs were selected, the bank personnel manager went out to the marketplace, specifically researching other banks in the area, and determined the exact market level pay for each one of the bank's positions.

Executives then compared the market information to their existing salaries. Several of their key postions were paid below the market rate. After the research and investigation, the bank decided to commit to a philosophy to pay at or above the marketplace.

It raised the salaries of those individuals whose performance was strong and who were paid below the market rate. Once that was completed, the bank set up a compensation system in which the market would be used to evaluate pay every year to ensure pay equity with the market. They developed a bank compensation policy and set up grades and ranges. Everyone was given a performance and salary review annually.

The following year, they reevaluated their turnover. It had dropped to just below 15 percent for officers and managers. They had slowed the process of losing good employees. By adopting a pay philosophy based on market pay, the bank had made a giant step forward in retaining talented employees.

Paying at market reduced turnover

Incorporate existing practices

Compensation Policy

The compensation policy is the written guideline your company follows in its wage and salary actions. The program should be written in clear and concise language so that a) employees can understand it; and b) it can be used in the training and development of supervisors. (A sample policy appears on page 271.)

In general, the development of a compensation policy should be simple and designed to cover all the basic information necessary to manage the process of hiring and increasing employees' salaries. This isn't esoteric stuff—it's practical information, such as how often you pay employees, the benefits you offer and how to deal with special issues like advances against salary.

A normal policy will cover the following subjects:

- the company's philosophy of pay
- responsibilities of administration
- communication channels
- position description information
- salary structure and grades
- hiring salary limits
- timing and frequency of salary increases
- timing of performance appraisals
- status definitions—promotions, etc.
- budgeting and financial considerations

Include hiring salaries, because if the hiring process is not consistent with internal compensation, there may be problems in internal equity.

A company initiating a new pay program should incorporate as much of the existing practices as possible into the new policies. We recommend retaining the timing of current increases if they are administered in a consistent manner. We also recommend incorporating the forms and procedures of the review process into the new program. The more of the historic process that can be incorporated into the new, the easier the training of supervisors and the acceptance of the program by employees.

What follows is a review of common elements of compensation policies.

Job Descriptions

Job content—an integral part of any pay system—is normally obtained by reviewing job descriptions. Job descriptions are written outlines of the duties in a given position. Job descriptions are used in training and coaching employees. A job description can be used to ensure both the employee and the supervisor understand what is expected in a job.

In many growing companies, job content changes constantly. Job descriptions are outdated before they are finalized. If there is constant job change, the job description process is too restrictive.

One effective approach: Have employees complete job questionnaires and use the questionnaire[2] to set up measured results. The job description process doesn't have to be cumbersome.

Benchmarking

To establish basic pay ranges, a company can select certain jobs to research in the market. These jobs are called benchmark jobs.

A benchmark job is a standard job common in most companies, and enables the surveyed companies to provide exact salary data. Benchmark positions should be compared easily from company to company. An example of a benchmark position is accounts receivable clerk. Almost all companies have an accounting clerk who keeps track of receivable cash or credit points.

Selecting benchmark jobs is not easy. Job content needs to be explored to ensure jobs are truly similar. Market survey data contains brief written explanations of job content. Because of the unique nature of some jobs and the individual ways firms title staff positions, using titles only will not guarantee effective matches. Job content is key to proper identification of salaries in the marketplace.

---

[2] A sample questionnaire appears on page 243.

Selecting benchmark jobs is not easy

Annual salary increases

General positions that have matches in other companies can be designated benchmark jobs. A benchmark position should be described in simple detail as part of the survey process. An example of a benchmark definition would be:

Accounts Receivable Clerk
Responsible for daily accounting, receivable processing, computer posting of general ledgers and subsidiary ledgers. Works in the accounting department. Two years experience in accounting, is required.

Every company has some unique job positions that are found only in that organization. Unique jobs cannot be matched in the marketplace, but need to be compared internally to equivalent jobs that can be benchmarked.

In selecting benchmark positions, companies should include jobs in all levels of responsibility, from a more senior position, like controller, to a very junior position, like receptionist.

When evaluating which jobs should be selected for survey benchmark, a company needs to consider responsibility ranking of the jobs, and also the major departments. A typical benchmark survey should include positions from accounting, administration, production, auditing or quality control, and marketing and sales. The benchmark positions are selected from a variety of responsibility levels and various departments of the company.

Evaluation and Pay Increases

In most pay plans, employees may receive salary increases annually based on job performance. You should consider market data as well as performance when increasing salaries.

About half the companies surveyed increase salaries based on a business cycle, and about half increase salaries at an employee's hire date anniversary. Both ways work, depending on the business strategy.

In most progressive pay plans, the amount as well as delivery of method of pay depends upon the relationship of the pay to market, as well as the performance.

The merit increase grid below illustrates how companies are deciding increase amounts. If an employee is below the market average and a strong performer, he or she will get a bigger increase than a strong performer paid at market.

With a larger increase, the below-market employee moves toward the market rate more quickly.

Employees paid above-market salaries would receive lump sum payouts and lower percentages to retain pay within market parameters. By providing a payout, the salary increases do not compound, and salaries remain at the same level while the market moves ahead yearly.

MARKET REVIEW INCREASE GUIDELINE

	Performance Level		
Range Salary Position	LOW	MEDIUM	HIGH
Below Market	2 to 4%	6 to 7%	8 to 9%
Market	1 to 2%	4 to 5%	6 to 7%
Above Market	0	2 to 3%	2 to 5%

Adjustment to Market

When companies complete a market survey, they often will find internal jobs at market, below market and above market. In many cases, there are clear reasons an internal pay rate will be off the market. If the internal rate is below the market, then the job incumbent could be new or a trainee, not fully seasoned or could have had performance problems in the past.

It might also be true that the internal job is not as complex or responsible as the surveyed positions. Likewise, an internal job may be paid more than surveys indicate because the incumbent has been in the position for several years, is an outstanding contributor or has some other tasks that are in addition to the job content of the surveyed position.

Unfortunately, it also may be true that the incumbent is over- or underpaid. If underpaid, an ad-

Let employees rate themselves

justment to the market should be made. If overpaid, normally a company will not lower a salary, but will freeze the salary. That means no more increases, until the market catches up.

A company can adjust salaries to market at once, or can increase salaries over time. When adjusting to market, normally a company considers a range of pay for a position.

Yearly, new surveys are conducted. As internal salaries are reviewed against the market, companies use the annual review process to increase salaries or give lump sum increases based on performance of incumbent, level of skill and market pay. In most companies, a compensation committee conducts the yearly surveys and provides the information to supervisors regarding the pay process.

Communication

Communication of pay policies is part of the ongoing responsibility of management. As new hires begin, they are told their salary, job title, the date they can expect a salary review for increase and the date they can expect a performance review.

Supervisors must be trained to evaluate performance and provide timely feedback to employees. Supervisors also must understand pay principles and market rates. They use the market rates to recommend hire salaries and annual increases.

Most companies use some type of feedback form to evaluate annual performance. The review of performance is documented on the form, and a copy is given to the employee by the direct supervisor. The document is also an opportunity to discuss performance and give necessary input back to the employee on his or her strengths, areas to improve and areas of training.

Progressive companies let the employees rate themselves on the form, as well as have the supervisor evaluate the employees. The supervisor and employee then review both forms to see when they differ and agree on performance issues. Only the supervisor's review is retained as the official review form for the period.

Compensation communication can be in the form of employee meetings, department meetings, company meetings or one-on-one explanations.

Written communication, such as handbooks and newsletters, also should convey pay philosophies and pay information.

Some companies communicate all areas of the compensation policy to employees, except individual salaries. In those companies, employees know the grades, ranges and market mid-points of positions within the company. Other companies provide little salary policy information to employees. The sophistication, education and competitive markets are used to determine how much information to provide employees.

Executive salary levels and market data are confidential and not shared. Confidentiality at top levels is vital to retaining executives and avoiding information leaks that spread this proprietary data among competitive companies.

KTLA was an independent TV station in a major market. It had grown from a low rating to being the top-rated independent station in the market. As a top-rated station, it could charge more for air time and use the additional revenue to train and upgrade its staff.

Executives discovered they were training their competitors. As they took loyal staff and trained them to know more, competitive stations would hire them away from KTLA. The station was losing the very talent that had helped it achieve its number one market status.

To combat this problem, the station established a pay policy that reviewed salaries every six months, and provided increases more often to employees who achieved results. They followed the processes described in the next chapter to adopt a market pay philosophy. By adopting a market pay plan, they kept their talented people, and base salaries stayed current with the marketplace at 5 percent above the average.

This philosophy was approved at the highest levels, and communicated to all employees:

They were training their competitors

The station retained skilled staff

KTLA Compensation Philosophy

KTLA will compensate all staff in a timely and effective manner. Base salary levels will be at least 5% above market for the incumbent's performance level, skills, responsibility and experience levels. Base salary will be augmented by benefits and cash incentive plans that provide above-market total compensation for all non-union staff members.

Performance level and salary reviews will occur every six months. This compensation policy will be administered with equal opportunity for all participants, and is based on performance, market data and position duties only.

Once the review process was set up and running, the station retained its skilled staff and turnover dropped. The staff benefited from more input from management about their performance, and the station retained talented professionals to contribute to its leadership position in the ratings.

Conclusion

Many employers hire outside consultants to help them establish compensation plans. This makes sense in many cases. But if you choose to hire a consultant—especially if you hire a consultant—you need to set up some basic parameters.

Some compensation consultants will suggest that you adapt a pay plan of their choosing and allow them to implement immediately. Others take the opposite approach, spending a lot of time and money surveying your employees and the marketplace in an effort to identify the plans and trends that apply to your business.

You can avoid both of these extremes by setting the terms you prefer from the beginning. Take the time to learn about what other companies in your field or your area do. If you hire a consultant, you can then tell him or her what you've seen and—in rough terms—what you want. This usually cuts down on the time the consultant spends learning about your business.

Of course, you don't have to hire a consultant. The rest of this book deals with the details of setting up a progressive compensation plan for yourself.

CHAPTER 3: ESTABLISHING MARKET BASE PAY

Introduction

Historically, most companies have established competitive pay structures in which employees vie against each other for salary increases. Supervisors rank employees according to subjective measurement—which can be difficult, as well as unpredictable.

When many so-called *merit* systems are examined closely, one common problem emerges: Most managers do not differentiate between employees when giving annual raises.

Merit pay systems usually produce rigid and vaguely military hierarchies within organizations. In some cases, the military connection isn't vague—it's explicit. And, in many cases, this result is intended.

While the military approach may work in certain situations (for instance, if you use many entry-level non-service employees), it gets in the way of such contemporary management goals as open communication, team building and total quality.

Traditional merit pay systems make other assumptions about the labor market that may be outdated. Like the military, they assume that most employees enter near the bottom of the pay scale and, over time, advance through the ranks. Clearly, this slow and steady progress doesn't reflect attitudes that contemporary employees have about their careers.

Market base pay, which can operate as a stand-alone system or as the foundation of an incentive pay plan, better reflects the realities of today's labor marketplace. Market base pay is objective. It takes into account both the performance of your employees and the wages your competitors are paying.

How base salaries work

In short, this kind of program compares your jobs to marketplace jobs and salaries. It uses the comparison to help determine how your employees should be paid. Finally, it provides a fair method for evaluating base pay of all employees and allows you to maximize the effectiveness of payroll dollars.

This chapter will explain the reasons many employers are moving to market base pay plans. It will then show you how to design and put into practice this kind of plan.

By following the steps outlined in this chapter, a successful market base pay compensation process can be customized for just about any organization. The plan will provide guidelines for establishing and increasing pay within economic boundaries that support organizational and personal growth.

Why Market Base Pay Works

Pay is the best tool you have for communicating direction and focus to employees. Compensation plans work best when they act like a continuum of reinforcement to achieve business results.

Market base pay is one effective method for pricing internal jobs, based on local market survey data, job evaluation and incumbent skill level. One survey conducted by a human resources consulting group[1] found that 50 percent of the large companies that responded had adapted a pay process that consistently conformed base pay to company philosophy, market rates and skill levels.

A market base pay plan can solve the constant fixed-salary increases that a maturing work force will demand. However, it solves this problem by making the increases a variable cost—which may be even more intimidating to some employers.

Base salaries for all employees are set to market standards on a regular basis—often annually. Merit increases and cost of living increases are replaced by market adjustments and—when needed—one-time lump sum increases.

Some form of variable pay usually offers additional, above-market compensation. The variable pay occurs when goals are met and business results achieved.

---

[1] American Compensation Association

So, a company can price its goods or services in a way that minimizes its fixed costs and cost increases.

Market comparisons are easy when jobs are common and comparable to available industry standards. They get more difficult when positions are unique to a company and cannot be compared to other positions or other companies.

This leads to a common complaint: Many business owners—and most employees—feel their circumstances are so particular that they defy comparison. The image called up is the *comparable pay* standards that political groups advocated in the 1970s and early 1980s. These standards made absurd comparisons between jobs traditionally held by men and jobs traditionally held by women. (It was much better to focus, instead, on getting rid of those *traditionally*s.)

But the practical truth is that most jobs can be compared effectively to others within a company or within an industry group. If you have any doubts, use the following questionnaire to get a general idea of whether a job can be adequately compared to others in your company or your competitors' companies. (Remember, jobs are compared using job content, not job title.)

JOB CONTENT QUESTIONNAIRE

1) Are the job duties more important or less important than those of other jobs to the effective success of the company?

2) Is the knowledge an employee must have to do the job successfully greater or lesser than for other positions?

3) Is the formal education required to perform the job higher or lower than for other positions?

4) Is previous experience needed to perform the job successfully? If so, is the amount and type of experience greater or lesser than for other positions?

5) Is the degree of responsibility, which includes impact on customers, company per-

Know the market rates for jobs

formance, assets and supervision, greater or lesser than for other positions?

6) How much impact does the job have on influencing results of the company? Is it more or less than other positions?

7) How much communication skill is necessary in the position? Does it require writtten and oral skills? Are those skills required more or less than for other positions in the company?

8) To what degree must the position coach, train, supervise and get work done through other people? Is the degree of supervision skills required less or more than for other jobs in the company?

9) How much physical, mental, and emotional effort does it take to do the job? Is the effort more or less than for other jobs?

10) How much direct contact with customers does the position have? How much influence over customers' decisions and expectations does the position have? Does the position impact customers more or less than other positions?

Of course, there are some jobs that really do defy comparison. For those positions, you may have to make a rough approximation, drawing from several positions—usually at other companies that do something like what your company does.

Beginning the Process

The foundation of a market base pay plan is reliable information. The fixed annual pay of each employee must be tied to competitive salaries measured by survey data. By knowing the market rates for critical jobs, you can better evaluate your pay levels. You can use market data to evaluate company performance and to establish where base ends and variable pay begins.

Most larger companies have come to recognize traditional hierarchical pay programs with rigid levels and standard cost of living adjustments as dinosaurs.

Under these systems, the dollars available to increase salaries were minuscule. Salary increase budgets were typically close to, or slightly higher than, wage inflation. Wage inflation was relatively low. This shackled everyone. Employees became stolid and bureaucratic; managers couldn't differentiate performance, because average increases were so low.

Today's frenetically changing business environment demands more effective ways of rewarding performance.

How can you encourage constant improvement, when supervisors control salary increase amounts? Because of the changing business requirements, jobs are changing constantly. When job content changes, companies cannot always give raises. Employees are expected to do more—but companies can't pay more.

The principle behind market base pay is similar to that of pricing a new product for the marketplace.

When you've developed a new product and want to price it for sale, you research the market to see how similar products are priced. Once you know the market, you price your product based on its quality level, your philosophy of the company and current market pricing of similar products.

Market base pay prices jobs the same way. A job is researched in the marketplace to see what others pay for the same duties. The research should match jobs based on content, location, size of business and type of industry. Then a company determines the fixed annual base pay of an employee based on performance and skill of the employee, company philosophy and market rates.

Market base pay sets salaries based on quantifiable market data.

Consider the case of a commercial real estate development company that needs to hire a mechanical engineer. A careful scan of job postings from local employers and surveys conducted by local engineering trade groups might show that a competent mechanical engineer with five years of experience is paid—on average—$45,000 per year.

Of course, *average pay* is around the middle of the

Rewarding performance in a changing environment

A formula for determining market rate

reported pay range. There will be engineers paid above and below the reported average. While there are many reasons why individual workers fall where they do in the pay spectrum, the most common distinction is experience. A less experienced engineer usually will be paid less than the market rate; a more experienced engineer usually will be paid more.

A caveat: Experience does not always correspond exactly with age. A younger employee can have worked with more focus and intensity—and therefore had more experience—than an older one.

The process of establishing a market rate is more consistent—if only within a single company—than relying on the broad ranges usually drawn from a company's internal employment experience. It also requires more work. The most common formula for determining a market rate is to compare three numbers:

- an average of salaries offered by comparable companies for comparable jobs, based on job postings (or classified ads) taken from random dates during the previous three months;

- pay scales, bands or averages compiled by the closest relevant trade organization or a recognized employment service or compensation consulting firm;

- random phone interviews with other comparable companies in the local area.

Even though gathering this data is a lot of work— many employers hire a contract consultant to do the research—it's well worth the effort. A market rate sets pay based on supply and demand of the regional and industry labor pool. It assures that the wages you offer aren't ever too high or low.

Once a market rate has been established, the development company can determine what level of pay is appropriate for its engineer employee based on performance, skill and tenure.

The development company looking for the engineer could begin by budgeting $45,000—whatever combination of fixed and variable pay that might entail. Offering the market rate salary, the company should expect to attract applicants from the middle to lower end of the career and experience range.

It's a basic reality of labor markets that employers attract job applicants with skills and experience at or below the level needed. But some employers forget this elementary fact. They cling to the notion that by offering an average salary, they can find diamonds in the rough or young geniuses who haven't yet made their marks. While both scenarios are possible, the more common result is a lot of work interviewing and considering applicants—just to find a competent employee.

If the commercial developer wants to attract a top-performing engineer, it may need to use the average market base pay as a foundation. And it also may need to offer some form of variable pay as an additional incentive.

With market base pay as the basis of a compensation package, salaries can increase based on both market rates and performance criteria. Rigid formulas for COLAs and subjective merit raises are eliminated. But top performers don't usually mind this exchange—in fact, they tend to prefer it.

Employees who prefer rigidity and subjectivity in a pay plan are usually looking for two primary characteristics in a job—stability and personal appeal. These things may be appropriate in some circumstances, but they're not what most employers consider the makings of cost-effective performers.

Using a Compensation Committee

Fairness—or, to be more precise, the perception of fairness—is an important issue when establishing market base pay. Once you've determined the market bases, you need to convey what you've found to your people in a way that makes them confident you're right. This is the place where many of the best-intentioned pay plans come undone.

There's no single thing you can do to create the perception of fairness. It requires a consistent management approach rather than specific tricks. Throughout this book, we consider the communications issues that help sustain progressive pay programs. Beyond that, there are some characteristics that usually indicate success.

Fairness—an important issue

Compensation committees play an important role

Employees trust compensation systems that fairly provide uniform treatment. A committee approach to decision making is usually perceived as less biased than an individual issuing edicts.

For these reasons, pay policy should be set by a compensation committee. In most small companies, this committee consists of the president, senior operations manager, controller and sales director. In larger companies, it might also include the human resources director, chief financial officer, middle managers and even rank-and-file employees. The committee either makes policy or recommends policy to the president, who then approves or disapproves of the recommendations.

In some companies, the committee reviews specific performance evaluations, increase recommendations and bonuses. This may be the most controversial role the committee plays but—in the long run—it's not the most important. Broader policy decisions have longer-term impact. The committee should focus carefully on changes in market or job data, keeping the compensation plan current and recommending adjustments in salary ranges.

You should work to keep the committee above local disputes. The strength of a committee within an organization is that it minimizes the effects of end runs, favoritism or bias. By meeting at a regularly scheduled time each month, a compensation committee gives the pay plan a system structure. It also supports whatever plan you end up using, by providing a channel for complaints and appeals. This takes some pressure off of line managers and division heads, who sometimes have to enforce unpopular wage issues.

Finally, a compensation committee can offer you a forum for testing your human resources (HR) management needs. The old rule of thumb is that a company doesn't need an HR manager until it has more than 100 employees. This may or may not be true for you. The ways in which the committee operates can help you make these decisions.

Often, an in-house compensation expert will emerge from a compensation committee. This individual will agree to spearhead change and recommend new ideas more often than others. He or she will stay current on labor trends, compensation administration and employee response.

Many companies grow their HR managers internally. A good communicator with a sense of fairness can be trained in HR by reading, attending seminars and staying current by interacting with peers in other companies or HR professional associations.

Case Study: Universal Studios Hollywood

The following illustration is useful because, in spite of the diversity of jobs and the complexity of the organization involved, the base compensation plan was remarkably simple. The plan can be copied in any organization by following several basic steps. Once a base compensation plan has been put in place, painful decisions involving hiring salaries, annual raises and promotional dollars become more simple. The decision-making process becomes fair and more objective. Having a uniform market base compensation system also allows companies to attract and retain strong individual performers.

Beginning in the 1940s, Universal Studios became one of the focal points of the Hollywood film industry. The busy movie lot in the northern suburbs of Los Angeles was home to hundreds of actors, directors and moguls. As the studio grew during the 1950s and 1960s, its interest as a tourist attraction increased. Tourists visiting Los Angeles would go to Universal Studios to get a behind-the-scenes look at how movies were made—and, possibly, a quick look at a movie star or two.

As a result, Universal Studios Tours Hollywood (USH) expanded into a separate profit center and division within the studio's corporate structure. It grew from a simple tram tour of the back lot into a fully functioning amusement park, which welcomes more than 10 million visitors a year.

During this transformation, MCA Inc.—the studio's corporate parent—made a commitment to expand the amusement park even further. With one eye on archrival Walt Disney Co.'s Disneyland, MCA invested millions in sophisticated rides and attractions. It developed stunt shows based on movies Universal produced. It built rides based on other

A uniform system attracts good workers

movies and television shows, including *Star Trek, King Kong* and *Jurassic Park.*

Historically, the studio tour division had been highly entrepreneurial. USH retained employees because it was an exciting and fast-paced work environment. Personnel problems were solved quickly with little fuss—and unions representing some workers remained cooperative during the rapid growth period.

In 1989, MCA launched Universal Studios Florida to take advantage of a low-cost East Coast location for producing movies, television shows and an amusement park. Many of USH's key executives were promoted and moved to the new location, near Orlando. MCA promoted the president of USH to supervise the operations of both theme parks—and look for other related projects.

An experienced theme park executive was brought in from a competitor to manage USH. The park began to streamline and formalize its internal policies. The new executive team felt strongly that the human resource function was key to running a successful entertainment business. A year after the new president arrived, he initiated a search for a top human resources professional to help design and manage the human resource function of the park.

Megan Barnett was hired away from a major soft drink company to be USH's new vice president of human resources. She was charged with professionalizing the process of hiring, firing and compensating non-union employees in the park. These employees included professionals and managers. (Most of the hourly employees were governed by union contracts.)

Barnett set about developing a strategic plan for human resources. She focused on key needs of the staff, which included succession planning and compensation planning.

The new president wanted to pay at market and to formalize compensation to attract and retain employees. As the theme park business grew steadily, the demand for strong people grew rapidly. Many promising young managers had been promoted to Florida, creating a drain on the West Coast.

The challenge of retaining and paying talented managers was ongoing—the issues became fires that needed to be put out daily. Barnett was constantly analyzing salaries and surveying the marketplace to ensure that USH's pay was competitive.

As individual managers were promoted, each promotion caused more salary questions. Barnett felt a compensation system that set market rates for all jobs would provide a solution to the constant questions.

Creating a market base pay plan for USH would be complex. It would include a variety of diverse professional jobs. Merchandisers ran retail operations that worked like mid-size department stores. Customer service and sales were more like the hotel or travel industries. Managers charged with park operations had jobs comparable to other amusement parks. Producers of stunt shows often came from the film or television industries—and were accustomed to those salaries. The engineering and facilities management were unique.

So, it wasn't such a surprise that complaints about compensation, market pay and salaries paid by competitors flowed into Barnett's office daily. To establish whether a new compensation plan was needed, Barnett and her staff conducted a series of interviews with key executives of all major departments of the organization.

One of their biggest concerns: Whether a traditionally entrepreneurial company could adapt easily to a more formal market pay compensation system.

Barnett met with each executive—starting with the president—and formally asked a series of questions to evaluate the need for change and the need for a market base compensation program. These interviews became a needs analysis to evaluate the need for a program.[2]

During the interviews, it became clear that the USH employees perceived the salary increase process as inconsistent. Once a year, management reviewed the budget, input salary changes and sent that information to the parent corporation. Several months later—usually sometime around March—the budget was approved and raises showed up in pay checks.

---

[2] A sample research questionnaire is found on page 307.

Adapting to a formal pay system

An executive from each department served on the committee

There was very little interaction between the manager and the supervisor and the individual receiving the increase. Some departments were good about scheduling regular, written performance reviews—but there was no consistency company-wide. In fact, many employees received increases in paychecks without even discussing performance with managers. This was a prime opportunity lost.

In general, the squeaky wheel got the financial grease. Employees who complained the loudest or brought in rival job offers got the best raises.

This ran against USH's stated philosophy, which was to pay salaries at market and use incentives to bring total compensation above market. It needed to keep its gate or admission price competitive. So, its philosophy would have to be formalized. A system of checks and balances needed to be developed to ensure consistent treatment and constant market evaluation.

Barnett concluded that a comprehensive market compensation system was the mechanism USH needed. This would guarantee that staff pay remained at or just above market average and that salary dollars were spent as efficiently as possible.

The next question was who would design the plan, write the policy and get the plan approved. Because of the size and complexity of the amusement park, every department wanted to ensure that its particular needs and talents would be considered. No one wanted to be left out of the planning process.

To satisfy these diverse constituencies, Barnett asked one executive from each major department to serve on a newly formed compensation committee. The committee would design and write the compensation policy. She didn't have any trouble getting people involved.

Vice presidents from the engineering, planning, sales, operations, entertainment, accounting, merchandising, food services and human resources departments joined the committee. The vice president of each major department reported to a senior executive. The senior executives would ultimately approve the plan.

By ensuring a vice president from each department

was on the committee, Barnett created an immediate liaison to the decision-makers. Each department participated and had a trusted spokesperson. Using a committee approach also ensured that, by the time the project had been completed, there would be a compensation expert in each department.

Barnett brought in an outside expert in compensation issues to facilitate the planning process. This consultant was able to train and direct the committee's activities. Committee members provided data and coordinated paperwork.

The committee members learned about the steps they would go through to develop a compensation program. They were given an existing compensation policy, examples and forms. The committee was asked to review a sample policy Barnett had written as well as her recommendations for a future policy.

In the first meeting of the compensation committee, Barnett presented an overview of her interviews with USH executives. In this meeting, the basic fundamental phases of development of a compensation plan were discussed with the committee and outlined.

The committee was asked to develop job descriptions in all areas of the company. Members went back to their departments, filled out job questionnaires for all key jobs and brought these back to the committee for review. The job questionnaire[3] was a form employees filled out, raising pointed issues about what they did and how they spent their time.

In order to establish the market value of each position, an external survey needed to be conducted. The survey would match existing internal jobs to outside salary levels.

Because of the variety of the jobs involved, each department was asked to help develop the survey. Each committee member selected four jobs in his or her department that were easily comparable to similar jobs in other companies. These jobs, representing different levels of authority and responsibility, were called benchmark jobs. Their salary lev-

Using the help of an outside expert

---

[3] A sample of this job questionnaire appears on page 241.

53

Jobs were ranked on responsibility, skills and complexity

els would predict the salary levels of other positions in the department.

Once benchmark jobs were selected, a one-paragraph simple job description was developed for each. By focusing on specific duties rather than job titles, the surveys would produce a better representation of true market values. If only titles were matched, results would be less useful—because the content of jobs can differ so widely from company to company.

Each executive then created a list of competing companies in his or her field to survey. The survey would obtain market information from published sources, as well as competitive information direct from the companies surveyed.

The competitive information from specific companies was obtained by phone. Some companies refused to participate—but those companies that did participate were given written results of the survey[4]. To get companies to participate, the survey data was accumulated in a confidential manner through a third-party consultant, so companies were not identified, and the total results were shared with survey participants.

Unique jobs found only at USH could not be matched. Other jobs, while not quite unique, were excluded because of time and budgetary constraints. The jobs that were not surveyed needed to fit in with the jobs that were in an objective way. The committee would then evaluate what pay rates the unsurveyed jobs should have.

The committee decided to rank all their jobs based on responsibility levels, skills and complexity. Once it had done this, the committee could use the survey market data to evaluate the market pay for surrounding unsurveyed jobs.

The method USH chose to evaluate jobs consisted of a numerical rating based on a point system. The committee selected seven factors to rate the importance of jobs. Each factor was given a numerical rating scale of 0 to 100.

The seven factors were a job's required:

- skill

---

[4] A sample of a survey appears on page 215.

- education
- previous experience
- level of responsibility
- effort
- customer interaction
- supervisory responsibilities.

Every position was evaluated[5] and a job list was generated from lowest to highest based on average points assigned by each committee member evaluating the job.

Each job was given a final score based on the averages of all the individual scores assigned to that job by committee members. The averaging minimized the effects of biases that individual members might have.

Once all the jobs were ranked, the committee reviewed the order. Some adjustments were made. Typically, each member only changed positions in his or her own department.

When the committee had agreed on the ranking, jobs were clustered into groups of similar average points. Each cluster became a grade and was assigned a market rate from the survey data. The market rate was the midpoint of the salary range for that grade. The range was defined by adding 20 percent to the market rate for the high end and subtracting 20 percent to establish the low end.

Once the grades and ranges were developed, each member of the committee was given his or her department to review. Members could evaluate how the positions ranked based on the group evaluation and compare actual salaries to the financial ranges.

At this point, each member was asked to make final position adjustments that affected his or her department. Members were required to explain their adjustments and justify the changes that occurred to the committee.

Once every department was approved, the total plan was presented to the committee. There was no actual salary information included in the final information—only job titles, grades and ranges.

---

[5] A sample of evaluation criteria appears on page 251.

Defining the salary range

Adjusting salaries to market

To adjust salaries to market would require an ongoing process. The committee would need to consider complicating issues, such as what would happen if a new job were created, if promotions changed a department's salary average, if market data needed to be updated, etc.

That last point was particularly important. USH needed a process to ensure salaries would stay at market. It also wanted to ensure consistent treatment of staff throughout the year in evaluating salary changes.

The committee developed a set of compensation guidelines or rules to follow in evaluating ongoing pay changes. These guidelines became the company's compensation policy.

As her internal research took place, Barnett called several companies and requested copies of their salary policies. After Barnett reviewed them, she developed a sample policy[6] for the committee to evaluate. She had designed the policy around the existing processes, so it would not require a radical change to the employees.

The committee then reviewed Barnett's draft and made changes.

Once the grades and ranges had been established, the committee analyzed which individual salaries were too low or too high to fit in the range. It evaluated the total cost of bringing all employees to minimum and also developed one-, two- and three-year plans to implement the changes.

Barnett presented the final plan and recommendations to senior executives from USH and its corporate parent. Financials and recommendations for increases for staff who were low in the ranges were included. Each executive received a packet of information to review before the meeting, which included the methodology, survey data, policy, ranges and financial recommendations.

Because vice presidents from each department had been involved in the plan from the beginning, there was little questioning of the results. The plan was approved quickly.

Barnett and the committee then had to design a

---

[6] A copy of a sample policy appears on page 271.

compensation communication process to explain the plan to key managers.

The committee decided to use the compensation plan as a guideline for managers. The communication effort would be directed at key managers first.

Fortunately, there was now a trained expert in each department. The vice president who had been on the committee understood the plan, policy and grades. Each vice president was assigned the task of training the managers in his or her department. The managers then were responsible for putting the plan into effect.

Every non-union employee was given a performance review by his or her supervisor. Based on market information, adjustments were made where employees were below market. The plan was used by supervisors and managers to ensure uniform treatment based on responsibility level, market rates and performance.

An incentive plan then was designed to provide additional rewards when the park met predetermined results. At the end of the process, USH had one complete plan that incorporated all of the complex jobs of the company. By using a variety of survey sources, the company was assured that its jobs were paid at market.

After the plan had been approved, Barnett's boss sent her a dozen long-stemmed roses—a non-cash reward for a job well done.

Conclusion

The foundation of today's incentive pay process is market base pay. The fixed portion of salary or hourly wage paid to an employee is more objective than in the past. Today's base pay is evaluated against what is paid for other similar jobs in the local area and/or industry.

There are six steps to developing a market base pay system.

Step one is **developing a pay philosophy**. This step requires research of past practices, as well as understanding how the company wants to pay employees to reflect market rates. Generally, companies with incentive plans want base pay to reflect

Communicating the plan

Developing a pay plan in six steps

the market—but total compensation to include incentive pay above market levels.

Step two is **establishing a compensation committee** to administer and develop the pay process. The committee acts as the champion of the compensation system and develops policies.

A compensation policy incorporates the pay philosophy and guidelines a company establishes to ensure similar treatment and consistence in salary administration. Generally, the policy is developed and controlled by a compensation committee.

Committees use a team approach to evaluate salaries to ensure fairness and also to ensure all areas of a company are represented. A team approach also is perceived by employees as having more legitimacy and less favoritism.

Step three is **conducting a market survey**. Base pay is established by market surveys. These surveys are conducted by the compensation committee and compared with internal salaries. Salaries are then increased, if necessary, based on market analysis and incumbent performance using uniform guidelines.

Step four is **evaluating the survey data** against internal jobs. In some companies, grades and ranges are developed to provide a framework to evaluate individual pay levels.

Step five is **adjusting salaries** that are significantly over or under the market. Salaries under the market are increased based on skill and performance levels of incumbents. Sometimes this process takes two to three years. Salaries that are over the market are increased very slowly—if at all—and strong performers are given lump-sum payouts until the market catches up to the internal salary levels.

One-time, lump sum payouts avoid the compounding effect of salary increases.

Step six is **communicating the plan**. There is a constant ongoing communication process necessary to explain philosophy, policy and procedure concerning the pay process. The communication takes place in company meetings, new hire orientation and supervisory training. Companies communicate little or all of the policy, depending on their culture, employee attitudes and competitive concerns.

The market base process is the foundation of an incentive program. The incentive must be set on a framework of base pay that is competitive and incorporates the company's pay philosophies. Market surveys help the pay process become less subjective and more related to business pricing strategy.

Controlling fixed salary costs through market base pay allows the employer to price products and services competitively, and also sets a base for incentive compensation to be paid when expected results are achieved. The employee makes more if the company succeeds; the company can succeed more effectively if fixed costs are competitive.

To attract and retain strong employees, a company should pay at market.

The work needed to design a market base compensation plan is the same work you do when evaluating the purchase of capital equipment. Most people don't buy capital equipment until they've surveyed the marketplace, considered alternatives, evaluated features and prices, and clarified company needs. You should take this kind of approach when you buy labor.

Labor costs are the single largest line item on most company balance sheets. They're worth pricing carefully.

CHAPTER 4:
DESIGNING A SIMPLE INCENTIVE PLAN

Introduction

Incentive plans can help growing companies stretch their labor costs by keeping base salaries at or near the market and using incentives to enhance the financial needs of every employee, you can support a productive attitude in an organization. As the company grows and succeeds, the employees find that they also are financially rewarded for their effort and contributions.

Informed employees have the ability to influence the sales and profits of an organization. Companies that acknowledge their support and contribution allow employees to have the same sense of ownership as the shareholders. Properly designed incentive programs tie the whole team together and focus on measurable results.

Every company is unique—and no two incentive plans are identical—but it is not necessary to reinvent the wheel each time out. Existing research on plan design in your industry and in your company's local area can be valuable in creating a plan for you. An easy way to start is by asking fellow employers, friends and business associates about incentive plans they have seen or used in the past.

By looking at various plan designs, companies can evaluate what works for them. Keep in mind incentives work best if a market-based pay process ensures base pay for employees is competitive.

If someone suggests a particularly good plan, ask for a copy of the plan document. Most employers save incentive plan information even after they've changed it substantially or moved to a different plan.

Another place to find plan designs is in the library.

The essentials for designing an incentive plan

Look at research material, as well as magazine articles. Trade magazines often have highlights of successful plans listed by industry.

The American Productivity and Quality Center in Houston, Texas is also a great resource for plan design. It has an extensive library of plans and can provide companies with copies through its service center. Other states have productivity centers that are helpful in researching what other companies do for reward systems.

Seven Basic Steps

By following seven basic steps, companies can design and communicate simple incentive plans that enhance performance and profitability. The seven steps are:

1) Identifying goals and pay philosophy. Companies need to identify clearly what significant accomplishments need to be achieved by employees in order to receive a reward. They also need to be clear on what levels they want to pay employees and how their pay compares to the marketplace.

2) Doing research. In any successful plan design, companies spend money researching what plan designs are available in the marketplace, how those designs relate to their business, what the marketplace and competitors are doing and how the marketplace and competitors are incentivizing employees. Just as companies spend time researching the purchase of an expensive asset, the research step is key to developing a quality plan design.

3) Working backward. Looking at key thresholds[1] and return to the shareholders is also important in designing a successful plan. This will protect the company and shareholders from moving cash if the minimum levels of performance are not obtained.

4) Designing a plan. Once the research is done and thresholds are clear, designing a plan is quite simple. Strategic advantage, as well as employee understanding, are key to de-

---

[1] A plan's threshold is the percent of profit or the revenue figure at which the company begins paying out incentives.

sign at this stage. Answering the simple questions outlined in this chapter can provide an excellent road map to finalizing plan design.

5) Using financial analysis. Once the design has been flushed out, financial analysis, and using *what-if* scenarios can provide additional refinement of plan design and threshold levels.

6) Reviewing for improvement. Once the plan is designed, looking at it from different perspectives can help to refine and improve the design. Brainstorming and review by others is an important step in this total process.

7) Mastering communication. The rollout of a plan and the communication of a plan are very important. How a plan is explained to employees—and the training process—can greatly enhance performance and efficiency.

Using Financials as a Standard

Common business goals, such as profitability and sales growth, can be measured in ratios, exact dollars, percentages and product units. The normal language of the business, communication levels of the organization and sophistication of the employee group are all factors that influence how a goal should be measured.

When designing the plan, keep in mind the strategic advantage of the firm. If flexibility and speed are advantages, you want to be sure to reward the behavior that will lead to these.

Financial ratios often are used to measure success in compensation plans. Some companies use a ratio of expense to sales to indicate profit. Others use labor cost to sales or expense to sales ratios for incentive goals.

One of the most important questions to ask in designing an incentive plan is: What do the stockholders need as a fair return on their investment and risk? The design plan depends on the financial resources that are available. Does the company need

Measuring goals with financials

Obtain annual information on your competitors

cash for research? Does it need to fund new marketing material? What are the anticipated future cash needs of the company? What kind of return is necessary to keep funding operations?

One of the first steps of plan design is establishing the line of investor return. No incentive plan can be established without a clear understanding of return on investment. All stakeholders—owners, management, employees—need to get a return for their investment. A return can determine how an incentive plan can be funded.

Various industries have different profit margins. For example, a distribution company generally has a very low profit margin, and a manufacturing company usually has a higher profit margin. It's usually necessary to determine what average return should be expected and is normal for a company in the same industry—and what results are necessary before the additional payout to staff members can occur.

To understand how your company does against the market, obtain the annual reports of your public competitors. If there are no public competitors, trade association or industry research can provide information on your market. If you have a unique market niche, simulate expected returns by a comparison to the closest match in the market that has published returns.

For example, a well-known public chain of specialty retail stores was showing very little profit. Although most chains in the industry showed a profit of 4-5 percent of sales, this company only produced 1-2 percent of sales yearly.

The company had an incentive plan that paid out 10 percent of profits from the first dollar as a bonus. The employees were all earning a bonus, but the company was not doing well in the marketplace when compared to competitors.

When the incentive plan was changed to share the profits over 4 percent, the company began to improve its profit margins. This change involved communication and training at all levels to explain the new company goals and how they were tied to beating the competition in the same industry.

The design of the plan also can be determined by the financials. In this scenario, the plan is finalized by the financial spreadsheets that work backward from the thresholds to simulate what the plan would pay out and cost the company if various business models are used.

Testing Your Theory

Once the basic concepts of the plan are determined, it is time to run some *what-if* scenarios. The most critical first step is to simulate the sales, costs and profitability of the company for the year of the plan. Several different forecasts should be developed that vary the profit and sales. These forecasts are used to determine thresholds and payout pools of cash.

Once the projections are complete, payouts according to the proposed new plan should be calculated. The calculations should be evaluated based on shareholder and employee needs. It also is helpful to calculate bonus payouts if the plan had been in place in the past. By using various payout targets and various company business scenarios, the appropriate targets can be identified.

Once the scenarios have been evaluated, the thresholds and payout targets can be finalized. Normally, a plan should pay out the equivalent of 1 or 2 percent of salary—at the minimum. This adjustment of payout targets is key to fitting the plan into the expectations of the shareholders, the management and the participants.

After finalizing the forecast for the year and the suggested payouts of bonuses, the plan can be conceptualized and tried out on paper. A spreadsheet is developed to allow us to use various bonus scenarios, and we play with the plan design itself until we find a plan that fits into the financial goals and shareholder needs.

Useful financial numbers and ratios from the last five years include long-term growth, profit, percent of cost of sales of each expense line and how those expenses as a percent of sales have varied over the five-year period. When looking at forecasts, evaluate how realistic the goal is. Is the goal achievable based on past performance, and how has labor cost influenced profit?

Determining if the goal is real

Examine plans of the past

Other key financial figures to review are the amounts of any cash bonuses paid in the past. If there was no incentive, but there was a pool of cash for discretionary bonuses in the past, how has that pool changed over five years, and how have the bonuses related to profit and sales growth in the past? Is the new plan consistent with the past payouts?

When evaluating payout levels, keep in mind the payouts of the past. If results are achieved, participants of a plan expect at least to be compensated at the same level as in the past. Plans that are most successful set targets that provide participants with better rewards than they would have gotten under a former plan, given the same or similar circumstances.

The design phase is not over when a draft plan is designed by the compensation committee and approved by you. Explaining the draft plan to other key advisors to adjust and get feedback is a critical step. Showing the plan to key executives can identify flaws in the plan and test the concepts and communication process. If the company has a CPA firm or another outside advisor, their input can also be quite helpful.

This step is important for two reasons:

1) it gives you more input and ideas for the plan, and

2) it allows the other managers to buy into the plan and feel that they have participated in the design phase.

Whenever people feel they have input, they are more receptive to the introduction of a new process. We will talk more about that in the sales incentive design.

Managers will be helping to communicate and reinforce the plan. Obtaining their input early can facilitate design, as well as communication.

If possible, also get the input of supervisors prior to finalizing the plan. They too feel a sense of ownership and pride in knowing about a potential plan before the employees. Requesting their input gives valuable feedback on how well your plan can be understood.

A small precision tooling company developed a spreadsheet on rework to show the employees how much money they were losing on overtime for rework. Management wanted to incentivize workers to do it right the first time. When discussing the plan with supervisors, it was determined that the spreadsheet was too complex for the employees to understand. It was changed to a simple bar chart. The plan was adopted, and the format proved to be much more understandable for the workers.

Issues to Consider

Before you implement a plan—even on a pilot basis—the following questions need to be answered.

How do you measure the goal?

The type of measurement applied to goals is important in plan design. When measuring profit, for example, most companies measure profit before taxes and before bonuses are paid. Some companies use cash to measure profitability; some companies use accrual basis accounting to measure the goals. It is important to clearly understand and measure goals based on the needs of the organization.

Quite often, companies need cash in hand in order to fund incentives. In these cases, goals should be based on cash—rather than on an accrual basis or on sales that have not been paid for.

It is also important to have credible measurement systems. In many companies, the computerized process for measuring sales, profitability or other incentivized goals, such as customer service or shipments, is questionable. Hand inputs and adjustments for various costs and returns can influence computerized numbers. When goals are set, the measurement process has to be clean and efficient. It also has to conform to the ultimate strategic advantage of the company. Employees will not trust an incentive plan based on questionable measurements.

Who will be in the plan? Who will be eligible?

With an alternative reward plan, generally, all employees are in the plan, unless they already have a different incentive. Sales personnel that are on com-

Payout timing is crucial

mission are usually not involved in reward plans. Temporary help, consultants and seasonal workers usually are not included, either. Employees often have to have been on staff for a period of time to become eligible for a reward, as well.

What is the size of award for the participants?

The pay philosophy of the company, market survey data and industry norms are all used in determining how much incentive to pay. Survey data can provide average industry bonuses based on job titles. Information on how bonuses were paid in the past is also useful.

The amount of bonus can be expressed in dollars, percentages of salary or salary mid-points. It also can be expressed in *days of pay*. A plan that pays out 2 percent annually is really paying out one week's pay. To most employees, one week's additional pay sounds better than 2 percent.

If you use percentages of salary, more highly paid employees receive more actual compensation than those who make less. This may be something you want, though most companies try to avoid the perception of preferring higher-ups. These companies often use salary averages to ensure all employees evaluated at the same level are paid the same bonus.

How often will the plan pay out to the participants?

Normally, plans pay out monthly, quarterly or yearly. Payout timing is often based on cash flow and salary levels. Seasonality of sales and profits determines quarterly or yearly payouts. For example, a ski store may lose money all year until Christmas and then make up the loss after Christmas. This company would probably have a yearly payout. A manufacturer that makes a steady monthly profit might have a monthly incentive.

A point to consider: If salaries are at or below market, payouts should be as often as possible.

What are the threshold numbers? What is the point where payout starts?

Some plans pay out at the first dollar of profit, others after some minimum level of return is met. If a plan is designed around a customer service standard—such as shipments made error-free and on time—the threshold can be more difficult to determine. In these cases, you may need to experiment with different thresholds during successive months or quarters.

A caveat: If you suspect you'll need to try different thresholds or standards, make this clear from the beginning. Otherwise, employees may grow impatient with what they perceive as manipulation.

Do employees need to be employed to receive payout? How fast can audited financials be produced?

Most cash plans require employees to be employed to collect a payout. This may lead to a small turnover rate. The timing of the payout is important in plan design.

What is the definition of salary? Does it include overtime? Other incentives?

Companies need to be very careful when they design incentive plans that they define the word "salary" properly. Most companies do not include severance pay or expenses, such as car allowances, in the definition of salary. If a company grants other types of bonuses or management incentives, those cash payouts normally are not included in incentive-pay calculations.

Federal law requires that incentive plans must include overtime hours in salary calculations for hourly workers. Some companies have gotten in trouble with the labor department for setting an incentive plan that requires extra work to pay out, and then eliminating paid overtime. Workers effectively work overtime, but don't put it on their time cards. This kind of manipulation of incentive plans is highly illegal. Most incentive plans include overtime worked as part of the payout process, and the payout is based on a percent of salary, including overtime.

Most definitions of salary do not include other cash types of additional payment. Normally only overtime and straight base salary are included in any kind of definition for plan design purposes.

The company's definition of salary

Testing the plan

Does everyone receive the same incentive, or is reward based on other criteria such as percent of salary or individual effort?

If employees receive a percentage of salary, everyone receives a different amount of money depending on their salary at the time.

When does the payout occur? Who is responsible for the calculations and communication? Who will administer the plan?

Plan communication is critical. Constant reinforcement of plan goals and timely information of activity is necessary. This responsibility needs to be assigned to an individual who has credibility and who can maintain a constant flow of data. The person assigned to communicate also handles procedure or policy issues relating to the plan. A neutral arbitrator is needed when plan designs require clarification.

Who measures performance?

This issue can be a red flag for trouble. The individual who is responsible for the measurement should not be involved in the plan he or she is measuring. Too often, the measurement can be manipulated.

For example, a company might reward the accounts receivable department for improved collections. Everyone in the department performs beyond quota and gets substantial payments from the incentive plan. Then, during a routine outside audit, it's discovered that there were several hundred thousand dollars in a suspense account.

The importance? The collections supervisor had moved uncollected funds into the new account to increase his bonus. By holding back payments or not crediting returns, a financial manager can inflate profitability numbers.

In many cases, it makes sense for an employer to exclude the controller or top financial manager from a plan—to ensure integrity of the underlying data. The financial person also should be incentivized, but by different criteria than the plan as a whole.

Will you pilot the plan?

When designing a plan, the first trial version is normally called a pilot. The pilot is usually tried on a division or a department for several months before determining to use the plan company-wide.

By developing a pilot, the company can test the plan design on a few employees and get feedback to improve the plan.

Does the plan pay out all monies due, or is there a hold back provision?

Some plans pay out partial rewards to participants in anticipation of future goals. For example, an annual plan with yearly goals can be divided into quarterly benchmarks. The plan can have an annual payout that is paid partially, as benchmarks are accomplished—but pays the total bonus after yearly goals have been achieved.

What is the life of the plan?

All plans need *sunsets*, or ends. The end should be announced when the plan is announced. This gives management the ability to adjust or change the plan periodically.

It's good to have a plan in place for one year at a time. It is important to clearly announce that the plan, thresholds and design will change as the business direction and needs of the organization change.

The Central Role of Communication

The communication process is as important as the plan design. Ensuring that employees understand how their behavior relates to an increase in reward is key to improving performance and achieving goals. The more often you announce how a plan is working, the more opportunity the employees have to change their behavior. How you communicate goals also will drive behavior, so it is important to communicate goals in such a way that all employees can identify with the target.

In many cases, companies need to train employees to understand profitability targets and how their behavior can directly impact the goals selected. A *champion* of the plan should be designated by the company. Since communication is ongoing, one individual, with rank and authority, needs to constantly communicate, monitor and announce plan activities. This champion should be an active par-

Discussion is important

ticipant in the application of the plan, ensure new hires understand the plan and constantly reinforce plan objectives.

All managers are responsible for ongoing communication but one manager needs to be responsible for the daily, weekly and monthly updates of the plan, goals and actual performance.

Communication of any type needs to highlight the behavior required to meet the goal. Recognition needs to support the communication of the plan.

Simplicity of design and communication are key. Consider the level of education and sophistication of the employees, then plan communication design for the most basic level employee. Often employees do not read or read at a grade school level. Bar charts, graphs and pictures are helpful in communicating goals and results.

Typically, a plan is introduced by the CEO or owner in an all-company meeting. The plan is usually in written form, and is passed out to the employees. Since the communication is also a training process, the commitment to ongoing communication is very important.

Once introduced, the plan needs to be discussed in department meetings and one-on-one with employees and supervisors.

Once the plan is rolled out, a key communicator—usually the CEO, HR manager or controller—meets with the supervisors and the employees in small groups to ensure that they understand the plan and the types of actions they need to take to meet the goals.

Meet often to discuss goals and results. Monthly meetings are a minimum requirement to facilitate training and establish understanding. Employees need examples of behavior that will result in the goals being met. Successful plans have very significant communication components.

Communication also may take the form of training. Most companies provide ongoing training for employees in their specific work areas. But training employees to understand the direct relationship between their activities and meeting or achieving goals is also important to plan success. The most successful companies provide ongoing training to all employees to constantly improve their efficiency and performance.

Case Study: Midnight Trucking

Midnight Trucking was a transportation company that had carved out a profitable niche for itself. It shipped fabric from the East Coast to the West Coast—and then shipped the finished garments back again to New York. It had more than $20 million in annual sales and employed about 80 people in various U.S. locations.

During the 1980s, deregulation helped Midnight emerge as a leader in shipping partial truckloads. The company grew under the leadership of Donald Green, who had left a life of social work to help his father run the business.

Green was a no-nonsense leader who had vision and a knack for computers. He used his talents to create a successful customer service program that gave Midnight a strategic advantage in the marketplace. But he had a gnawing problem with how he could pay his people.

Despite its success, Midnight was in a very competitive marketplace. The rates it charged customers were what determined its business. In order to keep rates down, the company could not pay market salaries to its employees.

The same federal deregulation that had helped the company gain market share within its niche had caused a steady drop in all trucking rates. As a non-union company, Midnight was in a position to steal business from the unionized carriers that could not adjust their rates quickly because of the costly union staff.

Green felt the secret to growth was in the continuance of low customer rates and excellent customer service. How could he keep good employees and still keep his labor costs down so he could maintain low rates for his customers?

The answer: Keep base salaries low and add an incentive to pay off when business was profitable. An incentive plan for his employees would increase

The keys to measuring results

their pay when the company was successful, but would not cost the company money during the seasonal dips of business. Green knew that additional pay in the form of an incentive could be useful for his company, but he wasn't sure how to begin.

Green's goals were clear. He wanted to grow and gain market share and, at the same time, maintain his profitability. After a return on his investment, he was willing to share some level of the profits with employees.

In designing an incentive, it is important to have the vision of where you want to go clearly in mind. Green had experienced good growth in the past, and expected continued growth in the future. It was logical that his growth would continue and his profit goals were reasonable based on past history.

In most surveys of incentive plans, sales, profit and service goals are the key to measuring results. This said, the key to a properly designed incentive plan is selecting reasonable goals.

Looking at financial information from the past can provide excellent insight. Plans that set goals that cannot be met fail miserably. Successful plans set goals that are within the bounds of past practices and marketplace changes.

When identifying goals, evaluate the annual and monthly financials for several years. Trends also can be used to identify goals. If a company has continued to improve 6 percent per year in sales, the trends indicate it will continue to improve 6 percent in sales. It also is useful to consider published achievement of other companies in setting goals.

Green looked at the strategic advantage of Midnight as a company, too. It was successful because of strong customer service, flexibility in the marketplace and quick response to the changing needs of the customer. In designing an incentive, he wanted to enhance, not detract from, his advantage in the marketplace.

Green identified three short-term business goals :

   1) sales growth of 10 percent per year,

   2) net profit margin of 10 percent, and

   3) improved customer service.

Whatever compensation he chose would need to encourage behavior that would accomplish these goals.

Sales volume was controlled by an outside sales force that worked on straight commission. The employees who participated in the plan would have little ability to influence sales directly. However, they had a lot of direct influence over the other two goals—profit and customer service.

Because his employees could control costs and service, Green wanted a simple measurement of these matters. Profit was selected as a goal for plan design—it would measure cost control. Repeat sales served as a simple measurement of service. Another part of setting business goals included setting up a pay philosophy.

As we've seen, pay philosophy is how a company decides to set up pay for different jobs. Some companies pay below market and some pay above market. The type of industry, competitive needs and supply and demand all enter into determining a pay philosophy.

Midnight decided to pay slightly below market for the experienced employee. Because of deregulation and resultant downsizing in the trucking industry, Midnight could hire experienced staff at several percentage points below market average.

Midnight decided to design a compensation program in which base pay was 5 percent below market rate. They hired a consultant to work with their controller to design a base compensation program. They established benchmark positions and went to the marketplace and obtained survey data to verify the market rates for those positions. Once those market rates were verified, they set up grades and ranges around a plan designed to be 5 percent below the market.

Once the plan was designed, all employee salaries were adjusted to fit into the plan. If any employee was significantly below the market, they were brought up close to 5 percent below the market. If the employee was paid over the market his or her salary was frozen until the market caught up to that pay rate.

Encouraging behavior that will accomplish goals

Researching other transportation companies

Green wanted to pay salaries below market and add cash bonuses tied to performance to bring total pay above market. He knew his company's benefits were below the market and hoped the incentive would offset the lack of benefits. The bonuses needed to have a cash value of at least 2.5 percent to ensure that employees' compensation (at least for those with the lowest wages) would be close to market when the company hit its minimum targeted goals.

Because Midnight was a privately held company, Green did not want to share details of the company's financial performance with his employees.

For Midnight's plan design, Green researched transportation company plans. There were very few companies that had any incentives in the U.S., but several plans had been used for airlines in Canada. The plans used financial ratios to trigger payout. In the plan Green liked best, an operating ratio—sales divided by the total expense of a company—was used to determine profitability. (An operating expense of 95 percent indicates that a company has a 5 percent profit.)

Many of the employees at Midnight were unskilled dock workers who did not speak much English. This meant that plan design and measurements had to be simple. In order for the design to work, profit had to be communicated in an easy-to-understand format.

Green also researched Midnight's competitors and other transportation companies in the local area. The information was useful in evaluating the market and comparing the company's payout levels against competitors' payouts.

When it came to using the financials as a standard, Green decided that he needed at least a 2.5 percent personal return on sales and 2.5 percent cash return to the company to reinvest in new technology and sales. He was willing to share additional returns with the employees. As the returns got larger, he could share more of the profits.

Green discussed these numbers with several people he trusted and concluded they reflected reasonable needs and expectations. He decided that he would share anything over 5 percent profit with his employees. The split of money to employees would be larger if higher profit targets were reached.

In compensation jargon, a profit of 5 percent became the **threshold** of the plan. If the threshold was not achieved, no incentive was paid.

A minimum sales volume required to generate a profit from both a dollar amount and a percentage also was established. Green decided Midnight needed to receive $2 million in sales per month before any payout could occur.

This minimum sales volume became the second threshold of the plan. If the minimum sales volume was not attained, the plan would not pay out.

Thresholds are an important part of plan design. They protect the shareholders from losing any cash if the minimum level of performance is not attained. Plan payout begins after thresholds are met or exceeded. Normally, plans have two thresholds: sales and profit.

Finally, it is important to know how sales are measured for financial effectiveness of a plan. Sales are usually measured by new business booked or sold, items shipped out the door and invoiced to the customer, or sales dollars collected.

In Midnight's case, Green needed current cash to fund the payout of the plan. He decided to define sales as cash received monthly. The sales threshold was a cash-in-the-door number.

Midnight decided to pay out monthly to offset the below-market salaries. For cash flow purposes, sales volume would be money received that month. Using actual money received as sales meant there always would be enough cash to pay the bonuses.

Green knew that the plan would be built around operating ratios of sales (cash received) to profit. He tried various payout levels at various ratios until he found the ones that fit the thresholds. He discovered, by trying various numbers, that at 5 percent profit he could afford to pay out 2 percent of salary to all employees. At this rate, he looked at the cash payout to each employee based on individual salary and determined that the payout would be around $20 at the low end and $100 at the management level.

Green wanted to continue to increase sales without adding staff. Cost control was very important

A monthly payout was best

A cash bonus plan

to his competitive advantage. This is the main reason he took a cue from the Canadian airline plans and paid a percent of the profits based on the company operating ratio.

The incentive plan was rolled out and explained to all employees. The controller, as well as Green, spent time explaining how each employee could improve profitability.

The first few months saw a slight improvement in costs. Occasionally, when temporary help was needed, the employees would pitch in and help to save costs. Simple savings, such as using both sides of a piece of paper and other small economies, occurred that helped push the company into a slightly more profitable position.

The breakthrough occurred six or seven months after the plan was initiated. The dock workers, who had historically been resistant to using a computerized system to evaluate loads and how to pack the trucks for maximum capacity, discovered that if they could put more weight on each truck by packing the crates with better care and more thought, they could eliminate every thirteenth truckload across the United States. This accomplished Green's goal. A major cost savings occurred when trucks were packed with more efficiency, and the company profitability improved dramatically.

This was not the end of the story for Green. He still uses incentives. His fixed labor costs are lower than his competitors', but his employees are all paid at or above the marketplace based on incentives. The company has doubled in size, and the incentive plan has helped contribute to the success of the organization.

Midnight's Bonus Plan

Midnight is proud to introduce the Cash Bonus Plan. This plan provides immediate rewards to the participants for increased productivity involved in assisting the company. Bonuses will be paid monthly if operating ratios are met. If the company operates at a ratio below 95 percent, and a revenue threshold of $2 million is met, the participants will be paid a cash bonus.

The objective of the Cash Bonus Plan is:

1) to improve the company profits and to increase employee compensation.

2) to create interdepartmental cooperation.

3) to provide additional incentive to employees to stay with the company.

How It Works

Each month the company will determine the operating ratio of the total organization. The operating ratio is a trucking industry standard comparison of sales to expenses. If the company, on a monthly basis, reaches an operating ratio level lower than 95 percent and has income of more than $2 million, the participants will share in the profitability of the company. All participating employees will be given a cash bonus based on the attached ratios.

The plan is a monthly cash plan. Those employees who are participants of the plan will be paid out at the end of the following month. The payout will be a check with the effective deductions for taxes taken out. Each month's evaluation of operating ratios will stand alone without carryover from other months.

Who Is Eligible

All regular employees who have been employed at Midnight one full year are eligible to participate in the plan. Employees must be employed at the end of the month in order to participate in the bonus.

Employees who leave the company prior to the payout, but who have completed the total month of service, will be eligible to receive a check. Those employees who complete a year of service during a month will be eligible to participate in the payout for the month in which they have their anniversary.

There are some exclusions based on job responsibilities. Commissioned salespeople, independent contractors, consultants, part-time employees, temporary employees, as well as summer help, will not be eligible to participate in the plan.

Allocation

The allocation formula is a percentage of a participant's monthly base pay, excluding overtime. Each month, the base pay of those employees in the plan will be upgraded if they had an increase or a promotion in that month. If an employee is sick or on vacation during part of the month, he/she still will be eligible for the whole month's payout. All bonuses will be paid out, and appropriate taxes will be deducted.

Rehires are subject to the same criteria as a new hire.

THE COMPANY HAS THE RIGHT TO UPDATE, MODIFY OR TERMINATE THE PLAN AT ANY TIME.

Midnight has created this program to benefit the employees and to assist in the further success of the organization.

Cash Bonus Plan Payout Formula

Participants will be paid out a percentage of their monthly salary based on the following formula:

Operating Ratio	Bonus Percent
95.0 & Above	0.0
94.9	2.0
94.8	2.1
94.7	2.2
94.6	2.3
94.5	2.4
94.4	2.5
93.9	3.0
93.5	3.4
92.9	4.0
92.5	4.4

Example: If the company has revenues of more than $2 million and operates at a ratio of 92.5, all participants would receive 4.4 percent additional monthly salary. If a participant's salary was $1,500 per month, he or she would receive $66 in bonus payout, less taxes.

A Second Case Study

ABC Custom Products is a small manufacturing company that manufactures injection-molded parts. All but two employees work in the factory. The owner wants an incentive plan that will help reduce errors and improve attendance. He's willing to incentivize his workers to produce higher-quality goods.

The ABC Custom Products plan is designed to protect the company with monthly minimum profit thresholds and quarterly minimum thresholds.

Midnight's plan was designed to pay out monthly; ABC Custom Products' plan was designed to pay out quarterly. Because of the cash flow of the manufacturing company and the timing of rejects and returns, a quarterly payout was more advantageous to protect the company from fluctuating sales and profit levels.

As you can see by this plan design, the owner has specific needs in mind. There are certain behaviors that he wants to drive using this plan. Attendance and quality are key issues. He followed the same steps we discussed earlier to design his plan, which is significantly different from Green's plan at Midight Trucking.

ABC Custom Products Ltd.

Bonus Program

Basic Outline

- Bonus pool based on monthly profit
- Bonus to be paid out quarterly through payroll
- Monthly minimum profit is $20,000.
- Quarterly minimum profit is $60,000.
- If monthly minimum is met, between 5 percent and 8 percent of profit amount will be put into bonus pool.
- If quarterly minimum is met, bonus pool will be decreased by company deductions (if any).

Using attendance as a key issue

- Adjusted bonus pool will be divided between all eligible employees quarterly.

- Each employee's bonus will be decreased by individual deductions (if any).

Company Deductions

- Rejects equal to greater than .5 percent of sales but less than 1 percent of sales: 25 percent deduction

- Rejects equal to 1 percent or more of sales: 50 percent deduction

Individual Deductions

- One unexcused absence: 25 percent deduction

- Two or more unexcused absences: 100 percent deduction

- Write-up—includes any rule violation and first report of injury: 25 percent deduction per write-up

- Quality—inferior-quality parts shipped or not shipped: deduction will be determined by the Material Review Board on a case-by-case basis.

Eligibility Requirements

- New hires must be employed as of the first day of the quarter to be eligible for a bonus for that quarter.

- Part-time employees must average 80 hours per month in the quarter to be eligible for 50 percent of the bonus for that quarter.

- Participants must be employed when bonus is paid out.

This program will be reviewed occasionally and is subject to change.

This is a simple plan designed by a company that wanted to drive quality. The owner designed a plan not only to pay out a percentage of the profit, but also to deduct payouts if rejects or attendance were involved.

Because ABC had few employees, it wanted to encourage good attendance. The first quarter that the plan was in place, the attendance remained as problematic as it had always been. There was no appreciable change. Once the payout occurred—and people who had poor attendance got smaller checks—attendance improved dramatically. The second quarter payout showed a 50-percent improvement in attendance. The quality of work improved in time, and rejects dropped to an insignificant level.

This bonus plan was divided into simple objectives, with deductions for individual and company problems, and everyone got the same amount of money.

In some plans, attendance is an add-on instead of a deduction; these plans pay out additional awards for achievement of attendance goals.

Companies need to look at the components of any compensation or benefit plan design to see who benefits. In a normal sick-pay program, an employee's pay is continued when he or she is unable to work for reasons of illness or emergency. Thus, the employee who is off work benefits from the plan. Surprisingly, few employers look at how to provide a benefit for an employee who has perfect attendance. A simple award program can solve this problem easily.

In many companies, attendance is an incentive process. Smart companies have developed an incentive bonus plan for attendance that pays out unused but earned vacation at full salary around the Christmas season. This allows employees who have good attendance to benefit from an attendance policy, as well as the employees that miss work due to family emergency or illness.

Incentive Design Questionnaire[2]

A design questionnaire is useful to begin the thinking process. Key executives or decision-makers should answer questions independently and

***

[2] An extensive questionnaire can be found on page 225.

then share their answers. By obtaining a variety of independent answers, more synergy is created—and there is more clarity on the strategic advantages of the firm.

Once the goals of the plan and the reward are established, research can begin.

1) How do you measure the goal?

2) Who will be in the plan?

3) What is the size of the award for participants?

4) How often will the plan pay out to the participants?

5) What are the threshold numbers?

6) Do employees need to be employed to receive payout?

7) What is the definition of salary?

8) Does everyone receive the same incentive?

9) When does the payout occur?

10) Who is responsible for the calculations and communications?

11) Who measures performance?

12) Will you pilot the plan?

13) Does the plan pay out all monies due, or is there a hold-back provision?

14) What is the life of the plan?

Conclusion

In this chapter, we have looked at two simple incentive programs. Both benefit all the employees of the company and are designed to focus behavior and efforts on a common goal. Midnight Trucking's incentive plan focused on cost saving through operating ratios. ABC Custom Products' plan focused on improved profits through improved quality, decreased rejects and better attendance.

Both plans are designed to benefit all employees and ensure cooperation as a team, and are predetermined and measured and pay for results. The incentive pay is determined based on the results achieved, and communication is constant and on-going.

Following the simple steps outlined in this chapter, you—or your management working as a committee—can design and implement a pilot program for your company.

The key to an effective alternative reward is to identify the goals of the organization that are strategic to the business. Goals must be measurable, clear and understandable to the employees. The goals also must complement the strategic advantage of the company. In addition, goals should ensure that employee behavior that leads to excellence in customer service is not minimized by plan design.

Once the goals are identified, a company needs to put energy and time into researching the information necessary to ensure that the design is effective. That research includes understanding how competitors pay, industry norms and reviewing the plan designs of other companies to incorporate the best ideas into the plan design process. Research can include formal surveys, industry comparisons and the simple process of talking to other employees and managers who have been involved in effective incentive plans in the past.

Once a company has completed the review of its goals and research, stakeholder considerations should be incorporated into the plan design. Return on investment is critical in setting thresholds and establishing minimum reward payouts. Working backward involves looking at the cash needed to continue effective operations, as well as to meet the future needs of marketing and research for an ongoing organization.

When looking at the financials, keep in mind the cash flow of the company, as well as the type of industry. The critical issues and needs of a company also can be taken into consideration in plan design.

The next step is to draft the actual plan design.

Once the design has been established, future financial scenarios must be developed to establish what would happen if the plan were in place and how much the plan would pay out based on vari-

Research is important

ous scenarios. Care should be taken at this stage to evaluate what payouts would have been received by employees if the plan had been in place in the past.

Once the financial scenarios have been tested, the plan needs to be reviewed for improvement. The draft plan should be shown to key contributors—as well as to any interested parties, such as boards, advisory boards and CPA firms—to gather opinions. Input from various individuals can be helpful in tweaking a plan in the design phase and making it more complementary to a business's objectives.

The final step and—probably the most important—is the communication and rollout of the plan to the employees.

Communication needs to be ongoing, so that employees are informed about targets and about results. Effective plans have a critical component of review incorporated into the design and the methodology of communication.

Results should be celebrated as goals are achieved. All employees can contribute to the success of the type of plans that were described in this chapter. Celebrating victory and recognizing employee contributions are key to empowering employees through these plans.

Successful reward plans follow basic steps and ultimately improve the understanding of everyone in the company. By using an incentive plan to alter behavior, companies have significantly better results than their marketplace competitors.

Chapter 5:
Non-Cash Rewards
and Recognition

Introduction

While cash is the most important aspect of any compensation plan, it isn't the only aspect. Rewards for results do not always show up in a paycheck.

There are no standard rewards that work all the time for all groups of employees. Diversity of employees, age and interests make each employee population unique. Frankly, money means more to some groups than others. As a progressive employer, you face the challenge of identifying your employees' needs—and experimenting with the kinds of compensation that works best for each.

Special acknowledgment and recognition can be meaningful to employees. Praise doesn't cost much—and it goes a long way toward celebrating the behavior that contributes to outstanding performance. Acknowledging extra effort in customer service or praising special accomplishments in front of a team reinforces productive behavior.

Companies that are successful in today's marketplace take full advantage of all types of rewards. Recognition in the form of employee awards, safety programs, letters of accomplishment and gifts goes a long way toward benefiting the employee and allowing the company some cash flexibility.

Every company's goals and strategies are particular to its industry, market share, financial condition and philosophy. However, the mechanics of non-cash rewards are similar in many companies. Companies that want to empower employees and improve teamwork use one of several recurring programs to focus employee interest and energy on improving the company—and improving the individuals.

Using rewards other than cash

Non-cash incentives can provide variety and support for a company's goals and results. Using rewards of recognition, services and products can support team development and business strategy. Recognition highlights the effort of those employees who behave in ways that enhance the strategic advantage and goals of the organization.

Most importantly: Non-cash rewards also can complement cash incentives and other forms of compensation.

This chapter highlights two unique plans that were developed without cash. We also discuss time off, recognition and service plans, as well as information on focus groups and how you can facilitate a meeting to get employee input. We will examine two examples of incentive programs that provide non-cash rewards—and then give you some examples of recognition and other types of benefit programs that could be helpful in your organization.

Case Study: Comco Inc.

In the 1960s, a manufacturer's representative made a decent living selling specialized machines and manufacturing tools. After a few years, the representative saw the need for a new product in his market. He found two partners—one who managed engineering and one, the rep's son, who managed operations.

Together, they designed and built small machines that deburred and cleaned industrial products and museum artifacts. Comco was started in 1968 to manufacture the machines and distribute them through representatives worldwide. The machines developed into the hand-held *micro blasters* used in many industrial and electronic applications.

In 1985, the father retired to do part-time research and development. His son, Neil Weightman, took over the business.

Weightman had worked for Comco in operations and sales for more than 20 years when he took over as CEO. He knew the business well and saw potential for growth. He was determined to run Comco according to a basic, yet strict, code of principles—and to treat his employees like family.

Weightman had been instrumental in developing more product. He diversified the product line and computerized the mechanical processes.

As the sales grew, Weightman wanted to create a feeling that profit came from results, and he wanted employees to see a direct reward for their efforts. Since he needed cash to grow the business, he had to create an incentive that would be non-cash, but would motivate his team.

Drawing from a variety of sources, Weightman came up with the following plan.

At the beginning of the fiscal year, Comco announced an aggressive sales plan. Weightman called an all-company meeting and outlined the monthly and annual sales goals. He projected sales growth based on backlogs, historic sales and best estimates. His figures were a stretch, but they were clearly stated and understandable. So, they had credibility with his employees.

The goals were posted in the lunch room, where everyone could see them. Goals were tracked every day against that day's actuals. If the company made its monthly goals, Weightman promised to provide homemade pizza for lunch to celebrate. If the company made its annual goal, he promised to take employees—and spouses or guests—on an all-expense-paid trip to Las Vegas.

Employee reaction was mixed: Some were excited and some were skeptical. The goals seemed high.

Comco had some 35 employees from all ethnic backgrounds. There were engineers and a few professionals but, for the most part, employees were assembly workers and customer service personnel.

Although most were only high school educated, they all understood Neil's explanation of sales goals and how each could contribute to achieving them.

The first month the sales goals were met, Weightman served pizzas and the whole company celebrated. Weightman thanked the staff and singled out key performers. He encouraged everyone to participate in improving sales.

Employee reaction began to change. They were getting into the sales goal push. Customer service could

Goals were posted and tracked every day

Increasing speed while maintaining quality

sell more during each call in to the company. Manufacturing needed to increase speed but maintain quality. Shipping could pack faster—getting more product out correctly was the key.

By the fourth month, everyone was working as a team. They enjoyed their once-a-month team meeting with pizza. The sales numbers grew and the mood of the company lightened. By the eleventh month of the program, Comco was already close to the annual projection.

One Monday morning, Weightman arrived at his office—as usual, at 7:00 a.m.—and found a yellow Post-It on his door. Shipping announced they had hit the annual sales target. A young shipping clerk knew the company had hit the sales target before the accounting department had tallied the numbers. That was a sure sign that the program had worked.

When the achievement was announced company-wide, there was loud celebration. Everyone began to discuss how they would enjoy their long weekend vacation.

A few weeks later, after the fiscal year had ended, Weightman closed the company early on Friday. He and his wife, his staff and assorted husbands, wives and guests piled into two chartered buses and headed for Las Vegas.

Weightman had planned everything ahead. He wanted the opportunity to get together over the weekend, while allowing time for everyone to do his or her own thing. Taking advantage of group discounts and package deals, he had hotel rooms, dinners, free gambling chips and a show ready for the group. He took time during the weekend to identify specific contributions and recognize efforts that contributed to Comco's success.

When on their own, his employees still ran into each other—and there was an air of celebration.

Weightman had created a successful bonus plan that was cost-effective. When his sales goals were exceeded, he was able to do more than just charter a bus and rent a bloc of rooms. He funded Comco's 401(k) plan with a portion of the increased profit.

Although Comco's employees received no cash di-

90

rectly, they did have a small vacation they might not have been able to afford. Building an event around company goals encouraged employees to work together for an easily identifiable common cause.

By including spouses, Weightman furthered his concept of family atmosphere and made the experience even more memorable. He created a sense of community with the trip, which complemented his commitment to team effort.

Case Study: Cal Swiss

Cal Swiss was a small precision manufacturer of metal parts based in Southern California. It had been founded in the 1940s by two Swiss instrument makers. Tom Martin, the CEO, directly supervised sales and operations. He also negotiated purchases.

The strategic advantage of the company was its ability to produce small machined parts with very tight tolerances. Its quality standards were well known, and the company had repeat business from most customers. It had an excellent reputation in the marketplace.

However, Cal Swiss had grown dependent on the aerospace industry—and was scrambling to diversify after the military downsizing of the late 1980s.

The diversification was making headway. A move into medical and dental instruments was generating growing sales.

Martin had cut administrative expenses to the bone during his lean years. He hadn't given raises in the years that Cal Swiss wasn't making money. Still, the highly skilled tool makers—who, despite the downturn, could have found work elsewhere—had stayed with him.

To reward this loyalty, Martin wanted to do something to improve their income. But it was too early to tell whether the new markets would continue to grow and turn profitable. Despite all this, Martin believed that an incentive plan could reward his staff without increasing the monthly fixed payroll costs of the firm.

Martin identified two big problems—rework and

Rewarding staff without an increase in payroll

Lowering rework as a goal

returns—that drove up his cost of goods sold. During the last two years, the company's rework labor hours had increased dramatically—from 50 hours to 200 hours per month. These hours were usually logged as overtime. Martin worried that a few employees were creating rework to supplement their incomes.

He also was concerned about returns. Once parts were sent out, they occasionally were rejected by his customers and sent back. This created more rework, but it also eroded the company's reputation for quality. Historically, the returns averaged less than 3 percent of sales—but that number was tracking higher.

He knew if he could lower the rework and return numbers, his labor costs would go down. To further analyze the problem, he reviewed all major jobs completed in the previous year. He identified certain machines and operators that had consistent errors and overtime. He posted this information on the shop floor.

Martin felt the posting—rather than creating morale problems—alerted employees of his intention to monitor rework.

This would protect Cal Swiss from downside risk. But what about lost opportunities? After four years of no raises, morale was certainly dropping. This would eventually take a toll on productivity—if it hadn't already. Martin hoped that an incentive plan would help to show the employees he was willing to share whatever profits the company could generate.

Cal Swiss's key business goals were sales increase, labor cost control and profit. Each of these goals was measurable and clear. However, Martin didn't want to share the company financials with the staff, so another method of measuring would be necessary.

Martin didn't spend much time researching other companies. He decided early on that he wanted to design his own plan. He also knew he wanted two people he trusted—his controller and his wife, who worked with him in the business—to evaluate the plan and help with the design.

Martin started the process by creating a hypothetical plan. This way, he was able to identify the important issues. What would it look like? Who would be included? What would the results accomplish? Once he'd considered these issues, Martin was ready to implement the real plan.

Clearly, rework was the major problem. Martin felt that a goal of fewer than 35 hours of rework a month was reasonable. The company had achieved those numbers—but it had been several years in the past.

Martin decided he could incentivize rework numbers right away. He told the employees that a pizza lunch would be provided on the month that the company logged fewer than 50 hours of rework. This was a positive reinforcement to balance the negative reinforcement of the posted problems.

The next positive reinforcement: Martin added a $25 grocery certificate to the mix. This would be awarded, in addition to the pizza lunch, to all employees when the company hit fewer than 40 hours of rework a month. And he offered to increase the certificate to $50 the first month the company hit fewer than 35 hours of rework.

The grocery certificates cost Cal Swiss only a couple thousand dollars a month. The employees would have a small increase in their buying power—but the company wouldn't have to absorb the compounding effect of increased payroll expense.

To communicate the plan to the employees, Martin met with employee supervisors first and then with employee groups. A series of simple bar charts were used to articulate the goals and track progress.

Within the first year of the plan, Cal Swiss had resolved its rework problems.

The Theory Behind Non-Cash Incentives

People work at jobs—and plan careers—for multiple reasons. The need to make a living is certainly chief among these. But there are other, less direct motivations that often determine what kind of work a person does or the company for which a person works. Chief among these is status.

Status can be difficult to define and predict. It's a concept that eternally bedevils sociologists and

Simple acts send signals on performance

anthropologists. For our purposes, it may suffice to say that status is the social position a job bestows on the person who takes it. This can be the social position a person has outside of work. But—more importantly—it also can be the position a person has at work.

It has always been true that people define themselves by the work they do and the recognition their coworkers give them. This is more true than ever as the Baby Boom generation dominates the workforce. Many Baby Boomers complain that work is the most stable factor in their lives. This kind of affirmation can be a major management advantage.

Each business or business unit division can be thought of as a small community. The employees are members of that community. They relate to one another on a more personal level than most people—even the employees themselves—often realize.

Recognition rituals and ceremonies may arise whether you, as the employer, are involved or not. So, it's a good idea to get involved and make sure the recognition rituals reinforce productivity.

Actually, the term *ritual* sounds more academic and heavy-handed than it needs to. These rituals are simple things—people eating lunch together in the kitchen or cafeteria, doughnuts and coffee in the morning or even the simple act of a manager handing out paychecks.

Even though the acts themselves are simple, the effects are serious. Companies send signals to employees in the manner in which they handle commonplace events. Recognition programs take advantage of these commonplace opportunities.

Recognition of performance is a significant, positive influence on behavior. Done well, it acknowledges productivity, efficiency and creativity and sends the message to employees that these things are important.

And—despite the cynicism that some people feel about these things—letters from a supervisor, plaques of achievement and certificates of accomplishment are important to employees. The objective is to reward behaviors that exemplify the values of an organization.

The rest of this chapter will focus on recognition programs that identify and encourage behavior that improves efficiency, service and excellence.

Employee of the Month

This is one of the common and most basic recognition programs. Like so many common things, it can be done well or badly.

An effective recognition program should be delivered in a timely manner and updated yearly. Often, these are the only awards that recognize good performance. You shouldn't devote all of your managerial effort to developing systems to isolate poor performers. These recognition programs can ensure that the employees who remain loyal and stick with the company are rewarded for their ongoing efforts.

A large nationally known restaurant chain with fast-food restaurants in almost every town in America has a formal Employee of the Month program in all of its branches. Each month, the manager selects an employee to honor—based on compliments by the customers, behavior that exemplifies going the extra mile to satisfy a customer or some other behavior that is directly linked to customer service.

The recognition centers around customer satisfaction and rewards results that improve customer service efforts. The manager has to write a few paragraphs about the employee's result. His written praise is put into a newsletter and distributed to all employees of that branch.

The recognized employee is sent to a photography studio to have a picture taken. One large color photo is given to the restaurant to display on the wall. The employee is given a set of photos as a gift from the restaurant. The employee also is recognized by the manager in a small ceremony in front of his or her peers.

The employee and his or her family have a keepsake that reminds everyone of that recognition. The restaurant displays the photo in a Plexiglas holder on the wall. The holder has a small plaque stating the employee's name and announcing that he or she was Employee of the Month.

An Employee of the Month award can be success-

Employee recognition ensures loyalty

Company products can be used as an incentive

ful only if you have a large number of employees, so you can rotate the award. Many large companies have employee awards that are generated by a committee, founded to identify and reward behavior that exceeds expectations. Typically, the CEO presents the award at an all-company meeting.

This same process can be used to recognize an employee of the quarter or year—or to give out other special rewards. It also can be a random award given when behavior dictates instead of a regular, ongoing basis.

In many companies, the employee of the month also gets the honored parking place, an imprinted shirt or cap, or other recognition gifts. Other employees are reminded constantly of the employee who was recognized and what the behavior was that triggered the award.

Tenure or Years of Service Awards

Many businesses recognize an employee's tenure with the company by giving him or her an anniversary gift. The gift varies based on years of service, with a bigger and better gift for each additional year of employment. Other companies recognize tenure with a thank you card from the CEO, small cash gifts, plaques or company clothing or jewelry.

Company clothing and jewelry can be an especially effective incentive. In Asia, many companies give service pins, rings or other jewelry to employees who reach specified seniority levels. Then, different or additional jewels are added for additional periods of service.

These gifts work well anywhere. In the late 1980s, one mid-size Wall Street investment bank gave watches adorned with its logo to junior level employees who'd worked for the bank for more than a year. Five years later, many of these employees still wore the watches—even after they'd moved on to other banks.

A caveat: Before you begin any formalized process of gift-giving, make sure the gifts you have in mind are appropriate. The interests and tastes of employees vary from company to company and place to place.

You can ask employees what they would value informally, through conversations, or formally, through focus groups.

Conducting a focus group is relatively easy. Select employees that represent a diversity of tenure, departments and opinions. Write a set of 10 to 15 open-ended questions that explore your topic. After explaining that you want help and input, ask the questions. Don't give any input. Just listen and take notes. The employees will do the rest.

Structuring a recognition gift program without doing some homework can be an expensive waste of time. One large computer manufacturing company provided gifts to employees for every five years of work with the company. The employee would receive a catalog and could select from silver, jewelry or crystal gifts. Once selected, the gift would appear three weeks later in the mail.

But the employees didn't appreciate the impersonal process. It defeated the very purpose of a recognition program. The company brought in a compensation consultant who found out—not surprisingly—that employees wanted personal recognition from their supervisors.

Also, your employees may not be interested in silver and crystal. Employees may prefer a useful gift that symbolizes tenure with the company and bestows status. Focus groups often discover that employees want job-related gifts, such as electronic gear and upgraded computers.

Time Off

A recent series of focus groups[1] considering reward and recognition singled out time off as the most valuable non-cash reward. In this hectic, fast-paced environment, employees want more time to spend with their families. Families, hobbies and sports can be enjoyed during extra time off. Most companies budget full salaries, so time off doesn't cost additional dollars. Today's employees want time off with pay to enjoy their families and leisure activities.

A large insurance brokerage set up an incentive plan that rewards all employees with every other Friday off—as long as the sales and profit goals are

---

[1] Jorgensen & Associates performed these tests as part of a compensation plan exercise for a large west coast employer.

The benefit of leaving early

met. The employees are enthusiastic about additional time off, and the company benefits from an incentive program that adds no additional payroll cost. The budgeted expense for the Friday salaries is already in the annual plan.

Generation X wants time off as a reward. Time off for good performance has been an excellent reward process for companies that work late on Fridays, or over the weekend, for many years. San Diego Trust Bank, a network bank with 23 branches, instituted a reward program that allowed the teller with the best balancing record for the month to go home early with pay on a Friday afternoon of her choice the next month. This reward process worked very effectively, did not cost the bank money and provided a real incentive for tellers to balance accurately. Each month, the reward was announced and the proud teller would select the Friday of her choice to leave at lunch. Since the bank was open 'til 7 on Fridays, it was a real treat to leave early. Not only did the teller get to leave early, but that individual got the acknowledgment of the branch and management for having performed the balancing requirements of his/her position effectively.

Many employers use the reward of additional time off instead of raises during periods when profits are slim. Instead of giving employees a raise, for example, they give one Friday off a month. The staff decides which employee takes which Friday. It can be a significant benefit that every employee wants.

Today's employees want to improve their lifestyle and have more leisure time for recreation, hobbies and family. Additional paid time off or unpaid time off is an excellent incentive.

Time off is a cheap way to recognize results. Providing 12 days off with pay each year gives employees the equivalent of a 5 percent increase.

Suggested Improvements

Like Employee of the Month programs, plans that recognize useful suggestions and input are as old as the industrial revolution. Again, the difference between a cliché and an effective program is how the old idea is executed.

To have a good suggestion system, you have to set

up a process to collect and evaluate suggestions. Normally, employees submit their suggestions and get feedback from a committee on the usefulness of the suggestion. The committee is made up of both managers and non-management personnel.

Suggestions can range from process improvements that increase efficiency to marketing slogans or new product ideas. Good ones are implemented to improve the company. Some rewards recognize the efforts of the participation of employees.

Normally, the formal process is rolled out and explained to all employees before the suggestion system is begun. Results are announced periodically in newsletters, handbooks and recognition ceremonies.

A caveat: Nothing is more discouraging to a person than submitting an idea and hearing nothing back. It's important to evaluate and respond to all submissions. A group of managers and employees should be designated to evaluate and respond to every suggestion. To succeed, this program must be continually supported, reinforced and sold.

The rewards for implementing a good idea can range from a small cash token to a significant portion of the yearly cost-efficiency improvement.

Some companies use a so-called *bounty system* that works like a commission. Employees who make useful decisions are given a percentage of the proceeds—costs saved or sales generated—for a limited period of time. This way, employees can receive as much as several thousand dollars for an idea that saves a company significant time or money.

Typically, this kind of reward is given in a ceremony with a speech and letter. Usually, the suggestion speech and reward is given by the CEO or president. A well-administered suggestion program[2] is an important part of a total quality or team-based management system.

Formal Supervisory Recognition

When a large entertainment company had been purchased by a Japanese holding company, the Japanese company had a recognition program avail-

---

[2] A typical suggestion policy appears in Appendix 31, with the forms used to receive and respond to suggestions.

An elaborate award dinner encourages socialization as well as recognition

able to use in the newly purchased division—but it wanted to find out what the employees thought first. Focus groups were conducted throughout the organization.

They discovered the gift was less important than recognition from management.

The employees overwhelmingly asked for recognition from their superiors and top management of the division. They wanted the company to hold luncheons or dinners at which key executives would recognize employees by name, present awards and be more visible with the employee population. They wanted personal recognition from their bosses.

It is interesting to see that, in many cases, employees want interaction with supervisors as much as they want an award itself. How a gift or award is presented is critical to the value of that award.

Supervisory recognition can be a letter in their file, open acknowledgment of accomplishments or a formal award as a part of a recognition ceremony.

Many organizations have annual dinners at year-end, at which executives recognize employee performance. Recognition awards and service awards are given, and spouses and guests participate. This type of dinner encourages friendships and helps facilitate team socialization. All company dinners are fun, as well as educational, so employees can better understand the company's goals and achievements.

One elaborate company award dinner was conducted by Leegin Leather. Leegin manufactures quality leather products and sells to specialty stores nationwide. For several months before the dinner, employees were encouraged in groups, usually departments, to design skits about their accomplishments. An experienced facilitator and script production manager were hired to develop an entire evening of entertainment based on various department skits and presentations.

The presentations were made using video, slides and other creative media, and each department designed and wrote its own small drama. The dramas portrayed the accomplishments of the department and were presented in a large auditorium that had been rented for the evening.

Salespeople were flown in from all over the United States with spouses—and all employees were invited to bring family or guests. The company executives presented the annual profit and sales information to the audience in tuxedos, and the program followed. All employees participated in some activities designed to recognize accomplishments. Once the formal presentation was complete, the employees and their families feasted on an elaborate buffet of shrimp, oysters and other delicacies. The company had a night to remember, the employees enjoyed the excitement of the evening, and the information shared reinforced the culture of the organization.

Keep in mind that the ceremony of a company determines—in part—the social culture and behavior of its employees. By highlighting specific contributions that enhance the productivity and strategic direction of the company, supervisors can go a long way toward supporting the goals of the organization in which they serve.

Education

Tuition reimbursement is a significant non-cash benefit. To establish an effective tuition program can cost a lot of money, though, so many employers shy away from liberal plans.

Of course, a tuition program doesn't have to mean sending your receptionist to Harvard.

Most employers have some sort of educational benefit for employees. Tuition reimbursement usually encourages an employee to take classes that complement his or her job skills[3]. You can agree to reimburse tuition, books and other expenses up to a maximum amount. Many employers cap their programs at $500 or $1,000 a year.

This kind of program can make economic sense for you, as well as for your employees. Employees become more valuable, through their learning experiences, and the employee benefits by learning and developing job skills.

The more highly skilled your workforce, the more important continuing education becomes. Numerous studies by software and engineering associations have established that talented professionals

---

[3] A sample of a reimbursement policy appears on page 299.

A company uses education as a reward

value education greatly. If a company can provide learning experiences for its professional staff, the chances of retaining strong experts is enhanced.

Conversely, bright employees often leave companies because they cannot grow or learn about new areas of their profession. Many technical professionals cite learning opportunity as the main reason that they change employers.

Simulation Science, a software development company in California, uses education as a reward for software and chemical engineers who finish projects on time and within budget.

The program works something like this: Most of the company's engineers want to attend professional conferences, seminars and continuing education classes. The company has developed awards that allow people to attend conferences and have support in writing research papers. As projects are completed within budget and on time, engineers earn paid attendance at conferences.

Top performers are given travel expenses and seminar registration to attend professional symposiums. The only requirements the company makes: Employees have to brief their co-workers on new ideas they pick up at the conferences and be willing to recruit new engineers for the firm. (Engineers attending conferences are encouraged to bring business cards back to the personnel department from those engineers who might be likely candidates for employment.)

So, the company stays current on technology and the engineers earn a right to attend conferences. In some cases, if the project results are above expectations, employees are encouraged to take a spouse or guest with them. The company thus combines work and pleasure—and gives successful engineers the chance to combine a mini-vacation with a learning experience.

Another way to consider continuing education is as training. (The latter may seem less extravagant than the former.) Whatever you call it, this is a standard on which the U.S. trails its global competitors. Japan spends 7 percent of its gross domestic product on training. The United States spends less than 2 percent.

Education is an important benefit that employers can provide to supplement employees' earnings and also contribute to the value of the employee to the organization.

Discount Products and Services

Like grocery scrip, discounts are a cash-equivalent incentive that doesn't have any compounding effect on payroll.

One interesting discount program was developed by Info Systems, a large computer distribution company. It sells computer systems to Fortune 1000 companies. As part of its standard employment package, the company allowed its employees to purchase up to $2,000 of computer products at a discount and on very favorable terms. The company considered the $2,000 a non-interest loan; employees who participated in the program signed a loan agreement. After two years of employment, the loan was forgiven, and the employee could keep the purchased items.

This plan[4] allows the employee to own good computer equipment and the employer to have a staff that actually uses the equipment it sells. The employee also can use the company's purchasing power to receive substantial discounts on any computer or software purchased as part of the program. It is an award program that works very effectively.

Retail employers and manufacturers often discount their products to the employee.

Leegin Leather, which manufactures belts and other apparel accessories, has a sale once a month of all inventory overruns and seconds (the apparel industry term for imperfect but still usable products). Employees are free to buy belts at dramatically discounted prices.

There is a mad scramble at that monthly sale to buy discounted belts for relatives and friends. This way, the employer uses up its surplus belts and the employees can wear the product proudly.

Bank and financial institutions often give discounted loans to their employees. They lower interest rates to help staff members purchase homes and cars with lower out-of-pocket expenses.

---

[4] The form for this process appears on page 293.

Discount products and services don't have an effect on the payroll

103

Structuring discounts

The hospitality and resort industries always have allowed employees to use the facilities at a discounted rate—or for free. Big Bear Mountain and Mammoth Mountain ski resorts attract skilled, highly educated young people with the promise of low-paying jobs—but as much free skiing as they want.

Likewise, many people work for private schools or universities because their tuition and their children's tuition is discounted.

Normally, there are some checks and balances to discounts, to ensure that employees don't take advantage of employers or take merchandise when it is not appropriate.

How you structure discounts should reflect your business and your workforce. Some department stores give discounts of up to 40 percent to employees for any merchandise that they purchase. Depending on the type of retail operation, that discount can be very helpful. These offers recognize the fact that many people who work in retail are second or third incomes in their household. Many times, this income is discretionary—and sometimes these employees will spend most of what they earn without leaving the store.

Food and Meals

Incentive plans quite often use meals in the celebration and recognition process. In the case studies we considered earlier in this chapter, both Comco and Cal Swiss used pizza lunches to encourage staff participation and goal achievements.

Many companies use luncheons, dinners or all-company parties to celebrate achievement of goals or other accomplishments. Basing these events on company performance—rather than external events—reinforces employees' notions of efficiency and productivity.

On the other hand, many companies give employees grocery scrip at holidays as a way of indicating the company's thanks for their contribution during the year. Grocery scrip can be exchanged like cash for groceries and other items and helps to supplement an employee's income.

Some companies still provide turkeys and hams during the holiday season. However, a growing number of employers are moving toward scrip as a replacement for the actual grocery items. Using scrip makes the clear distinction that a reward is given. Base pay is not increased, but a commodity similar to money is given out.

As we saw in the Cal Swiss case study, it is possible to link a grocery scrip award to the achievement of company performance goals. Some employers like scrip awards and use them at holidays and when goals have been achieved. If you have to choose between an award at the holidays and an award linked to company performance, you probably should choose the latter.

Letters and Plaques

Nothing can be more complimentary than a letter of praise. Letters from customers, from key executives and from management can help highlight behavior that is strategic to improving company performance.

Many companies will add letters to a personnel file, post letters on bulletin boards that compliment customer service accomplishments and use letters to recognize and praise performance.

A simple thank you note from the president is as welcome as a more complex certificate.

Plaques of achievement and awards that are visible are another effective means of recognizing goal contribution. These plaques can be purchased from a supplier and engraved for individual recognition.

Plaques and letters are only effective when senior management, owners and presidents really stand behind the process. Recognition by a high official in an organization is as important as a physical trophy, in many cases. In conducting focus groups, we have identified that letters of recognition, plaques and other kinds of recognition symbols are very important to employees if they are very important to management, also. The fact that they are displayed openly—commented on and recognized—is very important to enhancing the usefulness of these types of award programs.

The effectiveness of a "thank you"

Barbecues to build teamwork

Clothing

Many companies provide t-shirts, smocks, or jackets with company logos for their employees to wear.

Infinity Systems, a division of Harman that makes high-end stereo speakers, has T-shirts and polo shirts for all its employees and management. Visitors to the factory usually are greeted by employees proudly wearing the company logo.

Employees are encouraged to wear company shirts whenever they can. Management sets the standard by wearing polo and T-shirts. Every Friday is casual day, and employees usually wear logo items.

If clothing is used as a reward, make sure that there is no discrimination among departments in regard to who gets what kind of or how many items.

Group Activities

Companies use group activities to encourage employees to meet certain goals. Salespeople are given trips, and other awards are used to enhance goal activity. Often companies conduct picnics, dinners or other activities together to enhance the interaction of the group.

Ski trips, weekends at the lake, barbecues and other simple group activities help build teamwork and also provide non-cash incentives.

These types of incentives encourage communication, as well as recognizing achievements. Generally, group activities recognize the achievements of several people, rather than just isolated examples.

Free Benefits

There are many free benefits that can be offered to all employees in any organization. By combining talents and using total company clout, you can offer benefits that might not be available to an individual. Discount coupons to amusement parks, discount coupons to movies and company-wide discounts to various grocery and department stores can help to improve employees' standard of living, and the company doesn't have to pay out any cash.

One of the most important benefits that can be provided to a group—and which is normally free to the employer—is membership in a credit union. The credit union benefits by having immediate access to a group of potential customers. The employer wins because employees will get discount loans and services from an accredited financial institution, and employees obviously win, too.

Safety Awards

Many companies use incentives to drive safety programs. Safety awards can be very helpful in decreasing workers' compensation claims and in decreasing days lost due to industrial accidents.

There are as many types of safety awards as there are incentive plans. One of the more traditional plans is Safety Bingo, in which employees are given bingo numbers for the days on which there are no accidents. They then receive some significant award based on a winning bingo card. The only way to participate is by remaining accident-free.

These awards have been very helpful in focusing employees' efforts and interest in safety-consciousness. The actual awards can run up to thousands of dollars—and some big employers even include cars at the highest levels.

The effect of these awards on worker's compensation costs can be significant. Savings in comp claims or insurance premiums often fund the programs—and more.

Customer Nominations

Customer service is key to most successful operations. The best method to evaluate true service to the customer is to ask that customer.

Many companies conduct customer surveys on a regular basis. These companies usually will include programs that allow customers to recognize the service of outstanding employees.

One such program is Applause, Long Beach Memorial Hospital's method for allowing patients, visitors and volunteers to recognize special care they receive. This program consists of a recognition request and card that is given out to patients and families, as well as displayed in lobbies and in the cafeteria.

Ask customers about the service

Anyone can pick up a card, make a comment and give it to an employee or mail it to the customer service department. Postage for the card is prepaid.

Once received, the acknowledgement is recorded, an award is given to the employee, and the card is retained in the employee's file as evidence of excellent service. The employee is recognized by his peers and supervisor, as well as by the president of the hospital.

Employees Recognizing Other Employees

Norman Howe and Associates is a full-service marketing company that does marketing and advertising for the grocery and drug industry. The company is run with open communication and a value system that requires honesty. It uses a reward system called PADRE.

PADRE stands for *Producing A Desired Result Efficiently*. Its distinguishing feature is that it allows employees to recognize other employees. Employees are encouraged to recognize one another for behavior that is above and beyond the results expected. They must get approval from two supervisors.

Any employee can submit a recommendation[5]. The PADRE awards can range up to $100—and are usually made without disclosing the person who made the nomination. However, if the award is noteworthy, the employee who recommended it is invited to give a presentation in front of all employees at a monthly staff meeting.

In this way, the company is recognizing the behavior that leads to its strategic advantage. The stories and excitement generated by this award process have been synergistic. The employees feel that they are part of the evaluation process and that it is not merely a top-down system.

At Norman Howe, employees are empowered with the same type of compensation input that a manager at another company would have.

Focus Groups

Done well, recognition can be a cost-effective means of incentivizing your workforce. Done badly, it can

---

[5] A copy of the recommendation sheet and the policy appear on page 319.

breed tension—and even resentment—among departments and between staff and managers. The best way to avoid problems is to use a focus group to suggest forms of recognition that will work.

A focus group should be structured as 10 to 15 employees taken from various departments and management levels.

An interesting outcome of employee focus groups is that you learn directly from the employee what reward or acknowledgment is going to be meaningful to him or her.

Start the meeting by explaining there is no expected outcome or action. It is an information-gathering or fact-finding meeting. (This helps alleviate the problem of employees anticipating unwanted change.) Explain that the company wants to develop an understanding of what rewards would be significant to employees.

Say that you understand most employees want additional cash—but this meeting should focus on non-cash awards. It's intended to identify awards, not evaluate them. To ensure everyone contributes, no negative comments should be made. All ideas are accepted. Evaluation will be done later.

Encourage employees to participate (*brainstorm* is the overused buzzword) by asking such questions as:

1) What reward systems in this company are working now? Why?

2) What reward systems in this company are not working and what would you like to see changed?

3) What would you like to see change about the way we reward employees today?

4) If we could design a reward system that was not too costly, what gifts or other items do you think would be appropriate?

5) How do you think employees should be recognized in this company?

6) What recognition awards would be identified as helpful in designing a reward program?

7) Have you had recognition and/or non-cash awards at former companies? How were they designed? Did they work?

8) Any other thoughts on how to recognize and reward employees?

The focus group is designed to get the employees' perceptions so management input should be kept to a minimum. In some cases, you may want to use an outside facilitator—unknown to the participants. Someone should take notes or the meeting should be taped so that all suggestions can be reviewed later. No ideas should be evaluated at the meeting, or the free flow of ideas will be inhibited.

Focus groups are only a starting point for considering forms of non-cash compensation that you might use. However, they also are useful in identifying concepts to avoid.

Conclusion

Recognition is a powerful tool in identifying excellence and setting standards. Using stories and examples helps to clarify expectations and set the tone for future actions. Role models can be identified and copied for improved efficiencies.

Creative companies can identify reward systems that are not necessarily an expense to the organization. Company product, time off and supervisory recognition are key non-cash rewards that can go a long way toward enhancing an employee's work performance.

Focus groups and employee input can be very valuable in determining what type of awards companies should consider. Generally, when conducting focus groups, expense is not the issue. Practicality and usability are more important to today's employee.

Recognition programs tell a story of what type of behavior is acceptable in the organization. Open acknowledgment of successful contribution can help other employees better understand what they need to do to obtain recognition. Stories help develop company culture. Culture builds community. Teamwork is enhanced when people understand the behavior necessary to be successful in an organization. Recognition programs can highlight that behavior and help all employees to better understand the requirements and needs of the company. No company should overlook non-cash rewards as part of its ongoing and overall communication strategy and reward programs.

Employers should not feel that incentive plans cost a great deal of money. Creative ideas and uses of non-cash awards can focus effort and energy on achieving goals and improving performance without a significant increase in labor cost.

Companies traditionally have used non-cash awards to supplement short-term and long-term cash incentive plans.

Group activities, luncheons, dinners and supervisor recognition also can highlight the type of behavior necessary to achieve goals. Non-cash rewards can focus employees' efforts on the direction of improvement. The non-cash awards are a significant way to tell how to be successful in an organization.

Most organizations have non-cash awards. In many organizations, these awards are informal, or have been in place for so long that they have lost their impact. Companies should be diligent about looking at their non-cash award programs and ensuring that they are still viable in today's marketplace. Many companies that adopted creative programs years ago have found that traditional programs don't work with the diverse workforce in today's businesses.

Companies need to identify what employees' non-cash needs are, and what kinds of benefits will drive the behavior necessary to achieve improved profits and sales. By designing non-cash incentive programs and using them to highlight an employee's efforts, companies can celebrate contribution and find variety without burdensome additional labor costs.

The non-cash rewards highlighted in this chapter will lead to an enhanced employee understanding of how they can contribute to a company's strategic business objectives.

CHAPTER 6: TEAM INCENTIVES

Introduction

Early in the history of the United States, families, farmers and military personnel worked in teams. They found greater efficiency in cooperation than they could achieve alone. In these modern, jargon-filled times, this kind of advantage is called *synergy*.

Farmers learned early on—and still understand today—that there is synergy in marketing cooperatives. They would band together to sell crops, rather than take their chances as individual farmers. The co-ops were run by the farmers. By grouping together as a solid team, they were assured of the best price for their crops.

Students in the armed forces' Officer Candidacy School are encouraged to work together as a team. *Cooperate and Graduate* is a common theme. Soldiers must cooperate with each other to survive. The soldier who marches one day is the leader the next. To work effectively, each person must work with the others to ensure the whole unit passes inspection.

Unfortunately, creating teams is not as easy as it might seem. Knowledge, information, power and reward must be shared fairly among members of successful teams. It takes time to work out all four parameters to the entire team's satisfaction.

Teams aren't permanent. New members have to be trained as to how to behave and meet the group's expectations. They are given extensive training and drills, because they have to be trusted with shared power and responsibility.

The rewards of tight coordination are considerable.

Businesses reward individual performance

In the case of the farmers, marketing co-ops give them fair access to markets, at least (as in the case of the Sunkist citrus co-op)—and a highly profitable stranglehold on the market, at most (as in the case of the Sun-Diamond almond co-op).

In the case of the soldiers, the rewards are morale and—in some cases—the difference between life and death.

For years, business in the United States has rewarded individual performance. So has the traditional education system. Individual achievement always has been valued as most effective. Students work for grades and individual recognition. Teachers give special awards, privileges and honors to individuals who learn to excel above others. The students then move into the workplace—where they follow the same instincts for promotions and merit pay.

Intense individual competition may work for your company. If you have the controlling share of a static or shrinking market, you may simply set prices and sell furiously. If you sell commodity products in a marketplace driven solely by price, you may focus on the quick sale.

But, if you're in an expanding business that relies on proprietary technology, information or efficiencies to compete, you need to encourage cooperation. This is where most small, growth-oriented companies find themselves.

The days of individual achievement and top-down management are disappearing in the American workforce. Even great inventors can't be successful unless their processes become repeatable and others can copy them. The success of the individual has been replaced by coordinated team effort.

This chapter will deal with the compensation tools you can use to build teams.

What Teams Really Mean

If you read much management literature, you know the 1980s and 1990s have seen a flood of writing and talking about teams in the workplace. A lot of this is just trendy posturing.

According to *Training* magazine, 45 percent of the

United States workforce belongs to a permanent team, and 82 percent of the United States organizations have formal work teams.

Building teams requires some serious work—on a continuing basis. It also requires something that frightens many business owners: shared decision-making power. But shared power shouldn't be so frightening. In the information-driven marketplace, no single person can contain authority within an organization. You're sharing power with your employees—whether you know it or not.

Realizing this is the case changes many things. For the purposes of this book, we'll concentrate on one: how you pay people to encourage the best aspects of shared power.

Companies have three sources of competitive advantages: people, cash and technology. Most companies rely on people to provide their advantage. Better service, better knowledge and better team processes give one company an advantage over another. Task-focused cooperation—a good working definition of the word *teamwork*—provides the synergy to accomplish that advantage.

Teamwork can drive company efficiency and improve customer service. Effective teams have created competitive advantages for many businesses.

The transition from rewarding individual effort to rewarding team effort began in the 1980s. Such companies as Coca-Cola, Hewlett Packard and General Motors discovered team rewards led to better profits and customer service.

The major drivers that have required business to adapt team structure include global competition, the need to do more with less and the pressure for constant improvement in operating efficiency.

Companies are trying to reinvent themselves. Their change processes put more daily problem solving and performance improvement requirements on the average worker. The average worker recognizes the synergy of group decision making and sharing improvements. Organizations are realizing that workers banding together to accomplish multiple tasks are much more efficient than a workforce that conducts business with isolated members.

Team members need equal access to information

Much like other incentives, each team needs slightly different rewards for its particular characteristics. There is no specific model that fits all teams. Each plan must take into consideration the business climate and goals, team characteristics and individual diversity of tasks.

The Four Major Parameters

The four key parameters that must be present and shared by work teams are knowledge, information, power and rewards. All four must be present to have a productive work team. All four must be shared and—as we've seen in other compensation issues—must be *perceived* as shared.

Research on team incentives[1] shows performance improvements occur when 90 percent or more of the participant members perceive the parameters as equitably received.

Team knowledge is knowledge of the business, the process and the actual duties of workers who will contribute. It includes the communication skills and understanding to work together cooperatively. Most companies facilitate team interaction with formal training to ensure all members have similar knowledge. Much as a coach explains the game to players, you need to give workplace team members knowledge of the business, customer requirements, work function and raw material to successfully contribute as a group.

Team information is information about change, quality, costs, customer satisfaction, timing, competition and results. Team members all need equal access to information. A good team understands the game, but also understands the conditions, its competition and the strengths and weaknesses of its players. Members have to be selfless—knowing that the team scores most reliably when its assets are allocated most efficiently.

Team power is the ability to make changes immediately in work efficiency, materials, flow and process. The ability to make decisions regarding the team—its output and input—can't lie in a single person. Each team member must be able to take action to support team efficiencies when circumstances demand it.

---

[1] Edilberto Montemayor, "A Model for Aligning Teamwork and Pay," *American Compensation Association Journal* (Summer 1994).

A good team works together to win. All players support the action—even the bench players follow the game and cheer. The coach may be the emotional and intellectual leader—but he or she can't control what goes on in the game. The coach has to trust the players to make good decisions.

Team rewards are tied to results—improvements in quality, productivity, growth in capacity and other contributions. They may reflect certain outstanding individual performances, but they are given to the team as a unit and must be equally attainable for all members. They can be cash or non-cash, such as gifts and awards or recognition.

Before designing team incentives, you need to assess whether the first three parameters are available and provided uniformly to team members. Information and knowledge must be shared, or there will be an imbalance within the team structure. If this occurs, the team will become just a smaller hierarchy within a hierarchy.

The team also must have the ability to change the work flow—if only for itself. There must be a process of internal communication that ensures information and knowledge are received in an open, cooperative way in which all team members learn and no one member controls the process. There may be a link person, but that individual must support the team by acting as a conduit, rather than subjectively parceling out news.

Once there is equality of knowledge, information and power, a reward system can be designed to enhance cooperation and provide equal pay for accomplishing results.

Work Teams Pose Some Problems

You have to be careful not to disincentivize employees by excluding them from a reward system designed for a team. Careful consideration must be made in constructing team membership. Teams must include all the employees that work and support a team. Otherwise, resentments can fester.

A large, publicly traded biotech company that manufactured blood products had one work team that was causing a bottleneck in a 1200-person manufacturing plant. The manager of the plant had

Equal pay for accomplishing results

... a potential mutiny on his hands

tried to encourage increased output with this group, because it was causing timing problems for the entire plant. He looked for a way to incentivize the team to improve its output and quality.

He decided to incentivize the team that caused the bottleneck to work faster. He set up a cash bonus program that paid them a monthly award if they improved their output. This eliminated the bottleneck—but caused an uproar in the plant.

The problem was that employees not on the team—but who supported its activities—were angry. They were helping the team meet its goals, but weren't being included in the compensation for doing so.

The team of workers that preassembled components used by the incentivized team was angry because its workload was increasing—with no higher compensation. The shipping and quality-control workers on the receiving side of the line also had more work. They resented the incentivized team for receiving more money, while they got nothing for working harder.

The plant manager quickly saw that he had a potential mutiny on his hands, because he was rewarding one work team without rewarding the other members involved in the work process. Once the reward system was installed, the troubled team—and the whole facility—improved output and quantity significantly.

When considering team-based incentives, you need to make careful analysis of identifying, structuring and rewarding teams. Creating real work teams is difficult and time consuming. Ensuring that the four parameters are all present takes time. Turning a group of individuals into a productive team may cause some slowdowns, as employees adjust from individualistic habits to team dynamics.

From a manager's perspective, the best rule of thumb to use is *the bigger, the better*. If there is a question of who to include, the larger the cooperating team—and subsequent reward-recipient group—the better.

Most companies that use teams start out with total company rewards, and then refine team rewards once the larger group understands and uses measured results for reward payoff.

Types of Teams

Like many business owners, you may be at a loss about how to divide your company into teams that make sense. A department like customer service might work as a single team, while your marketing department might make sense as several—or many—teams.

That's fine. Not all teams look the same. In fact, there are several ways of structuring teams. Michigan State University management professor Edilberto Montemayor, who's done much research on team structure, identifies three fundamental types of teams.[2]

- **Pooled teams**. In these, employees have equivalent roles but do not necessarily relate to each other during their work. Team performance represents the sum of the individual performance. For example, a sales team may work individually—but the total sales effort is the sum of these individual sales. Members may have different territories and customers, but they are doing the same basic job functions. This team functions like a baseball team, where each player has a role that is equivalent to but different than the others.

- **Sequential teams**. In these, employees have roles that relate to each other in some prescribed order. Typically, a manufacturing operation has sequential teams working with input of raw material, assembly and shipping. Team performance is a result of all team members, but the total team result cannot exceed the slowest individual performance. This team functions like a football team, where each player has a different role that leads to scoring effectiveness of the team as a whole, and is dependent on all players' abilities. If one player is weak, then the team is only as good as the weak member.

- **Reciprocal teams**. In these, employees have complementary jobs. Team performance depends on ongoing, back-and-forth coordination of individual efforts. An ex-

One department might make sense as several teams

---

[2] Edilberto Montemayor, "A Model for Aligning Teamwork and Pay,"*American Compensation Association Journal* (Summer 1994).

Identifying team structure

ample of this type of team would be a customer service, sales and job-bidding team. A sale is achieved only if the customer service representative sets up the meeting, sales performs, and the job is bid well and in a timely manner. All areas contribute in different ways to a sale, and information must be coordinated by all three areas for a successful close. This team is similar to a basketball team, where players must take turns fielding the ball in no specific order to achieve a basket.

All three types of teams need equal access to knowledge, information and power. It is important to identify team structure to ensure all real team members are included in the reward process. If the plant manager in the case of the biotech firm we considered earlier had a sequential team, he would not have isolated part of the team from the reward process. Once the structure of the team is identified, then the real team members can be included in the reward design.

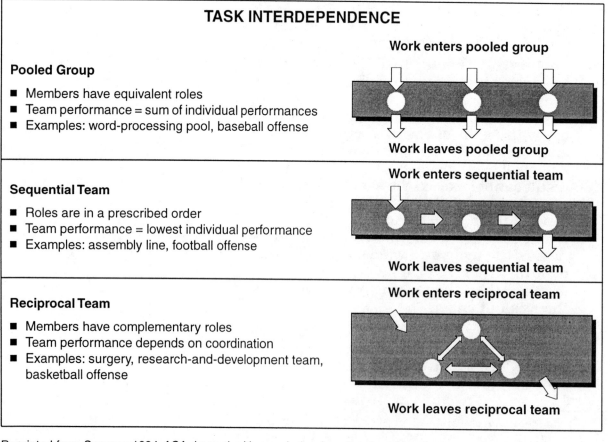

TASK INTERDEPENDENCE

Pooled Group
- Members have equivalent roles
- Team performance = sum of individual performances
- Examples: word-processing pool, baseball offense

Work enters pooled group
Work leaves pooled group

Sequential Team
- Roles are in a prescribed order
- Team performance = lowest individual performance
- Examples: assembly line, football offense

Work enters sequential team
Work leaves sequential team

Reciprocal Team
- Members have complementary roles
- Team performance depends on coordination
- Examples: surgery, research-and-development team, basketball offense

Work enters reciprocal team
Work leaves reciprocal team

Reprinted from Summer 1994 *ACA Journal*, with permission from the American Compensation Association (ACA), 14040 N. Northsight Blvd., Scottsdale, Arizona 85260 U.S.A.; telephone 602/951-9191; fax 602/483-8352.

In all three types of teams, the coordination of information, knowledge, power to act and reward is tied into coordinated success. The goals need to be clear and understood by all members. How each contributes to the whole is also a key point of understanding. The key to using rewards effectively in a team environment is ensuring a link between the team's performance and the payout.

Once again, this comes down to an issue of perception. Employees need to believe that if they perform as a group, the synergy of cooperating and excelling will provide adequate reward for their efforts—and they will be measured fairly and accurately by the organization.

Driving Team Performance

The key to effective team performance is linking effort to payout in such a way that all members cooperate and work to achieve the goal.

Effort —> Performance —> Measured Results —> Bonus Pool —> Payout

To link effort to payout, there must be a clear understanding of how performance can influence results. When dealing with team performance, each team member must recognize what he or she must contribute to affect results.

Knowledge and information, two of the four parameters found in all teams, must support individual and team understanding of the relationship between effort and reward.

Companies that want effective team performance must expend resources to train team members. The training coordinates the communication of knowledge and information to all members.

Knowledge of how performance links to success of the group, and how effort can improve performance, is *key* to the synergy of groups. Group communication of goals, performance and actual results must be timely and ongoing. A team is only as good as its weakest link—so the key to group effectiveness is getting everyone to perform and therefore push the group toward the goals.

The key is linking effort to payout

Goals need to be simple

To drive a team to excellence, you must ensure information and knowledge levels are constantly maintained through the communication and training process.

Effective team rewards demand ongoing, constant, open communication between team members, as well as communication about goals, results and business activities. A team must understand the product or service that is the output, work together to discuss efficiencies and communicate often on forward progress toward goals and results. Communication keeps all team members informed about progress; it also provides clarity on problem solving and customer needs.

In order for a team to be successful, it must function with a clear vision of expected results. All team members need to agree on the vision and results to truly pull together and create synergy. The vision of the team also must correspond to the ultimate vision of the company as a whole.

The plan, process and communication for a team must be understood by all members. Simplicity assures that both the best educated and the least knowledgeable employee understand the concepts, actions and directions of the team. Goals need to be simple to understand and simple to monitor.

Case Study: Sullivan & Curtis

Sullivan & Curtis was an insurance brokerage firm with 200 employees that had undergone some major changes. The firm had been started by three partners. As it grew, clashes over business philosophy caused one of the partners to leave. This had caused the firm to reevaluate both its mission and its values.

The remaining partners wanted to convey a new philosophy to the firm's employees. They wanted more teamwork—to give employees more autonomy in meeting customer needs.

The partners had several communication meetings with employees, but there was normal resistance to change. Although encouraged to be more empowered, employees constantly returned to the old, bureaucratic methods of doing business.

The partners realized that, in order to move forward, the company needed to change its operating style dramatically. They developed a strategic plan to increase sales and operating efficiency.

When the dust settled, the partners laid off several employees in an effort to reorganize and improve efficiency. They retrained clerical employees to support some new business directions. However, after the reorganization, there was an undercurrent of confusion and mistrust in the organization.

In an all-employee meeting, the partners rolled out the strategic goals for the organization: increase sales and profits, increase efficiencies by improving teamwork and improve cooperation between offices. The company would change from a bureaucratic mentality to a more creative, entrepreneurial environment.

The partners wanted to instill their clerical team with a commitment to a higher level of customer service. Each office had clerical teams that administered to client needs. These teams were responsible for the day-to-day maintenance of insurance contracts and follow-up with customer inquiries.

The clerical teams consisted of account representatives, insurance clerks and support staff that assisted in maintaining client files and coordinating information.

Both Sullivan & Curtis offices worked independently. They did not support each other effectively when there was need to interact to service an account. During peak workloads, one account manager might be very busy doing renewals, while the neighboring manager would have a light load. There was little cross-support for busy people who had heavy workloads.

Historically, the company had given all non-sales staff cost of living increases and year-end bonuses. The bonuses were based on effort, as evaluated by the executive management of the company. The employees were never sure how bonuses were calculated. Although the bonuses were tied to profit, individual employees couldn't ever be sure what their number would be.

The partners felt that there could be a more effec-

From a bureaucratic mentality to a creative environment

Employees' salaries were over market average

tive way of compensating employees. They wanted to more closely align the pay structure with the new direction of the firm. The goals of the compensation plan were simple: to encourage commitment to change, teamwork and quality customer service. A committee was formed to design the compensation plan.

The committee consisted of the operations manager and an outside consultant. Occasionally, the chief financial officer would participate. The committee developed ideas for a compensation plan that would complement the new goals of the organization.

The committee reviewed incentive plans from other insurance brokerages and carriers, as well as local organizations that provided reward based on measurable results. It also looked at current pay levels for clerical employees in the insurance business in general.

Next, the committee obtained an insurance industry salary survey that provided average base salaries of all the clerical jobs in the company. The survey was divided regionally, so the specific salary that the local market would pay could be identified. It also obtained current local average salaries by participating in a local salary survey.

Most of Sullivan & Curtis's employees' salaries were over market averages. The company was willing to pay over the market rate for an employee who was more skilled and had a good service tenure. Since the average tenure was several years of employment, the committee was confident the base pay was where it should be for a successful program.

The next step was more difficult. The team of clerical workers was a reciprocal team—each member had a specific job that complemented customer service and the generation of new business. The performance of the team depended on all members, but there was no real order of work. In reviewing other marketplace teams, there was no specific plan used by another company that would fit Sullivan & Curtis. The committee decided to design its own plan.

Based on its surveys of the marketplace, the committee concluded that the cost of living increase was not appropriate. It suggested that, rather than give COLAs, Sullivan & Curtis adopt a philosophy of constant improvement. In order to get a salary increase each year, an employee would have to improve performance in some tangible way.

The committee decided to use the same pool of money Sullivan & Curtis had traditionally reserved for discretionary bonuses to pay measurable bonuses based on results. The strategic plan required strong support of the change processes, continued performance of the daily work with quality and quantity standards, teamwork and improved efficiency.

The committee developed an annual review form that required measurable, stated goals each year[3]. Under this system, it was easy to measure progress and goal completion to consider salary adjustments at year-end.

The company decided to continue the process of paying the bonus at the end of the year, after the financials were evaluated. Employees would need to be employed to receive a bonus, and the bonus would be an earned percentage of the total profit pool available for payout based on the incentive plan.

The company also wanted to encourage growth and development. It agreed to pay additional money to employees who learned additional skills, took on additional work or became more valuable in some measured or objective way.

Once the plan was designed, it was given to the chief financial officer to review. He reviewed the math and strategy—and performed a what-if analysis to look for flaws.

Since the profit created a pool, and the payout was a percentage of the pool, there was no concern about the cost of the plan.

The developed draft plan was then shown to two senior team members for their input and suggestions. Their suggestions were added to the plan, and the draft was finalized for presentation to the partners.

The partners approved the draft plan,[4] and it was then ready to roll out.

---

[3] A copy of this form appears on page 321.
[4] Refer to pages 265-267.

Measurable, stated goals each year

Allowing employees to participate in the process

Communication Meeting

The communication process was critical to this plan. The company was introducing a totally new pay process. Most employees would not understand how to select improvement goals without some training. As mentioned before, the committee also wanted to introduce the concept of team evaluation. It needed buy-in from the staff about expectations of team behavior.

To provide the training necessary for the change in pay process, a half-day off-site training meeting was conducted with each team.

The operations manager discussed the goals of the organization. She specifically focused on how operations would support sales growth without adding additional resources.

The new performance review form and the improvement action form were explained. Then the team evaluation was explained, along with the incentive plan.

A draft of the review form was then explained in depth to each team, followed by a time for questions. The forms would be finalized one week after the meeting, so that employees would be able to comment or recommend changes.

By allowing employees to participate in the process of design, Sullivan & Curtis was able to gain better support and understanding of the whole process. Employees were encouraged to recommend changes before the draft of the forms and plan were finalized.

The incentive plan would be based on four measurable parameters, each equally weighted. The team as a whole would be measured on:

1) quality and quantity of work,

2) the rating on the team evaluation,

3) the participation on change committees or quality improvement committees, and

4) the actual completion of the improvement action plan.

Up to five points would be given for each of the four items. Each employee would be given points based on performance measures. The individual points over all points scored by the team would be multiplied by the pool to establish the exact amount of the cash incentive to be paid to an individual. It was possible to receive 20 points for a perfect score.

$$\frac{\text{individual points}}{\substack{\text{total points for} \\ \text{all team members}}} \times \text{cashpool} = \substack{\text{incentive} \\ \text{for each} \\ \text{team member}}$$

Once the incentive plan was explained, the training session focused on developing improvement action goals for the team members.

Individual goals had to support team goals. Team goals then supported operational goals. And operational goals supported the company's overall annual goals.

To identify goals, the group was broken into four randomly chosen smaller groups. Each group was given a flip chart to list its ideas and report back to the larger group. Each of the smaller groups was asked to identify:

1) What was working for their team?

2) What was not working?

3) What did they want to change?

4) What priority should be given to the change items?

Once the smaller groups had been given time to identify their issues, each shared its findings with the whole team. Each of the four smaller groups identified very similar areas of concern.

Then, individual team members were encouraged to select personal goals that would support the prioritized change process. One employee volunteered to document new customer input as her goal. Another employee volunteered to develop a desk manual, and another volunteered to collect and publish templates and shortcuts for using the application and claims software. Each employee then wrote his or her commitments into the improvement action form.

All employees were asked to complete the improve-

Selecting personal goals

Who would evaluate team performance?

ment action portion of their review form during the remaining training period. The operations manager and committee members helped each employee to develop ideas and goals.

Once the members had identified their goals in the workshop, they were asked to discuss them with their direct supervisor and finalize them.

During the training session, team members were told what they would be evaluated on in terms of personal goals in the upcoming year. They knew what to expect, and were given a road map of behavior necessary to meet company goals.

Historically, the review process had consisted of the employee meeting annually with his or her supervisor to discuss performance. That review was put in writing and retained in the personnel file. Because a growing number of employees had requested formal annual feedback, the review process was kept in place but revised.

Team Performance Review

One of the most difficult questions to answer was who would evaluate team performance under the new plan? Certainly, a supervisor could pass judgment—but this would not be as accurate as an evaluation by the team itself. The committee recommended introduction of a peer evaluation process.

To have the team evaluate itself, members needed to be trained in the evaluation process.

The committee spent time researching effective team behavior, and developed a list of individual behaviors necessary for effective teamwork.[5] They were:

- works effectively with others
- accepts assignments willingly
- friendly, cheerful disposition
- participates in group projects
- willingly trains others
- a problem solver
- enthusiastically motivates others
- follows up/follows through

---

[5] A general version of this form appears on page 267.

128

- demonstrates an awareness of cost effectiveness
- patiently listens
- readily assists others whenever necessary
- accepts criticism positively and without defensiveness
- demonstrates effective use of computer systems
- demonstrates professionalism under stress
- supports group decisions
- demonstrates pride in work and company
- accepts and adapts to change well
- identifies problems and offers solutions rather than complaining
- treats others with respect
- works without distracting group effort.

These were the standards against which members of the team were measured by their peers.

The new review process was based on specific behaviors identified by key managers and customers as important to Sullivan & Curtis. Problem solving, customer interaction and controlling emotions were all important in a busy service-oriented environment.

The review also was modified to add an improvement action step. This step required the employee and manager to agree on specific measurable activities that would improve skills, responsibility or efficiency.

Because the team evaluation process was new to the group, the operations manager suggested the team members rate each other at the beginning of the year. Each team member rated his or her fellow team members. The evaluations were given to the operations manager to tally.

Once tallied, the evaluations were discussed privately with each employee. The employee was shown his or her composite score and compared to the norm of the team. He or she was shown areas to improve in team interaction.

Problem solving, customer interaction and controlling emotions

Using multiple people to review an employee

Although the first ratings were not tied to the incentive plan scoring, one solid benefit occurred: Most team members improved their scores by the first year-end evaluation. Most employees worked on suggestions to improve their interactions during the year. The new system was working already.

360-Degree Review

The review system that Sullivan & Curtis used was part of what human resources experts call a 360-degree review process. Progressive employers use these assessments to evaluate behavior of individuals and teams from several perspectives. This means performance reviews are conducted not only by supervisors, but by other interested parties, such as co-workers, subordinates, customers, vendors and other department members.

Historically, supervisors have provided criteria for salary increases and job performance. Pay for results has changed that process. The subjectivity of a supervisor is avoided in the multiple-assessment measurement process. The 360-degree review provides an employee with unbiased feedback from several different sources.

To use multiple assessments, the employer identifies specific key individuals whose opinions should be incorporated into the review process, and obtains input on performance from those sources. This input is then fed back to the employee to help him develop better skills.

Independent studies have shown that employees take these reviews seriously and the reviews are not biased by friendships. Friends usually make good team members—so a social bias, channeled effectively, can help to identify supportive team members.

Leegin Leather provides an excellent example. The account representatives of Leegin perform a unique service to customers. An account representative team can approve new customers' credit, take orders, bill and collect payment from customers. Although the team has financial goals, customer service and team performance are critical.

The account representatives work in several self-directed teams. To evaluate performance, Leegin conducts customer surveys, sales surveys and team surveys of performance levels. The results of these surveys are fed back to the employees, and evaluations depend on specific scores achieved.

Customers are asked to rate team performance in service, follow-up, communication and accuracy. Sales personnel are asked to rate teams on sales support, response, follow-up and friendliness. The team members also rate each other on support, cooperation and follow-up.

This type of feedback is very effective in improving communication, cooperation and service. It identifies specific areas of strength and weakness.

An added benefit is that customers are impressed by a company that requests their input. Customers are contacted by phone, using a short script,[6] and are asked for any other suggestions.

Some companies use multiple assessments to give feedback to managers. Subordinates are asked to complete an evaluation and submit it to a third party, usually a personnel manager or consultant. The evaluations are tabulated, and general feedback is given to managers on communication, delegation, leadership and other coaching skills.

As self-directed work teams become more popular, 360-degree reviews also will gain popularity.

Conflicts Between Teams and Individuals

As we've seen, there are two major result areas incorporated into reward plan design for teams:

1) individual achievement, and

2) team achievement.

To some minds, these two interests are impossible to combine. Team incentives can be based solely on individual performance (such as sales commission plans), solely on team performance or on a combination of both.

How these two performance measures are mixed is important in directing cooperation between team members. The salesperson on straight commission is not likely to support the efforts of other salespeople. Straight commission causes competition, rather than cooperation. Where there is successful

---

[6] A copy of this script appears on page 261.

Get customers' feedback, too

Ways to measure creative teams' success

team cooperation and support, the individual reward becomes less important—which isn't the best motivation in every case.

To protect against this kind of bias, most team incentives have individual performance as a portion—usually 50 percent or less—of the total reward process.

Regardless of the logistical and communications challenges of team-based incentives, a growing number of small to mid-size companies are abandoning individual incentives and adopting a reward strategy focusing on team effort. Although there is still important criteria for individual results, progressive pay plans seem to weigh the results to be more team directed.

Creative Teams

Creative teams present a unique challenge. It's difficult to measure creativity. The time and energy necessary to create a new product or service are unpredictable. Results of creative effort are often difficult to evaluate until market introduction.

Research and development teams, artistic teams and engineering teams create particular difficulties when it comes to measuring results. How do you measure success? Start with the premise that all teams and all tasks can be measured by some means. It simply takes a different focus to measure creative teams.

The ultimate output is service or product. Looking at historic results can help set future goals.

With an engineering team, looking at past projects and results can help to set parameters on future expectations. Often, creative teams set up their own standards to be measured against. Timetables and benchmarks can be used to set up the reward process. If the ultimate outcome is service or product, the specific results of the creativity can be measured.

When Simulations Science, a company that develops software simulations for large oil refineries and other flow process plants, decided to design its own tool box, it took talented chemical engineers from several departments to participate on the design team. The company had a profit-sharing plan for all employees, but it wanted to incentivize the design team.

After the project plan was finalized, executives set up a cash reward for their design team that paid off if the final product was designed within the timeline parameters. All engineers on the team were equally incentivized, and they developed a very successful tool box. At the end of the project, the designers were awarded for their extra effort, and then moved back to their own departments.

The 360-degree review process also is useful for creative groups. Team discussions of behavior necessary to support success can result in a custom-designed assessment instrument to help evaluate individual contribution. Let the creative group assist in the design of the reward process.

Aeroenvironments is a company that designed the Impact electric car for General Motors. The design team was very creative, and worked together daily to plan and build a prototype.

After much thought, the company decided to let the engineering team rate members using a 360-degree approach. Management designed a review questionnaire that evaluated the team contribution of each engineer. They all rated each other, and feedback was given to each member by the personnel manager. The rated team member knew where to improve, but did not know which team member had rated him poorly in that category.

The members of the team took their roles as evaluators very seriously. Their feedback to each other helped to further develop the team and support each member's growth.

The team was given feedback through a third party, the personnel manager, and the 360-degree reviews determined the awards and increases for each team member.

Creative teams also can be measured by final deliverables and customer success, rather than the more esoteric or aesthetic standards. For example, an R&D group that designs five or six new products a year could be measured on general new product output numbers within a specific time standard.

Using a 360-degree approach

Increasing efficiency meant increasing billable hours

City Spaces, a nationally known corporate interior design firm, enjoyed excellent growth and employed top designers. But it was at a loss about compensating its creative types. Evaluating true creativity was impossible—but it was possible to evaluate the deliverable product of billable hours.

Although the designers were always busy, some seemed to produce more billable work than others. The firm recognized that if it could increase the efficiency of the design team, which meant increasing the billable hours, it could improve its business. Executives also felt it was critical to maintain quality and value to the customer. They set up an incentive to pay out when designers billed more than the average number of hours in a pay period. But they maintained quality. There was a quality control review for all work being billed to a client to ensure quality and customer need.

There also were rewards for bringing in new business, management incentives and total company rewards for all employees—creative and administrative. The company made itself highly incentivized on the business side—and remained able to attract top designers.

Conclusion

Rewarding teams is not easy. Teams are normally rewarded based on team performance and individual performance. The balance of how the reward is designed often will determine how cooperative the members of the team are.

The synergy of a team can manifest itself in results that are better as a group than the combined efforts of single employees. Most companies have teams, and many companies reward teams for measurable results.

This chapter has helped you identify team types, team behavior and team incentives. The design of a reward program can encourage synergy or cause disharmony.

In designing team incentives, team structure needs to be identified to ensure all real work team members are included. If any team members are excluded from pay for results, the reward process probably will not be successful.

In designing incentives, you usually need to allow teams to control equality, knowledge, information and power. Part of the design process includes an audit of these parameters to ensure they are available to members and new members are oriented into group knowledge and information. A formal training process often is used for this purpose.

More companies are turning to multiple assessments in designing team incentives. These are sometimes called 360-degree reviews. A 360-degree review allows the evaluations of the team members, customers, vendors and subordinates to be incorporated into the reward process. By providing feedback from several individuals that interact with an employee, the employee gets a unique picture of others' perceptions of his or her behavior. The employee will trust group evaluation more than a supervisor's opinion. Research has shown that multiple assessments can be very effective when incorporated into the reward process.

To bring reward systems into compatibility with self-directed work teams, re-engineering, total quality management and just-in-time manufacturing, team rewards need to be considered. Along with team rewards comes team evaluations. It is no longer the function of a supervisor to evaluate team contribution. Self-directed work teams evaluate each other.

Innovative rewards will include team rewards as a key ingredient. Team reward must focus on the behavior that will enhance the results of the team. The team itself can participate in the design and evaluation of the results and the rewards.

Employees will trust group evaluations

CHAPTER 7: PAYING FOR SALES RESULTS

Introduction

In some ways, sales is the easiest part of the business model to incentivize. It's easy to measure results. Despite this apparent ease—or maybe because of it—it doesn't take much experience to see that sales is the business function that most decision-makers incentivize poorly.

The dynamics of sales continue to change even faster than changing times. With a global economy, technological advances, business expansions and mergers, the sales function is constantly adapting to new ways of operation. Car phones, point of sale computers and telemarketing improve the sales effort and require new ways of doing business.

Sales, product development and service go hand in hand in hand. The customer expects more value for his or her dollar—and there appears to be more competition for that dollar. The sales function does not operate as independently as in the past. In fact, the sales function must work in close relationship with customer service, market research, engineering and advertising. A good salesperson knows how to expedite products and has important relationships within the company to get things done for customers.

Another new complication: Relationships have become key to the sales function. The emphasis in many businesses has shifted to a relationship sell. The salesperson must nurture relationships with existing customers who aren't ordering at the same time he or she is working with the customers who are ordering. In many cases, it takes more effort to close a sale. Businesses are more cautious about their spending. It takes more time to culminate the

Clearly identify and agree on objectives

sale. Customers and clients want to be convinced of value added and maximum return for their buying dollar.

All of these challenges can be overcome. In this chapter, we will consider some of the best tools for doing so.

Defining Goals and Philosophy

Clearly stated objectives are critical to developing sales team compensation. Do you want the compensation plan to encourage increased volume, specific products, profitability, new business, relationships or retention? The objectives of a sales plan should change at least yearly based on market opportunities, competition, new products and technology. Prior to developing any sales team incentives, the objectives must be clearly identified and agreed upon by all key executives.

Of course, strategic planning helps to support the company goal-setting process. Once the plan has been formulated, goals or quotas can be set for the total sales effort. Total company sales can then be divided by sales personnel, product line, services and geographical territory.

Beyond these categories, there are various goals for sales teams—including levels of service, sophisticated technical know-how, just-in-time delivery systems and a variety of other accountabilities.

Pay philosophy must take into account the technical know-how of the sales personnel, as well as the difficulty of the sale, training and risk of the business. A small business or a start-up is going to be riskier for a salesperson. An unknown product from a new company is harder to sell. The track record of performance is not established and, generally, small or new businesses have fewer benefits and sales support tools.

As a rule, smaller companies with less established products tend to pay sales personnel higher base salaries. Bigger, more established firms have lower base pay. The lower pay of big companies is offset by training, benefits, promotional opportunities, cars and trips.

Pay philosophy also must establish who constitutes

the sales team. What is the role of marketing, customer service, advertising or installation in the sales process? Are there non-sales functions that require time from the sales team, such as maintaining relationships, servicing accounts or providing technical information?

For sales team incentives to be effective, the whole sales area should fall under similar sales goals. Individual sales goals create competition, not cooperation. A company needs to evaluate how much reward or incentive should be tied to the total team. The trend in most industries is toward more team-related sales incentives.

Simple Sales Goals

Competitive pay practices are an important factor in evaluating and setting sales compensation. Researching what is happening in the industry, the expected average profits of other companies and predicted sales growth is very important.

In designing sales incentives, sales personnel input can be very valuable. Discussing goals and expectations with sales personnel also can help overcome their resistance to change. Of all types of work teams, the sales function understands reward processes the best. These team members usually have excellent input into what needs to change, how measurements can be improved and what team expectations need to be rewarded.

A sales incentive questionnaire[1] can be used to gather information from the sales force. This can be done one-on-one or in a focus group. All members of the sales team should participate.

Historic information on sales incentives should be reviewed as part of the ongoing research. The potential target of any new plan design must be greater than or equal to the old reward systems.

When rolling out a new sales plan, we recommend the new plan be designed to be more lucrative if goals are met than the old plan. We also feel that if you obtain sales input during the research phase, the actual rollout and acceptance of the plan will be easier.

---

[1] A sample sales incentive questionnaire appears on page 231.

Designing a Good Incentive Plan

Once the true sales team has been established, the company must design a plan that includes account-abilities and provides a fair base salary for carrying out the accountabilities. The reward is for effort and energy beyond the accountabilities. Although the reward could be based on MBO standards, appraisal or formula, good sales personnel will never be totally happy with basic targets.

Normally, management and sales personnel are in constant debate about reward levels. The key to a good design is to find the point when there are mutual benefits, equality with the market and some degree of support. Both the sales personnel and the company will compromise to find the best point of mutual satisfaction.

There are several additional specific areas to review when designing sales incentives. They include:

- **House Accounts**. You should proceed carefully when establishing what constitutes a house account—that may not be managed by a salesperson, but retained by the company to be serviced by a CEO, sales manager or other company representative. Generally, house account increases and profits are not part of a sales team's incentive formula, unless servicing is part of the team's accountability. There also should be clear definitions of what constitutes a house account, and how accounts or customers become house accounts.

- **Retained Business Increase vs. New Business**. Generally, it's easier to increase the sale of product or service to an existing customer than to identify, meet with and open an account with a new customer. Most companies differentiate between these two types of sales in their incentive plan. The growth of an ongoing account or the reorder of an existing customer may be incentivized differently than new business. Quite often, new business leads and accounts are rewarded by one-shot cash payouts immediately upon close of the sale. Ongoing business and new business sales profits are volume that would count toward a longer reward cycle, such as a yearly or quarterly payout. Normally, the incentive amount will be in proportion to the difficulty of the sale. New business often is rewarded at a higher rate than reorders because it's harder to obtain.

- **Territories and Transfers**. A sales compensation plan should be designed to equalize effort to reward. Territories need to be clearly defined if rewards are monitored by sales territories. Customers who may bridge territories or have offices in more than one territory also need to be assigned clearly to a specific territorial location. Sometimes, a company must move a salesperson from a well-developed territory to a new or less-developed territory. The compensation plan must be flexible to deal with modifications and allow transfers. You would not want a good salesperson to suffer a financial loss for helping to support company goals by taking on a weak territory that needs improvement. Typically, in a loss-of-income situation caused by a territory shift, the company would guarantee income for some period of mutually agreed upon time. Once the sales are improved, the transferred salesperson returns to the original sales incentives.

- **Sales Splits**. Occasionally, two or more salespeople participate in a sale. All team members who meet sales goals should be rewarded. The company needs a process to split account credits if two or more individuals participate in a sale. Nothing causes more friction than fighting over an account. If this has been an issue, the company needs to identify and define how splits occur. Normally, it is the sales manager's call, or there is some formula developed to deal with splits.

- **Price Changes and Economy**. Some sales increase will occur because of price increases, changes or business economics. Generally, if unit volume stays constant

Some increases are not rewarded

and sales increase because of price increases, the increased sales are not rewarded. Any good sales program incorporates price changes into the formula. Most companies publish a price list and update prices annually before new sales goals are finalized. It is important to investigate pricing as part of the design phase. Most plans are adjusted if a price adjustment occurs during a plan year. Typically, pricing is done outside the sales area with input from sales. Rest assured that sales will always feel the price is too high, while the company feels the price is too low.

- **New Products**. As part of the plan design consideration, the timing and amount of new product introduction should be reviewed. Introducing new products may take time away from the ongoing sales effort. New products, however, also may be the key to an ongoing sales effort. Many companies create special incentives for new product introduction that run concurrently with the existing sales compensation plan.

- **Returns and Uncollected Bills**. Another important consideration in designing sales plans is product returns and unpaid bills. Normally, sales has some relationship with collections. A good saleperson will support a company's efforts to get a customer to pay for goods and services promptly.

Many companies don't count a sale until the cash is received and the merchandise accepted. As part of the design process, clear guidelines on how a plan deals with the cost of returns or uncollected bills should be identified.

There is normally a two- to three-month time lag between receiving product and paying invoices for the product. It's hard to take money back from a salesperson once the reward has been paid. Many plans incorporate a time lag—and hold back a percentage of reward to compensate for returns.

After answering all the typical design questions, researching practices and using the questionnaire, the company must evaluate how much bonus to give a sales team based on various levels of goal attainment.

Changing Sales Plans Designs

Often, companies are faced with a dramatic change in business that affects sales compensation. Because customers, pricing or customer needs change, sales compensation must change to redirect sales efforts. Normally, dramatic changes in sales incentives occur because the company has not set clear beginnings and endings to all sales compensation programs. Sales plans should have a clear sunset or ending. Normally, no sales plan should be in effect for more than a year. Although sales plans have yearly terminations, companies use similar plans for about three years.[2]

Many companies have a yearly ending to sales plans, but do not modify their plan's design from year to year. Therefore, the plan becomes an entitlement to the salesperson. When the company tries to change the design, there is practically a mutiny by the sales force. It is recommended that sales plans be modified annually with some change in design, even if the change is minor.

In the United States, sales plans historically were designed around commissions. For several years, commissions played a key role in sales design. Recently, team efforts, relationships with the customers and profit margin have been much more influential in sales design than commissions. Many industries are moving from the commission base to a more mixed method of rewarding their salespeople.

Here is a case study that illustrates my point:

Smith Engineering was an old-line engineering company that sold industrial ovens. Its ovens baked off the residue left after steel was made. They were large, complex engineering marvels that could heat manufacturing plants, as well as eliminate industrial waste. As an old-line company, Smith Engineering had the same type of sales plan for more than 15 years. Its salesperson sold all over the United States, and sales volume had continued to increase. The problem with Smith Engineering was that it used commission to sell its ovens. Back in the '70s an industrial oven cost a buyer somewhere

---

[2] *Sales Compensation: A Changing Environment*, Hewitt Associates, 1993.

Input from customer service is the key to an effective plan

between $200,000 and $300,000. It was a very expensive piece of equipment. In the late 1980s, that same piece of equipment cost the buyer between $1,000,000 and $2,000,000. The commission plan had not changed for the salesmen. Although the sales were going up, the number of ovens sold was declining. This decline affected manufacturing, since manufacturing could not operate when building only a few ovens a year. The company was facing layoffs and serious financial problems. In looking at plan designs, it was easy to observe that salespeople who originally had to sell several ovens to live comfortably now had to sell only one or two to maintain the same living level.

Smith Engineering was faced with changing plan design quickly to salvage the organization. In changing plan design, the company was very careful to involve the salespeople and get their input. The company also changed the design over several years by adjusting it slightly each year, to ensure that it did not lose talented and knowledgeable salespeople in the process.

Sales Input

When changing sales plan design, it is very important to get input from the sales team. Because members are the initial contact with the customer in the field, their input is key to effective sales plan design. Typically, companies that are changing sales plans interview and discuss sales design with their salesman during the process.[3]

Often, the salespeople actually review the plan after design and negotiate final changes with the company. By involving salespeople in the actual design, the company has helped salespeople better understand the plan, the needs of the company and the goals of the organization.

Measuring Sales

It is critical for any company to have accurate, effective and trusted measurements of sales. Prior to designing a sales program, companies should ensure that their computer systems, customer service and order entry are able to capture data that reflects sales volume and profitability, and clearly differentiates which salesperson sold what.

---

[3] See the sales questionnaire on page 235.

Case Study

Fairfax was a company that sold document preparation and copying services to law firms and other firms that had a heavy paperwork process. The company had several salespeople, and each worked a different territory. The company had been profitable for many years, but slowly its profit margins were eroding. During the process it had kept the same incentive program on for the salespeople. Fairfax had an incentive program that paid straight commission and, naturally, the salespeople were selling the easiest product to sell. The easiest product had no profit margin. In fact, it cost the company to produce some of the documents involved in that product. The other products had significant profit margins, up to 40 percent. But, the salespeople were gravitating, based on commission, toward the easiest sales dollar.

After a new president had analyzed the product lines from a financial perspective, a consultant was called in to redesign the sales program to improve the profit margins. The consultant sat with the president and controller, and spent quite a bit of time reviewing the goals of the organization, the sales process and strategic information of the company. While talking to the controller, the consultant reviewed sales documentation, input and computer analysis of the sales effort. The consultant was assured that the information reviewed was accurate, and that the new computer program was a significant improvement over the old hand-calculation methodology.

The consultant then spent time with the sales manager. He echoed most of what the president and controller had said, but he added that the new information system had caused a significant problem with the salespeople. The salespeople mistrusted the information coming out of the computer, and were very upset with the quality and accuracy of the sales analysis. The sales analysis generated their commission.

As part of the process, the consultant also sat down with three of the top salespeople and discussed their ideas regarding changes in the incentive plan. During that discussion, it was discovered that the salespeople were so irate about the misrepresented sales figures that two of them were about to quit.

Quick payout reinforces behavior

Obviously, this company needed to improve its data processing prior to attempting to adjust its sales program. If salespeople do not trust the accuracy of reports that lead to their bonuses or incentives, they will not be as motivated as if they knew there was clear pay for results.

In the case of Fairfax, the salespeople also reported that they spent as many as two or three days reconciling the company reports to their sales territory input sheet. Because of all the adjustments to their sales activity, it was very difficult for them to evaluate where the changes were made. They were taking valuable time out of the field to follow up accounting on numerous mistakes and errors. Obviously, this was not the best time to redesign the incentive plan. The first step this company had to take was to guarantee the accuracy of the reports prior to finalizing any plan design.

Most sales incentives pay out quarterly or monthly. The quicker the sales cycle, the faster the payout. Since most sales personnel are goal-driven, quick results in the form of payout reinforce their behavior.

A simple team sales plan[4] would be financially analyzed as follows:

1) The strategic plan estimates the future sales volume, profit and/or other significant sales objectives. New business or new product goals also may be identified.

2) The minimum company-wide growth goal and the maximum possible growth also are determined. Normally, this is determined by the executives, finance, marketing and sales.

3) The base pay for each sales team member is set based on market, competition and skill. Many companies also evaluate other sales costs, such as car allowances and entertainment expense. These expenses are subtracted before bonuses are paid.

4) The target bonus amount is set based on research, company ability to pay and cost of sales. The maximum and minimum lev-

---

[4] A sample incentive plan for sales personnel appears on page 283.

els of bonus are determined for the sales personnel based on the total minimum and maximum profit, growth, new business or other goals.

5) The company develops a sliding scale of goals to individual incentives, from lowest estimated sales and target bonus to highest possible sales and highest bonuses. The amounts between minimum and maximum generate incremental rewards based on achieving some, part or all of the goals.

6) The plan is evaluated, written and communicated to the sales team.

Here is an example:

A. The company's expected maximum goals are 12 new accounts opened, and a profit of $500,000 based on sales of $5,000,000.

B. The minimum goals are six new accounts and profit of $200,000. (Again, the highest sales profit expected is $500,000.)

C. There are four sales team members, whose salaries average $30,000 apiece.

D. At a profit of $500,000 before bonus, the company will pay $120,000 in bonus, or $40,000 per salesperson. It will pay nothing if minimum is not reached. At the minimum goal, it will pay $30,000 in total bonus.

E. The sales team's annual goals become:

Profit	Team Bonus	Individual Bonus
$100,000	$0	$0
$200,000	$30,000	$10,000
$300,000	$60,000	$20,000
$400,000	$90,000	$30,000
$500,000	$120,000	$40,000

At each level, the team must open at least eight accounts or two per territory. For accounts over eight each involved salesperson receives $500. The company can pay out monthly, quarterly or semi-annually depending on cash flow. Typically, a bonus would be paid monthly, with 25 to 50 percent held back until the payment of sales is received.

F. In this plan, each salesperson can double his or her pay, or better, if new accounts are opened. There is also a higher percentage of profit shared with the sales team as the profit level of the company increases.

A Sales Plan

The following Account Representative Incentive Compensation Plan is designed to motivate outside sales personnel, create teamwork and reward effective efforts in achieving the company sales objectives. Base salaries are intended to provide normal living requirements. The incentive payments are added to salary to provide additional remuneration for increased effort in terms of specific, measurable results. The plan is based on the successful attainment of territorial sales goals, effective management of a territory and the success of the total sales effort based on profit and new account goals.

This company divided the sales effort into territories. Fifty percent of the bonus was based on individual territories' sales volumes and 50 percent was based on territory profit. Sales personnel could influence profit by selling products that produced better profit margins. They also worked together as a team to introduce new products, hold trade shows and work with customers that ordered from more than one territory.

The company wanted to encourage its sales personnel to improve profits. As part of this plan introduction, they trained sales personnel on profit margins in various products and encouraged them to work together as a team.

Each salesperson worked with the sales manager to set monthly sales goals for his/her territory. Once the sales goals were set, they were rolled up into company-wide goals and put into the plan. Sales and profits were monitored monthly.

Compensation Philosophy

The compensation philosophy is to provide account representatives with a total compensation program that is the best within our marketplace. We believe our desire to be a leader in our industry requires a highly motivated and skilled account representative group.

To accomplish this, the company will pay base salaries, benefits, perquisites and bonuses that enable account representatives to significantly increase cash compensation.

Sales Goals

- More profitable, higher-margin ordering
- Increased order volume with existing accounts
- Sell new accounts
- Gain a larger share of the market served

Total Compensation Program

Your total compensation program is made up of:

- Base salary
- Bonus
- Benefits
- Perquisites

Base salary is designed to provide you with a stable income and to reflect your individual experience in managing your territory and developing sales. The base salary provides for normal living requirements.

Your performance will be evaluated in writing, annually, around your anniversary date of hire, and will be based on:

- Orders and new business performance
- Customer service
- Problem management
- Communications
- Teamwork

Salary increases will be determined on the basis of performance and position in salary range. Salary ranges will be adjusted periodically to retain their competitiveness. Each account representative will be given a written performance review highlighting strengths, weaknesses and appraisal of the past year's job performance.

Bonus Incentive

The incentive compensation target for this plan is $2,500 per salesperson monthly. This incentive will be paid for meeting sales and profit goals and opening new accounts.

Half of the monthly maximum target of $2,500 will be based on territorial sales goals set by the vice president of sales and the account representative for the territory.

The other half of the monthly maximum target of $2,500 will be based on profit goals.

Cooperation between account representatives is key to obtaining company-wide results.

An additional incentive of $500 will be paid on any new account opened after the second new account in a year. A new account has not been ordered from our firm during the last five years.

How The Incentive Works

At the start of the plan, sales administration will develop individual territory business goals for each salesperson. The goals will be based on previous territory sales and profit, total company sales and profit goals, economic trends, and discretionary sales goals. Returns will be subtracted from monthly revenue and profit as they are incurred.

Individual Territory Goals

The individual monthly goals will be determined based on last year's orders and this year's anticipated growth. A dollar sales goal and profit goal will be set for each territory. The actual profit per territory will be determined, minus returns.

Incentive Formula

The amount of each account representative's incentive will be based on the achievement of individual sales goals, individual profit goals and new accounts opened.

Component 1: Sales Goals

- Account representatives who meet or exceed the net sales goals for their territory will receive $1,250.

- Those who do not meet the goal but are within 90 percent will recieve a bonus of $625.

- Those whose performance is below 90 percent will receive no compensation under this component.

Component 2: Profit Goals

- Account representatives who meet or exceed the profit goals for their territory will receive $1,250 per month.

- Those who are within 80 percent of the percentage profit will make $625.

- Those who are below 80 percent of the profit objective will receive no compensation under this component.

Component 3: New Accounts

- After the first two new accounts are opened, any new account opened in the territory will trigger a $500 cash award.

- If two account representatives work together to open a new account, the incentive will be split.

- The sales manager has the discretion to decide on all splits.

Benefits

Our comprehensive and highly competitive benefits package adds as much as 34 percent to your pay and includes:

- Medical
- Dental

- Life insurance
- Vacation and holidays
- Disability leaves
- LTD—Long-term disability
- STD—Short-term disability
- Individual benefit accounts

The company provides you with a competitive travel and expense budget, to allow you to achieve your territory account order goals.

Promotions and Transfers

A participant who is transferred or promoted into a new position during the plan year will participate on a pro-rated basis. If promoted from an account representative to a senior account representative, a base salary increase may occur.

Termination of Employment

An individual leaving the employment of the company for any reason will be entitled to all bonuses earned up to and including the date of termination.

Disability, Death or Retirement

If a participant is disabled by an accident or illness, and is disabled long enough to be placed on disability, his or her bonuses will be paid to the date of disability. No incentives shall be earned during the period on disability. In the event of retirement or death, the company will pay all incentives due to the participant or the estate of the participant.

Miscellaneous

The plan will not be deemed to give any participant the right to be retained in the employment of the company, nor will the plan interfere with the right of the company to discharge any participant at any time. The plan, as set forth in this document, represents the guidelines the company presently intends to utilize to determine what commissions, if any, will be paid.

Participation

Outside account representatives are immediately eligible for participation is this plan.

Effective Date

This plan supersedes all previous incentive compensation, commission or bonus plans. It became effective January 1, ____, subject to the company's rights as described below to amend, modify or discontinue the plan at any time during the specified period. The plan will remain in effect until December 31, ____.

Plan Administration

This plan is authorized and administered by the vice president of sales. Administration provides support for establishing and tracking sales goals and results. The vice president of sales has the sole authority to interpret the plan and to make or nullify any rules and procedures as necessary for proper plan administration. Any determination of the Vice President of Sales about the plan will be final and binding on all participants.

Plan Changes or Discontinuance

The company has developed this plan based on existing business, market and economic condition, current services and personnel assignments. The company may add to, amend, modify or discontinue any of the terms or conditions of the plan at any time during the plan's specified period.

Participation Agreement

I understand the plan does not constitute a contract of employment with any participant or to be consideration for the employment of any participant; rather, I understand that the company and I have a right to terminate my employment for any reason at any time, and that this policy may be modified only in a written document signed by the president/chief executive officer. I have read and reviewed the Account Representative Compensation Plan, including the Terms and Conditions, and understand their applicability.

Participant's Signature: _____

Date: _____

Sales is still a personal activity

Conclusion

Despite all the trends, the salesperson still controls the buy/sell transaction. Sales is still a personal activity.

Sales compensation has traditionally focused on commission and volume. Individual incentives create competition among sales personnel—which has historically been considered a good motivator.

The general trend toward a focus on team incentives, profit and relationships has diluted some of the personal intensity of sales management. Companies want to ensure that the sales compensation rewards behavior that complements long-term goals.

This can be tough, because the goal of the sales team changes as the business changes. In a start-up business, increasing volume is critical. In a more mature business, profit and relationship building become key.

Changing sales incentives is more complex than changing other types of compensation. It is critical to an organization that a strong sales force is not discouraged by the change process. Most companies do not want turnover in their sales force, and approach the sales compensation changes carefully.

Often, compensation consultants are brought in to a company and asked to change sales compensation because the CEO feels his or her sales force isn't performing effectively. Salespeople don't meet quota, don't work very long hours, don't offer solid explanations for their progress, etc.

The executive usually feels that changing compensation will motivate the sales force. In most cases, other things besides compensation need to change. A new sales compensation plan cannot improve a poor salesperson. And, just as with alternative and team rewards, an incentive plan cannot compensate for poor management.

If sales personnel have performance problems, the problems must be identified specifically and a discipline process should be used to improve performance. A good sales incentive motivates good performers, but it can't work miracles.

Sales Team Incentive Checklist

When developing incentives for your sales force, sit down with each salesperson (or key salespeople, in a large company) and discuss the following points. These discussions will help salespeople feel some ownership of the new plan, and will ease the rollout process. Employees' input also will help you create the most effective program for your company.

- Tell me about your job and what is generally expected of a successful salesperson.

- Describe the strategic advantages of this company.

- Tell me about the goals for this year.

- How are sales goals measured at this time?

- Do you think the measurement is fair? Why—or why not?

- Do you think the measurement tools the company uses are accurate? Why—or why not?

- What do you think should be measured for effective rewards?

- How much time do you spend not selling?

- Who supports the direct sales effort?

- Who should be on the "sales team"?

- Tell me about any other sales incentive plan that you have direct knowledge that has been successful.

- Describe the role of marketing, customer service, advertising and installation in the sales process.

- Is there a non-sales function that requires time to be successful on the sales team?

- If you were going to design a new sales incentive, what would it look like?

- How should sales splits be handled?

- How should returns be accounted for within the plan?

- Describe any things the company can change to improve the sales team's efficiency.

- Is there any training that could improve results?

- Do you have a suggestion for how best to communicate a new sales team incentive?

- Please tell me any other ideas or comments you have.

CHAPTER 8: MANAGEMENT INCENTIVE PLANS

Introduction

A *management incentive* is a reward provided to managers of a company that is not paid to all employees. It is normally paid out in cash after the end of a business year. Payout occurs if a manager has contributed to the success and profitability of a business. A management bonus can be discretionary, based on meeting performance objectives.

Discretionary bonuses are paid based on subjective judgment rather than objective results. With discretionary bonuses, managers never know how they are perceived until the check is in their hands. That can be very uncomfortable for a manager who may not trust subjective evaluations. Typically, discretionary bonuses are rewarded after the financials are complete, and normally are part of a "thank you" process for a job well done.

The management incentive is paid out based on how well managers have accomplished predetermined and agreed-upon goals. The goals can be either team goals or individual goals.

Management incentive plans that pay out based on reaching predetermined objectives are better measures of management talent. Managers can measure their progress and results. They know exactly how their behavior and efforts influence goal attainment. They are able to understand how to increase their effectiveness, and thus increase the possibility and amount of reward.

If goals are set correctly, the management incentive encourages managers to perform based on a plan, and motivates them to even more solid performance. This chapter explains how management

Entire management team is incentivized as a group

incentives are structured with goals, specific payouts and measurable results.

A management incentive is not an alternative reward, because it is only for the managers of a firm and not a reward given to all employees. A management incentive plan is normally working successfully in a company before an alternative reward process is put into place. Strong, talented managers expect to be paid additional cash when a company is successful. They are visible and vocal about rewards.

Many management incentive plans originate in the hire process. As new managers interview for a job, they will bargain for more money than they received in their last position. The company wants to pay a new executive as little as possible until performance is successful. A compromise is struck by the manager's taking a lower salary and agreeing to an incentive plan that would tie additional compensation to performance. The additional pay is at-risk. The new manager wins because his or her total pay package has improved if performance goals are met. Once one manager has an incentive, the entire management team usually is incentivized as a group. Smart companies tie results to increased efficiency, cost control, or profit. The increase in results then is used to fund the bonus.

In this chapter, we will discuss management incentives, current cash bonus plans developed only for those employees who are in supervisory, professional or executive positions of authority with a company. Managers are included in any company-wide plan, but also may have a separate plan designed specifically for them. Research has shown incentives provided at the management level are present in companies that perform above the market. When companies have management incentives, part of a manager's total pay is at-risk. Although there is a standard base pay, any additional pay is "at-risk" based on meeting objectives. At-risk pay contributes to better profitability, and protects a company against paying too much for a manager when the company is not performing.

We will look at the specifics of two management incentive plans. The first plan is Nylon Molding's Goals and Bonus Plan. It is a plan for the managers reporting directly to the president of a mid-market distribution and manufacturing company. The second plan is a Profit Center Incentive Plan that was used by a large public service company to compensate managers that supervised sales offices throughout the U.S.

Why Have Management Incentive Plans?

Most managers are self-motivated. They don't necessarily need cash rewards in order to perform. However, consistently strong managers measure success by their compensation. They demand constantly increasing compensation. Because all companies need skilled management, supply and demand creates a market for proven management talent. In today's economic environment, companies cannot afford to pay key managers additional compensation unless they perform above the marketplace. Companies rely on a management incentive system to provide additional incentives for managers when company profit and sales results are successful. By using incentive plans, companies can be guaranteed that management pay will not negatively impact fixed costs of a company, but will vary and reward managers when company results are achieved.

In any organization, teamwork, especially teamwork of managers, is critical to the success of an ongoing viable business. By creating a uniform reward system for managers, a company can strengthen its management team. Since an incentive plan is also a communication process, a management incentive plan can go a long way toward improving communication between managers.

By mutual goal setting and clear planning, an organization can take advantage of the talent of all its managers and focus activity on the goals of the organization. By careful design, the management incentive plan can enhance teamwork by allowing managers to support each other. A management incentive plan is a strong communication tool. A good management incentive forces managers to discuss with each other what results are expected, and how managers play individual parts in achieving results.

A uniform management incentive is critical for success

Incentives clarify roles and expectations

Setting up specific individual goals can help clarify the roles and responsibilities of the participants. Sharing goals at the management level can help managers to better understand the interaction of other departments.

Management incentives help managers feel ownership in a business. If the business is successful, the manager also will be financially successful. This is part of the American dream. Empowering managers to work beyond the boundaries of their day-to-day jobs to accomplish goals and achieve personal rewards complements the notion of business partnership. By sharing the wealth of the company, through incentives, key managers share with shareholders in a business's success.

A well-designed incentive plan also can motivate a key manager. In most studies, compensation satisfies a financial need for family support, lifestyle and future.

Compensation is a measure of worth and job performance. Companies that are realistic recognize that managers use compensation to benchmark their success. An effective manager is going to use his salary as a measure of his or her achievement. An efficient manager is competitive in the marketplace with his or her peer groups.

A company can use an incentive plan to motivate executives to stretch beyond their normal activities and push the organization into better performance than their peers in the industry. There is a direct correlation between successful companies and management incentive plans. Companies do better when they provide some sort of a reward to their managers based on expected results.

A management incentive plan is a coaching tool. Just as a good coach has a game plan, a good president has a business plan for an organization. A coach can use trophies and ribbons to reward his players. A president uses incentive plans. An incentive plan can be used very effectively by a president to coach his players to top performance.

An incentive plan is a progressive way of clarifying roles and expectations. Although job descriptions are prevalent at a senior level, a clear business plan supplemented by an incentive plan can be very instrumental in assisting a president in developing and coaching a management team. Setting objectives that are difficult to achieve and clear to the participants at a company can send a signal to a manager as to what results and behavior are expected. Thus, the incentive plan becomes a useful tool on the part of presidents to control the behavior of the managers they supervise.

It would be very difficult to put a manager on probation for poor performance. It is much easier to manipulate performance by using an incentive plan designed to ensure managers clearly understand what results they need. Failure of a plan to achieve results identifies a weak manager and becomes clear documentation of performance shortcomings. The incentive plan thus offers self-identification of performance achievements for all management participants.

Management By Objective

Although discretionary rewards are prevalent, managers prefer rewards that are based on tangible results and are linked to business strategy. Many companies set individual objectives, as well as team goals, for managers. These plans are called management by objectives, or MBO, systems. Surveys show that successful organizations provide MBO systems that allow managers to increase their reward based on performance effectiveness.

An MBO system links the reward of the participant to the predetermined goals of the individual, team or organization.

An MBO system has four components. The first and most important component is determining the expectations or predetermined results that are anticipated at the end of an evaluation period. Typically, a manager and CEO will set the expectation or goals together.

Once the expectations are set, the company must provide the second component: resources to the manager to meet the expectations. Resources could include staff, computers, budgets and/or other aids that will help the manager accomplish the goal. Typically, a manager and his or her boss will agree at the beginning of the year on the cost, timing and availability of resources to accomplish goals.

Clearly define the goals to achieve

MBOs come in many variations

Third, if the resources are available and the expectations are set, follow-up must occur, so the manager is given feedback and is evaluated based on how the expectations are being met. The follow-up needs to occur often, and in a timely manner, on success points that have been predetermined.

Fourth, the reward must be tied directly to the results expected. This type of a system is extremely prevalent in the United States. An MBO system complements the communication process between managers and executives. An MBO system also is a strong communication tool for managers.

The MBO process takes on many characteristics, forms and variations based on the type of business, the industry and the personality of the individuals within the organization. Management incentive payout can be long-term or short-term, and can involve goal-setting with the managers, as well as the executives. Or they can be simple plans that set goals without participation or discussion.

Long-Term Management Incentives

Executives can be paid for achieving results with current cash at the end of the business cycle, or they may be paid in non-qualified long-term benefits that pay out upon retirement. Some long-term plans can be five or 10 years in duration. They provide managers with financial incentives to stay with a company and work toward long-term profitability.

Some types of long-term management incentive plans include stock option plans, stock bonus plans and supplementary retirement plans. All of these plans are designed to assist managers in accumulating wealth and off-setting retirement costs based on contributing to the ongoing success of an organization.

A stock option plan ties an individual's bonus to the movement of the stock over time. An option is granted at a specific stock value, and as the stock price increases, the manager earns the right over time to purchase the stock at the original value. If managers contribute to a company's success, the price of the stock will grow over time, and the executives will have accumulated a significant asset at the end of the time period. The manager could then purchase the stock at the lower original price and sell it at the higher market price—or keep it to anticipate further appreciation. Many stock plans allow managers to roll their old options into a new stock option plan and thus continue to accumulate cash based on the growth of the company. These types of plans are at-risk, however, because if the stock does not grow or, worse yet, the stock price decreases, the option has no value to the manager. Options that are granted and have no value because the stock decreases are *under water.*

A stock bonus plan is also a long-term plan. Based on the evaluation of a manager's performance and results, stock is granted rather than cash. Normally, there is some requirement for the manager to retain the stock for some period of time. Thus, a company can provide a bonus to a manager without paying current cash. If stock is granted to the manager directly, the manager is responsible for paying taxes based on the value of the stock received as a bonus.

Many plans provide stock to an executive, but do not allow for constructive receipt. Constructive receipt means the actual receiving of the ownership of the shares. In many cases, bonus plans are constructed so that the stock is not conveyed to the manager, but remains in some sort of a formal trust, so the manager does not receive the stock until the bonus plan matures.

Supplementary retirement plans are long-term incentive plans that are designed to allow managers to accumulate retirement cash over time. These are special retirement plans designed only for managers. They are not qualified by the Internal Revenue Service, which means that there is no special kind of taxation allowed for these plans. Payments to the manager would be at-risk until the plan vested, or matured.

Normally these types of plans are 10-year plans. They are funded annually, based on a manager meeting certain goals or objectives that are long-term goals, and they vest over time. Vesting means the manager gains the right to own the funds over time. As soon as the manager receives the funds, they are taxed. This brief overview is not complete;

Granting stock to management

Rewards are critical to performance

however, our remaining information is about short-term current-cash management plans.

Short-Term Incentives

In the United States, entrepreneurship is highly prized. Managers are successful when they show ability to move ahead, make decisions and improve operations. Those same managers have a need to improve themselves, as well as their financial position. Most organizations reward successful leadership through management incentive plans.

Successful American businesses recognize that rewarding key managers is critical to their overall performance. Management incentives take a variety of forms and are closely controlled by tax laws, as well as SEC reporting. Large companies have very complex management reward systems that cascade down in an organization to front-line managers. Smaller organizations normally provide some sort of incentive for executives that report directly to the president or the owner.

Management incentive plans drive cooperative behavior of key executives and pay for results. The plans can encourage teamwork or competition, depending on design. Discretion can be minimized or can drive a plan, based on how much control the president needs. Successful plans create synergy and communication between key managers. Often, the managers are involved in designing the plan or in designing the strategy that the plan supports. By understanding the goals and objectives of other managers, key executives can work together more cooperatively.

Setting Goals

In MBO plans, participants set individual goals for themselves. The goals must be measurable and quantifiable.

To initiate a goal-setting process, the president of the company and his key direct-reports design the strategic plan for the year. That plan includes a certain increase in sales goals, profitability, customer service and customer retention. The strategic plan sets the direction for the company and provides a road map for managers to then set goals individually. The overall direction of the company must be set prior to department managers initiating their goals. All department goals and management goals must fold into the strategic plan and work together to propel the company forward. Ultimately, the president and his key direct-reports must approve all goals for that plan year.

Selecting goals is one of the most important aspects of any incentive plan. Participants need to consider what they hope to accomplish for the year outside normal job routine and job descriptions. Goals must be measurable.

Goals must be clear and explicit. Both the employee and the supervisor must participate in determining goals, which must not be too difficult to complete or too easily accomplished.

Individual goals must be linked to overall organizational goals. Strategic planning helps to link goals together.

The time period for goal accomplishment should be specific. All goals should not have target dates of completion at year-end. Goals should be spaced to be accomplished throughout the Award Year. In setting timetables, a plan should be developed to indicate levels of accomplishment and benchmarks should be set to ensure projects are on target. For example, there should be a specific time for planning, preparing, getting started, completing points of partial progress and entirely completing a goal.

Goals should be flexible. For example, installing a computerized system should include time for unknown changes and business procedure changes that occur during the course of the award year.

Goals should include a plan of action.

Goals should include costs. These costs should outline manpower costs (both internal and consultative), purchasing costs, travel costs, development costs, etc. If there are savings to be monitored, the savings monitoring process should be explained and initiated.

Once goals have been determined mutually, they become the standard against which participant performance is evaluated. Level of performance is directly related to how completely and how well a

Time allotment for goals should be specific

Weighting goals by difficulty

goal is accomplished. The formal evaluation or overall rating is expressed numerically, and represents a subjective estimate of both goal difficulty and degree of attainment. An extremely difficult goal, when completed, would be given an overall better evaluation rating than a less important goal or one that was easier to accomplish.

Weighting

To emphasize difficulty, goals can be weighted by the participant. If there is a particularly important project that far outweighs the other goals, that goal carries more importance than the others. The weights should equal 100 percent as a total.

So, if there are four goals, one goal could be 40 percent and the remaining three 20 percent each. The 40-percent weight would be evaluated as twice as difficult as the other three.

The weighting needs to be agreed upon with the participant's supervisor and indicated on a statement of goals.[1]

The statement of goals is to be used initially and quarterly for reporting purposes.

A goal worksheet,[2] with additional attachments if necessary, needs to be completed initially by the participant to discuss possible goals with his or her supervisor. A participant should initially develop more than four goals for discussion with the supervisor.

Once a goal or objective is selected, it can be modified or changed with the approval of the supervisor. Changing goals or extending timetables may affect the final overall annual evaluation.

Once goals are agreed upon, they should be communicated to other managers to coordinate company teamwork on the objectives.

If, for some business-related reason, a goal must be changed, it can be changed or replaced by the participant and supervisor by resubmitting the goal worksheet and statement to the president for approval. If approved, the goal can be adjusted. The change may or may not affect bonus payout, depending on the nature and necessity of the change and the timeliness of the accomplishment.

---

[1] A sample form appears on page 263.
[2] A sample of this worksheet appears on page 269.

Case Study: Nylon Molding

Doug Stephen founded his company in the 1970s. As a salesperson for a manufacturer of fasteners, he noticed that there was a market opportunity in selling to the smaller accounts in the western United States. The manufacturer could not service the small orders efficiently. Stephen saw an opportunity in bundling small orders and consolidating them into one large order to obtain discounts. He persuaded several large manufacturers to let him represent their lines exclusively in the West. He started a fast-growing distribution business called Fastening Systems.

Fastening Systems was successful. As the business grew, Doug was able to purchase one of the manufacturers he represented. Nylon Molding became the umbrella company that absorbed Fastening Systems.

By the mid-1980s, Stephen's company had grown to about $5 million in sales. He was growing at 10 to 15 percent per year and had just hired a controller. With the addition of a controller, his management team was complete. He had an operations manager, sales manager, purchasing manager and controller reporting directly to him.

Stephen was a great salesperson, and an aggressive entrepreneur. His business had grown by the sheer force of his personality. Now it was time to plan for the future. He decided to conduct a strategic planning session with his managers.

At the planning retreat, he would set the sales and profit objectives—but he would need the input of his managers to develop a business plan to achieve desired results.

The strategic planning session was more effective than he had expected. His managers had some excellent ideas and set up an aggressive plan of action. If successful, the company would meet their objectives and profit predictions.

Stephen had always given discretionary bonuses to his managers. At the end of the year, he would evaluate the contribution of each manager and give bonuses based on his judgments.

The senior managers at the planning session re-

Bring in outside help to facilitate

quested an incentive plan. Stephen felt with a structured business plan, he could pay out bonuses based on how well the management team achieved the results it had predicted.

Stephen wanted to create a team. At the same time, he believed a feeling of risk and reward would motivate them to perform at their highest level. He felt an incentive plan would help drive his business leaders in a direction that would support the growth of his organization.

In the past, Stephen created sales goals based on previous-year revenue. Then the organization followed behind, supporting his projections with customer service, invoicing and warehouse operation projections.

For the first time, Stephen and his managers talked about a company-wide business plan that would design the strategy for the upcoming business year. Strategic planning would help ensure that all managers were clear on the direction of the organization. There would be agreement on the key management responsibilities and duties of each manager. Finally, with a business plan, the company could benchmark itself against the expected results and evaluate the performance of the organization.

Each manager had a different idea of how the business plan should look and feel. Doug took an aggressive approach. The other managers seemed not as willing to stretch.

Stephen decided to take his managers off-site and complete some strategic planning as a group. He hired a facilitator—and he and his key managers spent two days discussing business objectives.

They talked about what was not working in the organization, what was working and what they wanted to change. They then prioritized the change. They also talked about the threats and opportunities facing Nylon Molding. They evaluated the best business direction based on external economic and internal resource conditions. Once they had agreed upon a plan, it was documented and refined. The documentation process flowed into the incentive plan process in a very simple and easy manner. Once the business plan or results were clear, each manager's role in producing those results was identified. Once those roles were identified, specific measurable objectives could be set for each manager that directly related to his or her contributions.

As part of the strategic plan, the pay philosophy of Nylon Molding was defined. Stephen wanted to pay his managers above market based on top performance. He knew the company could not afford to pay managers above market unless the company was successful; therefore, some compromise needed to be made between market pay and the resources of Nylon Molding. Stephen decided he wanted to emulate the market rates for base pay. He was willing to provide pay, benefits and incentives that were similar to the total average package in the marketplace. His philosophy as a small company was to pay at market, and to reward his managers with additional cash if the company was profitable. He was willing to give managers a bonus as big as his competitors' for their contributions if his company met its projected sales and profit goals.

Stephen next surveyed the marketplace to find out exactly what the pay programs were for similar companies that operated in his geographical area. He called various business leaders, he obtained survey data, and he sent for national distribution industry statistics to give him clarity on the specific pay rates for managers with similar responsibilities.

While conducting his research, Stephen also obtained information on MBO systems and incentive plans that other companies provided to their managers. He read industry information regarding incentive plans and was able to identify some characteristics he wanted to put into the plan design. He decided to adopt a simple plan design in which his managers would all be paid a cash bonus at or above the marketplace if the sales and profit performance goals were met. Stephen decided that he wanted a portion of the bonus to be based on individual contributions and a portion on effective team performance. He wanted to set specific measurable goals for each one of his key managers, based on their jobs. At the same time, he wanted all his managers' bonuses to tie in with group attainment of business objectives.

Survey the marketplace for other pay programs

Payout only when thresholds are met

Plan design came fairly simply once Stephen worked backward and determined payout levels that he could afford. The plan was designed around a sharing of profit when individual goals and company goals were achieved. Basically, Stephen wanted all of his supervisors and managers to participate in the plan. He answered the same questions for his management incentive plan as we ask for designing group incentive rewards.

The following questions needed to be answered:

How do you measure the goal?

Strategic planning set the annual goals. Stephen expected a certain level of sales and profit. He designed the plan around those goals.

Who will be in the plan?

The plan would cover all supervisors and managers.

What is the size of award for the participants?

Supervisors would get between 0 and 10 percent, administration managers between 0 and 15 percent and his top managers between 0 and 20 percent. These were based on survey data of similar companies.

How often will the plan pay out to the participants?

Annually. Because results were not final until year-end, the plan would pay out after the year-end financials were complete.

What are the threshold numbers?

Stephen decided that if his sales and profit thresholds were not met, he did not want to pay incentives. The total awards for the participants could be determined mathematically—if everyone met their individual objectives.

Once he determined the total cost of all bonuses, Stephen was able to work backward to evaluate what actual projected sales and profitability would be necessary to fund a plan based on individuals meeting their goals. He also took into his evaluation the business's needs for ongoing cash and return on investment to the shareholders.

It was determined that a sales volume of $6.75

million would be necessary to provide the cash flow and profitability to fund a plan. The $6.75 million then became a threshold that had to be met to fund the plan.

Do employees need to be employed to receive the payout?

Most cash plans require employees to be employed to collect a payout. Nylon Molding felt that it, too, wanted managers to be employed to collect a bonus. The bonus would tie the manager to the company for the whole plan year.

What is the definition of salary? Does it include overtime? Other incentives?

It was decided straight salary would not include overtime or other cash payments.

Does everyone receive the same incentive, or is reward based on other criteria, such as percent of salary or individual effort?

Supervisors and managers received the same percent of salary, so everyone was receiving a different amount of incentive based on their salary. There were two levels of payment, based on seniority.

Who is responsible for the calculations and communication?

The controller was selected to announce ongoing results. Stephen would be the champion of the plan and explain it to his management staff.

Who measures performance?

Stephen would measure performance under this plan based on the financials. He had the right to change the plan, add or subtract participants, and evaluate goal achievements.

Will you pilot the plan?

Because this was a plan for a year, there was no pilot—instead the total plan was rolled out. The company was small enough that there was no appropriate subgroup to try a pilot.

Does the plan pay out all monies due, or is there a hold-back provision?

Stephen only paid out after final year-end results, so he did not hold back any of the largest reward.

The bonus was raised if the company achieved more than its goal

What is the life of the plan?

This plan had a beginning and an end. It began at the beginning of the fiscal year and ended at year-end. When Stephen announced the plan, he also announced that the plan was only for the year and there might not be another plan. He was trying the concept and would decide if it worked before he announced another plan.

Stephen took the type of discretionary bonus pool money that had been distributed in the past, and designed a plan around the same payout based on the future success of his organization.

He also determined that if managers met all of their objectives, they would get 100 percent of their target. If they met most, but not all, of the objectives, they'd get between 50 and 80 percent of the target. Managers not meeting most of their goals—but who were competent—might earn somewhere between 0 and 50 percent of their bonus.

Stephen then leveraged the bonus plan by raising the bonus if the company achieved more than its goal. By agreeing that if the sales volume was higher than he predicted, at $6.75 million, he would add additional incentives to his managers. Therefore, managers could make up to 150 percent of their target award during the plan year. The award level would start at $6.25 million, where participants would be paid out at least half of their target if the company was successful. Based on company success, the target would be set. Individual performance would determine the evaluation of each individual payout level.

Stephen also set parameters for individual goals. The individual goals needed to support the strategic plan and be a stretch for the participants.

Quarterly, the participants would report in writing on their progress toward the goal. (A copy of the plan is furnished on page 311.)

The financial analysis was fairly simple. By designing a plan around the maximum payout possible with everyone achieving 100 percent of their goals, Stephen was able to determine what the thresholds would be. In this case, the profitability and the sales figures, as well as the cash necessary to provide working capital and return on investment, really projected the level at which payout could occur. This was done by first funding return on investment and working capital, then developing a pool of cash that would fund the management incentive plan.

Stephen wrote out the plan and set it up for review with the managers. He allowed the key direct-reports to review the plan and give feedback on plan design. He discussed at length quantifiable, measurable results and how to submit their goals for review. He wanted to ensure that the goals were clear, measurable and unique to the individual. He also wanted to make sure that goals could be accomplished without the need of support.

Communication Is Key

The communication process for Nylon Molding's Goals and Bonus Program was more complex than the communication for a simple incentive plan. Once the plan was complete and managers had given their input, Stephen finalized the plan and handed it out to the supervisors and managers in a meeting. He explained the goal-setting process.

When rolling out the plan, Stephen explained the sales and profit margins he expected, and spent time explaining the strategic plan. Although his key direct-reports had been involved in the strategic planning process, several supervisors were hearing the plan for the first time. By explaining the plan in depth to all of his supervisors and managers, Stephen was able to lay the groundwork for their individual goal-setting.

Each manager and supervisor was asked to set four goals that were in addition to their day-to-day work schedule. These goals had to support the strategic plan for the year and be within the control of the participant selecting the goals. Stephen explained that the goal-setting was one of the most important aspects of the plan, that each manager would be evaluated at the end of the plan year on the attainment of his or her selected goals and overall contributions to the company, and that achieving goals contributed to achieving the goals of the company.

After the plan is finalized it is communicated

Worksheets— part of the goal setting process

The goals were required to be outside the normal scope of a manager's daily and weekly job responsibilities. Stephen used his new controller as an example. In the controller's job description, she was to be responsible for MIS and financials. However, to meet the strategic plan, a new computer system was to be installed. The controller had asked Stephen if installing the new computer system could be one of her goals. A computer installation was well beyond the scope of her daily activities. To accomplish an installation within budget and within the time frame allotted for the transition would be a major accomplishment. It is not easy to convert to a new software program. Stephen knew the controller would be stretched to accomplish the task within the agreed-upon parameters.

Stephen explained how goals would be measured. Goals needed to be clear and explicit. Both he and the manager or supervisor would agree together on the four goals. He encouraged the supervisors to develop goals on their own and then present them to him. He provided worksheets for each supervisor to complete in order to clarify the goal-setting process. He explained that the time commitments must be specific, as should any resources or costs. Goals should be flexible and include a plan of action. Timetables were an important part of the goal-setting process.

Stephen also explained that the goals could be weighted. The difficulty in installing a computer system is significant. That particular goal would account for 50 percent of the controller's bonus potential. This particular project also was more important to the company than the other projects; therefore, it carried a larger percentage of the whole. Bonus plan weights add up to 100 percent. So, in this case, the other three goals would account for 50 percent of the controller's target bonus.

Stephen explained to the group that he would follow up quarterly. Each quarter, the manager and Stephen would sit down and review goals and benchmarks, evaluate progress and discuss performance. Participants would have an opportunity quarterly to explain their actions and discuss goal attainment. At each quarterly meeting, Stephen was willing to modify or adjust goals if the direction or requirements of the company had changed. Sometimes, with a management incentive plan, it is difficult to project exactly what the needs will be over a year period. Quarterly updates allowed Stephen the flexibility of adjusting goals if business plans altered based on economic or competitive marketplace changes.

If goals changed because major business objectives changed, the manager or supervisor would be required to resubmit the goal worksheet and statement to Stephen for approval.

Typically, a management incentive plan, or MBO plan requires more frequent follow-ups and one-on-one meetings than a company-wide incentive plan. Although financials are still posted as frequently as possible, managers with individual goals need to report on progress frequently.[3]

Sandbagging

One of the historic problems of goal-setting is that participants select easily achievable goals. Because of self-interest issues, some managers will consciously select easy goals. Other managers that have less interest in financial gain and are focused on the challenge of performance will select goals that are difficult to accomplish. In all MBO-type plans, there needs to be a central neutral party who can examine all goals and ensure fairness of the plan.

Normally, the company president also helps define and set goal criteria. The president is responsible for equalizing the difficulty of the individual goals, and can adjust goals, increase expectations or require additional effort. As part of any individual management goal selection, the president would review the goals and ensure equality.

Sometimes it is difficult to judge the ease with which a goal can be achieved. This is the reason for the quarterly follow-ups. At the quarterly follow-ups, goals can be reevaluated, changed or adjusted. Both the individual manager and the president work together to initiate the change. The president must use some judgment in determining goal selection, so his or her judgment must be credible. Plan participants need to trust the business judgment of the central party in adjusting or changing goals.

---

[3] See Nylon Molding's incentive plan on page 311.

Self-interest can lead to less challenging goals

Non-competitive vs. competitive team goals

Individual vs. Team Goals

In about 50 percent of management incentive plans, there is some type of MBO component. This component identifies individual goals required to be met for participant payout. There is normally also a component of team goals or company goals that need to be accomplished. How the individual goals and team goals are used sends a signal to the managers on how important team accomplishment is versus individual accomplishment.

Some companies only incentivize managers on total-company or total-team performance. Managers all receive the same target payouts depending on company success. An example of a total-team bonus would be a plan in which managers divide a percentage of the company's profits after alternative rewards, but before taxes. All managers' risk is equal, and all are equally incentivized to meet company goals. If the company fails to perform, no one gets a bonus. There is no competition in this type of design. There is also synergy in the total team focusing on the same simple business objectives.

At the other end of the scale, an MBO plan may totally tie a payout to the individual achievements of the participants. This type of plan does not encourage cooperation and is competitive in design. Competition in reward systems drives behavior that does not complement teamwork. An example of a plan that encourages individual goals would be a sales commission plan in which each salesperson is incentivized to maximize sales efforts. Often, these types of plans discourage sharing of customer information and support. They are effective only for business growth that does not require support between sales personnel to effectively sell and service clients or customers.

Typically, most MBO-type plans are heavily weighted toward total-team goals. Most plans use team performance to set thresholds and to reward group performance. If teamwork and constant improvement are company goals, this should be reflected in the design of the compensation systems.

Setting Target Amounts

The target amount of a management incentive plan

normally depends upon the market, industry and local economy, as well as the company pay philosophy. Just as we researched pay rates in setting base pay levels, survey data also can provide incentive or bonus pay target information.

The survey bonus amounts differ based on the seniority and job of the incumbent. Executive management has higher bonus potential than mid-level managers. Mid-level managers have higher bonus potential than line managers. Sales and operations normally get better bonus pay than administrative functions. Supply and demand may account for variations in bonus amounts, also.

Once the research is obtained, companies evaluate payout targets based on their corporate value systems. Some companies want to pay all managers the same, some different. The target award has to be large enough to change behavior and be perceived as a reward, but also needs to conform to the financial abilities of companies to pay.

Target amounts can be presented as a percentage of base pay or a fixed dollar amount. Some MBO plans establish a pool of money as a target, and managers split the pool based on a mathematical formula.

Self-interest enters into the analysis of setting bonus amounts if executives are designing the plan. Adherence to market data can help alleviate problems of self-interest. The design team should be considering company needs and values first in setting payout targets.

Target amounts of a management bonus normally depend on the philosophy of the company toward base pay and at-risk pay. At-risk pay is another name for variable or bonus pay. Because the bonus is linked to the business plan or results expected, the payout depends upon achievement of results. No results means no payout, therefore, that portion of the manager's compensation is at-risk. Incentive pay is called at-risk pay because it is not guaranteed. Payment depends on results. If results are not achieved, there is not additional reward. The incentive pay is exposed to the chance of loss if the results are not achieved.

It is important to establish the base market pay

Research is a key factor in setting the payout target

At-risk pay is dependent upon achievement

rates for the management positions found in a company. Once market pay rates are researched, then evaluation of current pay levels can be made. Bonus amounts are paid after the payment of base pay, so the base pay must be appropriate or the incentive won't be effective.

The amount of management incentives paid are normally based on job responsibility level, size of business, location and industry. As in base compensation, survey data can be obtained to give owners a clear understanding of what other similar businesses pay. A general rule of thumb is the incentive target amount is 5 - 10 percent for first line supervisors, 10 - 20 percent for mid-management and 20 - 30 percent for managers. In large companies, executive management incentives can equal up to a year's pay. The larger the company and more senior the manager, the higher the percentage of at-risk pay.

Case Study: Profit Center Management

This chapter's second case study is a profit center manager bonus plan for a service organization. This was a national company that had offices in major cities throughout the United States. Their offices were called profit centers, and sales managers were promoted to profit center managers. Profit center managers (PCMs) did not get commission, and they were on a bonus plan based on profitability of the office.

The company had paid bonuses based on profit center activity, and it had never adjusted bonuses based on company results. The company had not achieved average or above average results for several years, although it was paying out substantial bonuses to its managers. At the time that we redesigned the company's plan, the company was not profitable, although its peer group was experiencing between 6 and 10 percent profitability per year.

The company wanted to change direction, improve teamwork and tie managers to total-company performance. Senior management redesigned the incentive based on teamwork and total-company performance factors.

To redesign this plan, a questionnaire was developed for the profit center managers' input.[4] They were asked to discuss their evaluation of the current plan, what results should be evaluated in a new plan and how overall profits should be incorporated into plan design. Each manager was quick to give input, and all the suggestions were evaluated.

A marketplace survey of both competitor plans and bonus amounts also was used to brainstorm plan design. Senior management also used published salary surveys to make certain that base salaries were at market. Geographical location and asset size of the office determined base salary in this industry.

Target bonus amounts were established based on sales volume of the profit centers. Larger offices were perceived as harder to run and of more value to the company. By setting bonus amounts based on sales volume of profit centers, managers could see the potential of more income as their offices grew. Using a sliding scale also ensured that all managers with similar-size offices were treated the same. By increasing the target amounts, the company weighted the larger payouts to the larger offices.

The problem was adjusting the bonus plan, which historically had paid the successful managers substantial bonuses, to a plan that incorporated the overall company objective. By tying the bonus plan to company objectives, the profit center managers would be more cooperative with each other. Several of their large clients had important dealings with many offices throughout the nation and, as part of the research, senior management discovered those offices were uncooperative with each other, and therefore did not provide the quality of customer service that could be achieved with more teamwork. A company-wide plan would help encourage offices to cooperate with each other.

Under the old plan, each office was expected to achieve varying levels of profitability. Some of the offices' profit center managers were given bonuses for very low percentages of the profit, and some offices were given bonuses for very high percentages.

---

[4] A copy of this questionnaire appears on page 239.

Target amounts were based on sales volume

Managers examined the labor-to-sales ratios

Senior management carefully investigated historic bonus payouts to ensure that the new plan would be equal to or better than the old plan.

Senior management also discovered that in one major division of the organization, a very standardized bonus program had been developed that set the profit requirement at 12 percent. The division that senior management reviewed had been profitable historically, and managers had found that 12 percent was an achievable profit margin.

Finally, this company had historically had problems controlling labor costs, so one of the goals of the plan was to require managers to look at their labor-to-sales ratios. All PCMs were encouraged to do at least as well as their competitors in the marketplace—with a 57 percent labor-to-sales ratio. This was a very labor intensive-type sales operation.

A formalized bonus plan[5] was a result of cooperation of the profit center managers themselves. Because the company had an established philosophy and strategic plan, the first step in designing a plan was to interview the regional vice presidents and profit center managers.

A standard list of questions was asked to evaluate their historic plans, as well as to develop ideas and suggestions for the new plan. As each manager answered the questions, new ideas and suggestions were encouraged to help design an even better vehicle. Three of the managers were new to the organization and had excellent incentive plans at prior companies. These plans were reviewed in depth to determine if the design or part of the design would be practical to incorporate into the new plan document.

As part of the historic planning process, each office was evaluated for profit, and a total company sales, expense and profit projection was developed. The thresholds were set based on the development of the total company projections. The threshold for this plan was set at a company-wide operating profit of 3 percent at the beginning of the year. This threshold was developed by working backward in terms of how to pay out the plan, as well as by the expected results based on the prior year's activity.

---

[5] A copy of this plan appears on page 279.

Each profit center was given varying requirements of profits to achieve. Some centers could operate as high as 20 percent. Several of the new centers were at 0 percent because of start-up costs. A standard amount of profit expected from the offices was 12 percent. The standard amount of operating profit (12 percent) from each profit center generated a target standard bonus amount of 100 percent.

The standard bonus amount was leveraged, so that the higher the sales volume (i.e., the more complex the transactions and supervision of the office), the higher the potential target standard bonus amount would be for the profit center managers. An office revenue up to $2.5 million would generate $15,000 in bonus, and for more than $10 million, the standard bonus amount was $45,000. This amount varied depending on how well the manager met his or her operating objective. If managers met actual profitability of more than 12 percent, they then had an opportunity to increase their standard bonus amount up to 240 percent.

The reward was divided so that 40 percent was based on the profits of each individual office, and 30 percent was based on MBO criteria and 30 percent total company operating profits. In order for an office to have a full 100 percent of its bonus, both the profit center and the company as a whole would need to meet profit objectives. By requiring a 30-percent payout based on company profitability, the managers were tied to team results, not just individual office accomplishments.

As with most plans, this plan had a sunset of one year, and superseded all previous short-term incentive compensation plans.

Unlike at Nylon Molding, managers in this plan were incentivized for individual effort as a profit center manager, as well as company effort. Typically, a small company will tie achievements to team efforts whereas a larger company will start individualizing its management incentive plan to emulate the management by objective plan for each individual.

It has been found that when you make changes to an MBO plan for managers, the changes should be gradual over time. In this case, the profit center managers had historically been paid 100 percent

Bonuses were tied to individual center and total company profits

of the standard bonus amount based on their individual profit center's achievement. By going to a 40/30 percent split, the company sent a signal to the managers that total company results were important. The potential for the same bonus amount was calculated for all profit center managers, and based on the formula developed, each profit center manager still would be able to achieve standard bonus results similar to what they had in the past, but they would receive enhanced benefits if the company performed *and* their MBO criteria was met.

This plan equalized the expectations for all profit center managers. Twelve percent was made the uniform profit expectation. Traditionally, in this company, various sales managers had a variety of deals. By making the incentive plan uniform, all former incentive plans were superseded and the historic deals given specifically for various profit centers were eliminated. By putting all PCMs on a level playing field, there was less perception of favoritism. This plan is found at the end of the chapter.

Conclusion

Management incentive plans are popular in most large companies. Managers have pay at-risk, which becomes additional pay when they meet the strategic goals of the organization. Occasionally, there will be a discretionary plan, but typically plans require that managers perform specific duties in order to collect additional cash. Companies use management incentive plans to motivate managers, coach them to understand how they can perform more successfully to meet company objectives and communicate strategic information on how their departments interact.

Management incentive plan design is very similar to alternative rewards design however, the plans are only for a select group of employees. Typically, only top management and those managers reporting directly to a president are in a management incentive plan. In large companies, incentives go down to the first line manager or supervisory level.

We have covered the steps necessary to create a management incentive plan within this chapter. The steps are similar to a company-wide incentive plan.

First, the company management needs to develop a strategic plan and a pay philosophy that includes how they are going to pay both monthly wages and incentive bonus. The strategic plan provides the vision, or road map, for the company, team and individual goals that must be achieved to fund the plan.

Next, research and surveys will provide information on incentive design and target amounts for similar companies that would be competing in the marketplace for managers. The research process is an important one, and provides information that can be used later in the design of the plan.

The third step is plan design. In this chapter, we covered the 14 questions asked during the design phase. With management incentive plans, the selection of both team goals and individual goals is critical. Individual goals must be measurable, achievable and able to be completed without the support of other areas of the company.

The fourth step is reviewing the plan with experienced professionals who can provide input on improvement of plan design. Professionals might be managers who will be using the plan, outside CPAs or a board of directors. Once their input is obtained, the draft plan is further refined for rollout to participants.

The fifth step is communication. Management incentive plans are communicated slightly differently from overall company plans. There still needs to be a champion to reinforce goal attainment, but the communication process usually includes individual goal setting, which is a slightly more complex process than in a company-wide incentive plan.

We also have discussed goal-setting at length. It is important that if an MBO process is used, goals are set to enhance the strategy of the company. Individuals setting goals need to be responsible for the timing, the costs and the resources necessary to set goals. Time and cost benchmarks often are used in goal setting to ensure that managers are on the right track with their goal activity. Goals can be weighted. The most important goals carry heavier consideration and thus more financial impact on the payout bonus.

Research provides information that can be used when designing a plan

Input is important to the development of a "team"

Communication is ongoing and continuous. The communication process serves as a coaching device for managers, and allows them to better understand business strategies and how their behavior can support those business objectives.

Strategic planning is an important process in managing a successful business. Obtaining input from managers on business objectives, obstacles and potential helps clarify vision. Clear vision is critical in establishing credible and achievable results. Companies conducting strategic planning with their managers create synergy. The combined efforts of several people's ideas, knowledge and energy creates a more effective business plan than a CEO's isolated endeavors.

Having team input on expected business results helps solidify the team, develops better understanding and establishes buy-in. Managers that participate in the business planning process feel a sense of ownership. Group planning allows managers to voice their concerns and opinions, which overcomes resistance as the business continues to change to meet the changing needs of the marketplace.

In this chapter, we gave you two examples of management incentive plans—one a simple MBO system, the other a more complex plan that incentivized profit center managers. In designing an incentive plan for managers, a question of team versus individual goals must be addressed. Typically, management plans have company-wide goals, as well as individual goals within the structure of the plan. In identifying goals, benchmarks, timetables and costs need to be planned out carefully. Clear, concise goals that are individually identified and easily measured are the backbone for success within a management incentive plan.

Management incentive plans are here to stay. Based on the economy and the structure of compensation, managers in today's global environment will continue to demand additional compensation, especially those managers that are the superstars of tomorrow. Management incentive plans perform an important function. They help companies coordinate a team effort, encourage strategic planning and provide at-risk pay to key management personnel.

Profit Center Manager Bonus Plan

1. Purpose

The purpose of the plan is to provide additional incentive to the Profit Center Managers to meet individual goals and company operating plan objectives.

2. Standard Bonus

The standard bonus amount is $15,000 to $45,000, based on office revenues for achievement of objectives. The operating profit objective is 12% margin without interest income.

Office Revenue	Bonus
$ 0 - 2.5 million	$15,000
$2.5 - 5 million	$22,500
$ 5 - 7.5 million	$30,000
$7.5 - 10 million	$37,500
Over 10 million	$45,000

The standard amount will vary depending upon how well the manager meets the objective.

3. Calculation of Bonus

The award will be governed by the Profit Centers' total operating profits and by individual performance relative to MBO goals. The standard bonus for the manager's position is divided as follows: 40% of the bonus is based on operating profit to your office, 30% on MBO and 30% on company profitability.

4. The 40% standard amount operating profit portion

This amount is leveraged as follows:

Operating Profit	Standard Bonus Amount
20% +	240%
19% +	220%
17% +	200%
16% +	180%
15% +	160%
14% +	140%
13% +	120%
12% +	100%
11% +	75%
10% +	50%
Below 10%	0%

5. 30% MBO Portion

The company must make its budgeted operating profit of 3% in a given year as set at the beginning of the year for this MBO to be payable.

All MBO goals must measurable, approved in writing, and submitted through the regional to the Executive Committee for final approval. Once approved, they cannot be changed without authorization.

Below is an example of measurable, individual MBO goals:

- 50% revenue targets or total sales growth;

- 25% ratio of staff costs to sales at 57% or less;

- 25% new business exceeding annual goals.

The MBO portion of the bonus will be funded only if the company achieves its goal or forecast of 3% profit before tax and bonuses.

If the company makes its profit goal and all MBO goals are not achieved, a percentage equivalent to the results will be paid. For example, if a new business goal was 25% growth but only 8% was achieved, only 8/25 of that portion of the MBO was achieved.

6. 30% Company Profit Portion

If the company achieves 3% profit, this portion will be funded at the level of standard operating profit as in Item 4. If the company exceeded 3% profit, this portion will increase based on the percentage of profit over 3%. For example, at 3.5%, this portion would be funded at 1.16% times the leveraged amount.

7. Application of Formula to Fiscal Year and Future Years

The plan parameters are for this fiscal year only. The plan parameters will be reviewed and will be modified for the following year based on change in overall financial goals.

8. Other Provisions

A. The tables above indicate various references for determining the bonus award that will be payable if particular levels of performance are reached. Intermediate awards will be determined by straight-line interpolation between the pertinent references. All awards should be rounded to the nearest $100.

B. Incentive awards are payable in lump sum early in the next year, immediately following the determination of profit performance and completion of year-end audit.

C. The eligibility of an employee who is discharged or resigns during the plan year will be automatically cancelled. Managers must be employed to collect a bonus. Bonuses are prorated for new hires or transfers.

D. The plan will not be deemed to give any participant the right to be retained in the employment of the company.

E. This plan supersedes all previous short-term incentive compensation plans, unless a written contract exists.

CHAPTER 9: ARE YOU READY FOR AN INCENTIVE PLAN?

Introduction

Although alternative rewards offer excellent benefits to a company and employees, not all organizations are ready for incentive plans. To evaluate whether incentive plans are appropriate, we have provided a list of factors to consider. To determine whether your company is ready for an incentive plan, the company should be assessed against the questions that follow.

Assessment of readiness should include identifying requirements that are needed in a company to ensure an incentive plan's success. There are eight core questions that can identify readiness. Companies that can answer all eight questions affirmatively are in the best position to benefit from an incentive plan.

What the Questions Mean

If you can answer *yes* to these eight questions, you're probably ready for an incentive plan.

If companies meet the criteria set out by these questions, then incentive plans will enhance organizational objectives and performance. In most cases, plans fail because one of these eight factors is not established or present in the organization.

A caveat: The answers to these eight questions may not be immediately apparent. It may take some research to evaluate whether you can answer all the questions effectively.

Your company may not be ready

1) Are There Clear Goals?

You need to be able to clearly predict results necessary to drive the reward process. Strategic planning is used to develop business objectives. Business objectives normally are measured in sales volume, expenses, profitability and such customer service measurements as customer satisfaction surveys, shipped-on-time delivery numbers and percent of rejected work. There should be an internal management process that can predict future business activity levels with some level of reliability.

Many companies fail at incentives because they do not have a planning process that is able to capture a vision of the future. Employees do not believe in their goals, and plans lack credibility.

Start-up companies often fall into this category. It's difficult to predict cash flow or market share of an emerging company. Often, mistakes are made by designing incentive plans that give away too much or not enough. It is very difficult to accurately set goals and targets when a company is new in the marketplace or the marketplace is very volatile.

For example, a satellite transmission company was starting up in the United States. Its goal: to transfer live broadcasts overseas. The company had designed an incentive plan that shared revenue with employees based on a limited time in the marketplace. Unexpectedly, the company obtained a major contract to transmit international soccer events. The new business translated to 40 percent bonuses for staff who had been loyal to the small struggling company.

Unfortunately, the huge bonuses were only given to staff with tenure of one year. New staff hired because of the increased workload were not eligible until they had worked a year. This caused friction between the new and old employees.

When employees were hired, they were told about the outstanding bonus plan. The new hires anticipated great bonuses after they had met the eligibility criteria.

Because they had such a great year and grew so dramatically, the company changed the plan in year two. Raising the thresholds and expectations set up a major complaint from existing staff. By raising the thresholds, the new staff members who joined the plan felt they were getting cheated out of the dazzling bonuses of the prior year. Everyone got mad. Several employees quit, and the company suffered because it had installed a plan before it was ready.

In this case, the company had just begun to develop its culture and trust in each other. Premature plan adoption caused more harm than good. The company's ability to envision the future was impaired by its lack of experience in the marketplace.

Companies that have fluctuations in sales, major changes going on in the organization or unpredictable exterior/interior characteristics will find it hard to develop reasonable goals. In designing an incentive plan, the employees must believe that the goals can be obtained. Plans that are developed by companies that have unreasonable expectations—or that have experienced unpredictable results will find that employees are not motivated to meet the plan's goals.

Companies cannot predict results if there is business inconsistency. If companies are merging or organizational change is dynamic, it will be difficult to predict goals and, therefore, incentive plans may not be effective vehicles of compensation. Companies that have high turnover or other changes occurring will need to address those issues prior to implementing a plan design, too. Consistency of strategy, measurement and communication are key to successful communication of a plan.

There needs to be clarity of the goals, as well. That top management must be in agreement that the goals are clear and predictable. If strategic planning cannot identify clear, predictable goals, incentive plans are a waste of energy.

2) Is the Climate Right for Pay for Results?

Incentive plans cannot solve problems of mistrust, low morale or disharmony. The success or failure of most businesses depends on the effective performance of the employee. Incentive plans cannot fix management problems. If a company is not run-

Goals need to be clarified

ning effectively, and the communication between staff and management is not functional, incentives will not work.

For example, a mid-size pharmaceutical company that had recently changed presidents was looking for a new compensation plan. The company had a founder who had managed the business successfully for more than 40 years. He was a father figure—and treated his employees like family. But he had been ill for several years. The company continued to run, leaderless, slowly contributing less and less profit. The customer service department was old-fashioned and had never been computerized.

When the old owner died, his widow hired a professional manager as president. The new president was a young MBA—intensely *professional*. His expectations were based on several years' experience in the very aggressive airline industry. He immediately installed computers, dismissed long-term managers and set up rigid performance expectations. He brought in two new managers who were equally businesslike and aggressive and had high expectations. The remaining managers were very worried.

The company was reeling from culture shock. The remaining employees were constantly complaining about the new president. There was a culture split between the new professional managers and the old tenured employees. "We never did it that way," was a constant complaint.

On an instinctual level, the employees had no trust in the new management. There was significant resistance to change. The company did not set up an incentive for the employees. It decided instead to work on communication and teamwork first. The most important goal was to stabilize the staffing. Once the company stabilized and there was less resistance to change, a plan could be considered.

This was an environment in which an incentive plan would not work. Where there is such strong resistance to change and mistrust, other methods of motivation need to be used to change the climate before incentives can be effective.

Incentive plans won't work where employees have not been expected to perform based on measured results. Training and coaching are necessary to formulate a link between behavior and results. The companies that implement successful plans already have a culture or climate that encourages focusing on results. Those companies are not focusing on seniority, tenure or personality, but looking at the actual output of performance in evaluating employees' contributions.

The climate also has to be right for the shareholders. Incentive plans are only successful if shareholders are willing to provide additional compensation for additional effort. If there is a supportive environment, in which management works with stakeholders to enhance the value of an organization, and the shareholders are willing to reward that increase in value, incentive plans can be successful.

In companies experiencing change, resources are used up by the change process. Stakeholders do not see expected results. Trust must be established between management and staff, but also between the company and its stakeholders for plans to work effectively.

Organizations must have a level of trust in order to implement any type of incentive plan. Alternative rewards are based on adult communication. If companies don't communicate effectively, then incentive plans break down because of the barriers between management and the employee. Effective communication is key to any plan design. And those organizations that have communication issues and problems should first resolve those problems before exploring communication changes.

3) Is There a Credible Measurement Process?

Organizations that cannot measure results in a clear and timely manner need to focus on implementing measurement processes that work successfully, prior to installing incentive plans.

Several years ago, a national computer distribution company that supplied computer networks to Fortune 1000 businesses increased sales and market share yearly but had an all-too-common problem: As it was growing, its profits were decreasing. The president wanted to change the sales incentive plan. During our initial meeting, he bragged about

Trust—a key factor in implementing an incentive plan

his sophisticated computer processes and his up-to-date accounting system. A number of key executives echoed his feelings. The CFO was very boastful and claimed a very extensive MIS background.

Surprisingly, the sales manager identified accounting as a major problem. He had trouble tracking sales by territory and by individual salesperson. His sales reports were always late, and there was a month between sales action and reporting numbers.

Given the slightest opportunity, the company's salespeople made bitter, angry comments about their commissions and the accounting procedures. Accounting had to hand calculate each salesperson's incentive. One bookkeeper kept track of each sales contract and completed incentive calculations one by one. Each salesperson had a different sales agreement, with a different percent of commission based on selling to different customers.

To grow the company, the president had hired existing sales personnel who already had a customer base. He negotiated a different deal with each person. Each salesperson had an agreement that separated old and new business. The poor bookkeeper was going crazy trying to calculate monthly incentives, while the salespeople constantly interrupted—asking for special favors, when they would get their checks, etc. Everyone was upset by the system.

Once a sale was generated and entered into the computer, there were hand adjustments for shipping charges, volume discounts that overrode territorial costing and technical support fees. The salesperson that counted commission by sales in the territory became angry, and mistrusting since commissions were less than expected because of major adjustments.

The adjustments to commissions were done by hand—and never explained. When the salespeople complained, they were told to "just trust accounting—it was too complicated to explain." They were constantly interrupting accounting to get answers.

The plan participants felt the measurement of sales results was not reliable. It was perceived as untrue by sales personnel. The first step in considering changing incentives was to develop a credible measurement process. Developing a better measurement system also would build trust between sales and administration. After the measurements were accurate, the company could set reasonable goals and get clean data.

Incentive plans fail if management and employees do not believe in the reliability of reported results. Many organizations have unreliable measurement systems. Incentive plans are effective only if the infrastructure, policies and procedures of a company will support the measurement used in designing incentives.

4) Is There a Champion to Drive the Plan?

An articulate manager or CEO must be available to drive the communication process of the plan. The administration of the plan is important, but the key to success is its communication to the employees. Do you have a champion who can link individual performance to the strategic goals of the organization, and clearly represent to the employees how they can improve their efficiency to meet company-wide objectives?

Once a plan is designed, the communication process becomes critical. Incentive plans are not successful unless there is commitment to constant coaching—and training regarding paying for results. Just as our education system depends on constant repetition in the learning process, organizations must constantly reinforce an incentive process.

Many times, a CEO will roll out a new incentive plan by announcing it once and expecting all employees to understand it. A successful implementation doesn't come that easy. Communication never stops. A good CEO reinforces the plan at every meeting, both with staff and managers. A CEO must be committed to constantly reinforcing the goals, the plan and the behavior necessary to reach the goals.

That reinforcement must come in the form of employee recognition, stories that compliment behavior necessary to achieve results and an emphasis on measured output to evaluate performance.

Management is needed to drive the plan

5) Is Compensation at Market?

Organizations must be prepared to seriously look at their compensation levels prior to plan implementation and design. Incentive compensation is only successful if the staff is compensated competitively. Increased turnover will result if compensation levels are not kept at market. Constructing an incentive plan on top of base salaries that are not appropriate will lead to mistrust of a plan. Employees quickly recognize incentive plans as a subterfuge if base salaries are not competitive.

Companies sometimes think that creating incentives can decrease their commitment to market pay. Companies must maintain pay at market, then recognize performance differences with merit increases. Increases should be for performance and market.

Companies are made up of three types of employees: value builders, value adders and value maintainers. Value builders are the superstars that build the sales and profits of a company. They are found in sales, research and development. These are the bright, aggressive top performers companies can't afford to lose. They should be compensated significantly above the market with base and incentives. The value adders are the staff members that do their job and contribute value added to the company. They implement new efficient procedures, up-sell, and provide improved customer service. They should be paid above market with base and incentive pay. The maintainers are the workers that get things done. Most employees are maintainers. They should be paid at the market. All three are valuable to an organization, and the builders and adders know their worth in the marketplace.

Base pay practices should not be lowered unless there are serious business problems. Employees depend on a level of income to meet their basic needs and secure a certain standard of living for their families.

A good incentive plan always starts with ensuring base salaries meet the pay philosophy of the organization. Adjustments are sometimes made over several years, but a good plan complements weekly and monthly pay practices.

6) Is There a Commitment to an Incentive Plan?

Organizations that are committed to measuring results, paying for results and monitoring results will be successful in implementing incentive plans. If there is not a commitment to quantifiable measurement, an organization will fail at designing and using incentives to motivate employees.

All areas and departments must be committed to measurable results, and all executives must be committed to reinforcing and coaching employees to meet strategic objectives. If one department or one faction of an organization is not committed, then an organization-wide plan will not work.

The commitment must be a long-term commitment to the process. New plans take time, energy and constant fine tuning. The introduction of a plan is a change for the organization. When introducing change, there is always resistance. It takes time to overcome resistance to change. When changing compensation or changing an existing plan parameter, several months or even years may be required to see results.

A caveat: Don't expect instant acceptance. It takes time to integrate an incentive plan into the culture of an organization. It takes time to change behavior patterns. The commitment to incentives means that you must recognize the difficulties in introducing new ideas—and be willing to continue support until the organization has institutionalized the incentive change process.

7) Is There Effective Communication?

This point simply can't be stressed enough.

In order to facilitate the installment of an incentive process, communication has to be ongoing and effective. In rolling out a new incentive plan, employees have to understand the plan and change their behavior based on the communication of the goals of the plan.

In the example of the pharmaceutical company cited above, the employees were upset by major changes that had occurred in the organization. The new

Introduction means change and resistance

president coming into the organization had not been received well, and the communication process between management and the employees had broken down. At that point, it would have been dangerous to install an incentive plan. The company was not effective in communicating strategy and goals to employees.

In communicating plan design, the champion should ensure that all levels of the company thoroughly understand the plan and the goals. If communication is an issue in other areas of the organization, it will be difficult to avoid communication problems in plan design. If 10 percent or more of the workforce speaks another language, then an interpreter is necessary.

The communication process must work on paper, one-on-one and in group meetings. Research prior to designing a plan can establish whether the communication in an organization is working.

8) Is There Consistency?

Consistency in business strategy is important in evaluating success and clarifying a vision for the future. It is difficult to set goals and to establish expected results if the company has constant turnover, changes in management and strategic direction changes. Consistency of management and of process needs to be established as a base before an incentive plan design can be added.

The basics of an organization need to be formulated. Process and procedures for communication, developing business strategy and customer service need to be in place. In companies that are going through dramatic change; mergers and re-engineering, it is difficult to measure goals. Better timing for an incentive plan will be after the re-engineering process has occurred and the organization has settled down into a more predictable and established process.

Consistency also is important in looking at the compensation processes of the past. If the company has historically tried various types of incentive programs, there will be mistrust and misunderstanding on the part of participants. Previous compensation processes also need to have established consistency so new plans that are pyramided on top of current organizational structure will have credibility.

Other Issues to Consider

Once the questions have been answered, there are few other issues to consider.

Group incentives can complement performance of organizations. Those companies that have used group incentives or alternative rewards over the last several years have proven to be more successful than those that don't use incentives. Group incentives give employees clear direction for their jobs and behavior, and provide them with a clear road map to success. Only companies that are ready for incentive plans will be effective in motivating employees based on paying for results.

Successful companies are established companies that can provide current cash incentives to employees and also predict with some reasonableness the results necessary to drive the company's success. Although there are always changes occurring in the marketplace, a company's ability to strategically plan for those changes and effectively communicate its plans will be more likely to experience above-average results.

Success Factors

There are characteristics of successful incentive plans that are common and recurring. Plans that have these characteristics tend to be effective. They meet the needs of business owners, employees and other stakeholders. And they act as a stimulus, propelling a company forward toward its goals.

(These eight characteristics correspond, roughly, with the eight questions that we just considered.)

Clear Vision

The only way an incentive plan can be successful is if it supports achieving company goals. A plan should encourage employees to behave in a way that complements the forward movement of a company. To move forward in the marketplace, companies need to have a road map showing how to move

Format is important

Focus is on achieving company goals

ahead. Clear vision of direction, future growth and organizational change is key to developing a successful incentive plan. Vision may be intuitive for a true entrepreneur but, more often, it involves planning. The planning process that creates vision is often called strategic planning.

Strategic planning is a must for all successful incentive plans. Strategic planning involves the key management of a company. The management must work together to evaluate the past performance of the company, look at the marketplace opportunities that are available and formulate a plan for the future.

The vision then must be distilled and presented to employees in such a way that they can embody the goals. Clear vision leads to clear goals that can be used as a road map for action. Employees can then focus effort and energy on attaining common goals and vision.

Many incentive plans fail because the goals and objectives of the plan are not attainable. Plans are rolled out with fanfare, and then die because the employee perceives the goals as impossible. Part of success is the vision to know what is doable—and how the results are going to be achieved. Convincing others of a plan's credibility is part of the vision.

If a company is moving quickly and the marketplace is shifting rapidly, the management cannot have a vision that projects goals one year out. In those cases, quarterly or half-year planning can help to clarify vision.

Clear vision must precede plan design, so you can set attainable goals and have the necessary credibility with employees to focus synergistic effort on results.

Timely and Ongoing Communication

Once the vision is established, communicating it in a way that employees understand and respond to is critical. Employees need to be initiated into an incentive plan with repeat training. Employees need to clearly understand how their behavior ties into achieving results. Employees need frequent feedback about their behavior and results. Successful

200

plans spend time and effort communicating timely results.

An incentive plan is designed to change behavior so all employees are focused on attaining company goals. It takes repeat exposure and training to change employees' behavior.

Employees learn at different speeds and with different levels of understanding. A good incentive plan communicates the desired results in many ways, so that every employee can understand goals and measurements. Some employees will learn by spreadsheets, some will learn by graphs and pictures, and some will learn by watching others. Whatever the level of understanding in an organization, a successful plan will link all the employees to a common goal and understanding.

When a company rolls out its plan, the CEO should meet with all staff and explain the guidelines and goals. He or she should give concrete examples of how employees can do specific jobs more effectively to achieve goals.

Supervisors should meet regularly with their departments to review achievements and future efforts. The CEO should schedule regular *state of the company* talks, at which he or she discusses specific goals, achievements and shortcomings.

Your employees know what affects sales volume and profitability—even if they don't think in financial terms. The purpose of an incentive plan is to formalize their thinking.

Track Success

Successful plans track success on a daily basis. Tracking does not have to be complex. A simple board in the lunchroom or a chalkboard in the factory can suffice. Tracking needs to take place as quickly after the event as possible. Plans cannot be successful if accounting departments have a several-day lag from posting to final figures.

Communication is the most important characteristic of a good incentive plan. In order to truly get people behind the objectives of a plan they must understand how their behavior can affect the goals. They must see a direct relationship between their individual results and the payback they receive.

Tracking must be timely & consistent

Simplicity obtains expected results

Simplify

Employees need to understand the goal and results. A complex plan confuses employees and makes them skeptical about being able to obtain results. Keep the plan and expected results simple and clear. If you are introducing an incentive plan for the first time, it should be as simple as possible. More goals and refinements can be added with the next plan, as employees begin to understand the process.

For example, a large tire manufacturer set up a reward system for its warehouse workers. The reward system was designed around average number of tires shipped.

The warehouse workers needed a very simple visual to track success. To encourage goal attainment, the company posted three large thermometers in the warehouse, one on the shipping dock, one by the time clock and one in the lunchroom. The temperature on the thermometer increased daily to indicate the volume of tires out the door. The employees knew if the thermometers hit the top, they would get two days additional pay. They could see the progress daily. Although the warehouse workers had varying levels of education and diverse ethnic backgrounds, they all could identify with the temperature level as it related to volume and reward.

Diagrams seem to work best with all levels of employees. Pictures are easier to understand and evaluate than words for most people. So keep it simple—graphs, thermometers and bar charts work well.

Then, reinforce the goals regularly in meetings, reviews and any publications sent out to employees.

Establish a Sunset

Every plan needs a beginning and an ending. A sunset, or an ending, needs to be clearly announced at the beginning of the plan. Plans need to change annually. As results are achieved, there will be new challenges and goals. It is important that participants understand at the outset of the plan that there will be new goals, new parameters and new expectations when the plan is over. A new plan design may be totally different, or there may be only minor adjustments.

A Test Run

If you are developing incentives for the first time, we recommend that you start with a pilot. A pilot is a temporary plan that is being tested, much like a maiden flight. By rolling out a pilot, you are not locked into any specific follow-up. Often, incentive plans are piloted with one group or division of a company before they are rolled out in the whole company. That way, the management has time to refine and change the plan to improve results.

For instance, a manufacturing company that sold industrial packaging equipment had a serious problem. The company had several capable engineers selling its products throughout the United States. The sales force had been in place for several years. But packaging equipment that was sold in the 1970s for about $100,000 was selling in the 1990s for more than a million dollars.

The commission schedule had never been changed—a salesperson needed to sell only one machine to equal the same income he or she had made by selling 10 machines in the past. Sales figures were increasing because of pricing—but the actual number of units sold had dropped dramatically.

The company had not reevaluated its incentives yearly, although it had changed the product pricing. The plan needed to be adjusted yearly to align with the strategy of the business. Had the commission plan ended each year with a sunset, the small adjustments would have been much easier to take than the huge change the company was forced to make after the commission plan had been in place for several years.

The sales staff had come to think of the fat commission structure as an entitlement.

This is a common problem: Plans without sunsets become entitlement. Many sales incentive plans have been in existence for years. When the market changes, pricing shifts or customer needs change, it is very difficult to change the plan if you have not had annual sunsets that allow slight alterations in plan parameters.

All plans should have an end

Announce and reinforce

Encourage Employees to Participate

A good incentive plan allows participants to change their behavior to achieve better results. The staff has some ability to influence sales, profit or other expect results. Employees have discretion over their output. Employees can effectively improve efficiencies. A good incentive plan must be achievable, but it also must be based on goals the employees can directly influence.

In some companies, employees cannot influence sales goals directly. But they can influence customer service, costs and efficiencies.

Separate Incentive Pay from Base Pay

There needs to be a distinct separation between base pay and incentive reward. Most companies pay incentives in a separate check—and often at a different time—than the payroll.

Employees also begin to feel the incentive is an entitlement if they regularly get a bonus and it is in their paycheck. They forget it is variable and at-risk.

Incentive pay needs to be reinforced and announced often. One of my clients had a very generous monthly bonus that the company paid to employees. There was no celebrating or announcement; the staff just got it in their normal monthly paycheck. Even though the employees had a 40-percent increase in pay with their bonuses, they complained about not getting a salary increase. They were very upset when the next year's new plan set new and higher goals. The management had not communicated clearly about the plan, its sunset and the monthly payout. So, the employees began to expect more pay.

Celebrate Successes

Achievement of a goal is a win. The win should be celebrated with the participants. A company is a community—and celebration of a goal gives the community a chance to come together in a non-problem-solving setting to interact in a risk-free environment. Celebration also reinforces efficiency and productivity.

Renn Zaphiropoulos was a top executive at a Xerox division, versatec. He had run a profitable division for several years. The company rewrote the parameters of the incentive plan for all divisions, extending the incentive plan payout three years. There was a very long and leveraged profit goal for each division. Divisions had to make their goal for three years to get a payout. His was the only division to make the goal. His division consistently made a 6 percent profit for three years.

Reluctantly, the company sent Renn his bonus check in the mail for several hundred thousand dollars. He opened the envelope and found a check. He was appalled that, after three years, there was no thank you—no words of acknowledgment. He was determined that he would not treat his employees the same way.

To give them their checks, he hired a marching band and rented a large warehouse. On the day of the celebration, he closed his factory, closed the nearby streets and had all the employees walk across the street to the warehouse with the marching band playing in full uniform.

Inside the decorated warehouse, the employees watched the president riding on a 2½ ton live elephant with a huge *6 percent* painted on its side. The warehouse was decorated for a festival. The president thanked the employees and then told them to find their supervisors. Each employee was personally handed a bonus check from his or her supervisor with a thank you.

Those checks were soon spent—but years later the employees still remembered the 6 percent and Renn riding an elephant.

Psychologists say that individuals learn faster when positive feedback reinforces behavior that leads to success. Incentive plans are no different. The more you can celebrate success and highlight behavior that leads to the goal, the more the goal is reinforced.

Successful plans reinforce the goal direction with regular tracking and attention. Senior management is aware and involved in every aspect of the tracking and communicating. There are constant celebrations of the little and big victories.

Make the success a "known" success

CONCLUSION: SOME FINAL POINTS TO CONSIDER

Incentive pay is emerging as the solution to the financial dilemmas facing today's businesses.

More and more companies in the United States are using alternative rewards or group incentives to reinforce teamwork, improve productivity and enhance the communication in an organization.

Historically, companies have paid salary increases based on tenure. In the 1970s and 1980s, salaries were increased based on cost of living and market changes. In the 1990s, as the economy tightened, companies could no longer afford to increase salaries based on tenure alone.

In today's competitive environment, companies are caught between the customer demanding more product or service for the same or discounted prices, and their staff demanding increased compensation. The solution that U.S. employers have found is market-based pay with alternative rewards.

Alternative rewards provide variable pay to employees based on individual, group and company performance. As the company, individual and groups meet their measured goals, the employees are provided additional compensation. This compensation can be in the form of cash or non-cash rewards. These rewards enhance the lifestyle of the American worker. Alternative rewards are company-wide incentive plans that include the rank-and-file employees, as well as managers. The incentive is preannounced and linked to company performance. The incentive is typically tied to profit, sales or customer service goals.

As we've seen, alternative rewards can be cash or non-cash. Some companies use gifts, trips or time off as incentives. The important feature is that an

Rewards are received if goals are met

alternative reward is not discretionary. There is no judgment to evaluate payout. Employees receive rewards if they accomplish predetermined results. The plans are not qualified plans, so they are not long-term and have no special tax benefit. They are taxed as earnings.

Studies for the American Compensation Association[1] conducted over the last several years have indicated that market-based pay and incentive plans are growing in popularity. About 50 percent of U.S. companies have general incentive plans—90 to 95 percent of those companies have some form of management incentive plan. Most of these plans have been installed after the 1980s. Fifty percent of all large companies in recent Fortune 500 surveys indicate market-based pay approaches are becoming far more important in today's economy.

Companies that use group incentives successfully find short-term incentives drive behavior that enhances company goals and productivity. Linking compensation to the strategic business direction of a company can enhance success and, at the same time, provide additional compensation to employees. Successful plans measure results, deliver the payout in a timely manner and allow for ongoing review and adjustment.

Finally, all rewards are linked to the business goals of the organization. Successful plans in today's diverse work environments link pay directly to results and avoid subjective evaluation on the part of management.

In this chapter, we will consider how the characteristics of a successful compensation plan relate to specific issues you—as an employer—face. This chapter should be a kind of master diagnostic checklist to determine whether you're ready to install an incentive plan.

Market Pay Process

Incentives are not guarantees. They are paid out as at-risk pay when company performance goals are met. The foundation for a successful incentive program is a base salary that is competitive with the market. Although the incentive pay is flexible or variable, the base pay is a fixed cost to a company.

---

[1] Edilberto Montemayor, *A Model for Aligning Teamwork and Pay,* American Compensation Association Journal, (Summer 1994).

The incentive pay is additional pay above the base salary if results are met.

The base pay is the fixed hourly, daily or weekly rate a person is paid. It is paid regardless of contribution, effort or performance. Once the base pay has been established, then incentive pay provides additional compensation.

Unlike base pay, incentive pay is "at-risk." The additional pay is a reward for accomplishing measurable results.

The fixed salary cost should be enough to satisfy and compensate the workforce. The salary cost also should be in line with other industry salary costs to protect the long-term viability of the company. If fixed salary costs are too high, the company must price its products or services higher than its competitors. Occasionally, companies can get away with higher-priced products, but it is not a strategy that is successful if demand drops. So careful research and assessment of base pay levels is critical to the incentive process.

The first step in designing a reward process is to determine appropriate base pay levels. This step includes designing total pay philosophies for your company based on its unique business strategy. You need to be ready—and your employees need to be willing—to scrutinize how you pay people. You have to be prepared to dedicate time and resources to developing a new system.

Finally, you need to realize that some employees may never be fully reconciled to an incentivized pay plan. These people will see only the risks (usually, of not getting steady raises) and not the advantages. Incentives do require a different attitude toward risk and reward than some employees are willing to adopt.

To determine effective pay levels, other jobs doing similar tasks need to be surveyed. This is the second step in designing an alternative reward. Position surveys can be obtained from published information, or a custom survey can be done to establish the average pay for a position in a business marketplace.

Once market data has been obtained, the skill level, tenure and performance of an incumbent will be

First determine base pay

① Base Pay

survey other jobs

① market data
② skill leve
③ tensru
④ performa

Understand return on investment and how it applies to the shareholders & owners

used to determine how he or she is paid against the market. Uniform guidelines on how pay is determined are called pay policies. They isolate a company's pay philosophy into concrete pay rates. Policies ensure consistency between divisions, departments and employee groups.

Overview of Incentive Plan Design

The design steps necessary to create an incentive plan are fairly simple. They have been explained with many examples in this book. The first step requires a company to evaluate its business and determine goals that will enhance value in the marketplace. The measurable objectives of a company include not only profit and sales goals, but also the strategy and philosophy for paying employees.

Once goals are determined through strategic planning, research is conducted to evaluate pay alternatives, market rates and competitive incentive plans. The research includes market pay surveys, analysis of local pay practices and an evaluation of industry standards. Knowing what your competition is doing is critical to designing a successful incentive plan.

Once the research has been completed and market evaluations have been reviewed, the company can work backward from the sales and profit goals to design a plan that meets the needs of its own organization. Working backward will keep a company's stockholders happy and establish thresholds that initiate the incentive payout process. Key to working backward is understanding return on investment and the needs of the shareholders and owners. Plan design is simple, once a company has profiled its needs.

Financial Review

Once a plan is designed, in the next step, financial scenarios need to be developed. These scenarios will provide information about the financial impact of the reward program. As financial impacts are evaluated, the design can be adjusted to meet the needs of the employees, as well as other shareholders.

Once a design has been agreed upon, it can be enhanced by review and comments from key executives, your CPA firm or other interested parties—such as advisory boards or boards of directors. Compensation plans are something advisors always should review.

Once the draft plan has been improved and adjusted, the next step is communicating the plan to the employees. New plans are sometimes tried for a specific time frame or in a specific division. Trial plans are called pilot plans. The initial communication process is called a rollout.

Communication is one of the most critical parts of an incentive plan. Explaining plan design to all employees in a way that every employee understands is important. Employees also must understand what their contribution must be to meet company goals. The communication process needs to highlight the behavior necessary from each employee to move the company forward toward the goals. The communication process is not just a one-time rollout. It consists of reinforcing information on an ongoing basis and providing company results constantly to enhance the focus on goals.

Getting Started

There is a simple way to begin the design of your own company's incentive plan. Ask yourself a few questions. Is your company ready adopt a variable pay program? Do you have the climate, consistency, champion and commitment to successfully develop and implement an incentive plan? Once these things have been determined and your company is committed to use incentives as a reward process, you're ready to begin.

Market pay is a result of internal and external equity. Researching survey data will give a company information on market rates for various benchmark positions. Those positions then will translate back to individual jobs within the hierarchy of the company. Market pay ensures that people have adequate base compensation. Variable pay plans can be successful only if the underlying base pay is at market.

The next step is to clarify goals. The goals of an incentive plan drive the plan itself. Looking at your

Make sure that each employee knows their "role"

211

Review the plan for improvement

strategic direction and your strategic advantage in the marketplace will help facilitate goal development. Part of evaluating goals is ensuring that you have a pay philosophy that supports your business strategy. Most variable pay plans are developed after a market pay program is in place.

Research of incentive plans can help a company determine design and compensation strategy. The research should include information about direct competitors, industry activity and local competitors or labor in the marketplace.

Once the goals and the research are clear, you can design your plan by working backward from shareholders' needs to set payout levels. Thresholds help to ensure that your pay for results program does not impinge upon the cash needs of the company or the return on investment to the shareholders.

Variable pay design then follows from the type of goals, the research and findings, as well as the needs of the organization and the shareholders.

Once a simple design is in place, an accountant or other financial expert needs to provide financial and *what-if* analysis, based on historic and projected business results. Looking at the financials can determine how much of a payout the organization can afford—and verify that thresholds are appropriate.

Once a plan is designed, it needs to be reviewed for improvement by interested parties that know something about the organization. Typically, this is done by key executives or a board of directors. They study the draft plan to find any weaknesses in plan design. Allowing key managers to see a plan in the design stage can help them buy into the plan itself. If they participate, they feel much more part of the process and in control.

Finally, in order to effectively design a plan, the communication process has to start at the beginning. A champion needs to be selected that will be responsible for communicating plan activity, both upward and downward. This individual needs to provide ongoing information that helps employees understand results, as well as how their behavior affects results.

A good incentive plan is really a communication

plan. It helps organizations clarify goals, focus and synergize the energy of the employees toward the strategic direction of the organization.

We have looked at several variations of variable pay or incentive plans.

The key to a plan design is remembering the acronym MALT: a good plan *measures results, avoids judgment* of individuals on a subjective basis, *links pay* to the strategic results of the business and is done in a *timely manner*—with sunsets to end plans and start new ones.

Successful companies will find that effective variable pay programs can contribute to the growth and development of business objectives. Success or failure of any business, to a large extent, depends on the caliber of its employees.

Successful firms want to attract and retain star performers. Rewards and pay are major factors in successful staffing. Balancing staff costs with product pricing is an art in today's global economy.

Incentives provide maximum flexibility for companies' product pricing, while sending a powerful message of empowerment to employees. Incentive plans are key to effective business performance. They help provide vision, communication and clarity to companies by paying for results. Incentives influence behavior by motivating employees to achieve goals and reinforcing the desired action. Incentives provide equity and fairness, and allow shareholders both inside and outside the business to share the wealth of success.

APPENDICES

APPENDIX ONE

SALARY SURVEY LETTER AND QUESTIONNAIRE

Dear Survey Participant:

Our Client has asked us to assist in a Salary Survey in your industry. Your organization has been identified as a key industry participant and is considered a valuable resource for compensation in these areas.

In exchange for your participation, we will be providing you with a copy of the completed survey as soon as the information is compiled. As always, the information will be formatted to assure company confidentiality.

We ask that the information be returned to us by July 14, 1995

We would very much appreciate your participation in the survey. Please don't hesitate to call our office if you have any questions.

Sincerely,

Karen Jorgensen
President

APPENDIX ONE

1. ___ Single location organization
    ___ Division or subsidiary location
    ___ Other:

2. Number of employees (reporting entity): _____

3. Type of industry: _____

4. Annual dollar sales volume of this location: $ _____

5. If you use a salary range structure, by what percentage did you increase your ranges in 1995?
    Exempt _____   Non-Exempt _____
    Effective Date of Structure Adjustment _____

6. What was your merit increase budget for 1995? _____
    Effective Date: _____

7. Do you provide medical insurance for employees?
    PPO? _____   HMO? _____
    Indemnity?_____   Employee cost? _____
    Deductible Amt.? _____   Dependent coverage paid by? _____

8. Do you provide dental insurance?_____
    Who pays premium? _____

9. Do you have a retirement plan? _____
    If yes, funded at what percent of salary? _____

10. Do you have a profit sharing plan? _____
    What percent of salary was paid in 1994? _____

11. Do you pay bonuses? _____ Discretionary? _____
    About what % of salary? _____
    Other (explain): _____

	After:	1yr.	2yrs.	3yrs.	5yrs.	10yrs.
12. *Non-exempt* Number of vacation days per year?		___	___	___	___	___
Employees Number of sick days per year?		___	___	___	___	___
Exempt Number of vacation days per year?		___	___	___	___	___
Employees Number of sick days per year?		___	___	___	___	___

13. Do you provide compensationary time off for exempt employees? _____

   If yes, please explain when:

   For weekend work? _____

   For USA travel? _____

   For international travel? _____

   Any other benefits or time off? _____

Submitted By (name of organization): _____

Name & Title of Respondent:_____

Return Address: _____

_____

   Phone: _____

DATA INPUT SHEET

Job Title: Accounts Payable Clerk

Duties: Process all accounts payable, ensuring all billings are correct, paid timely and authorized. Takes full advantage of discounts and avoids finance charges. Works independently to organize work for accuracy, efficiency and attention to detail. 2 years job specific experience.

Geographic Location	# of Incumbents in Position	Minimum	Salary Ranges Midpoint	Maximum	Average Salary

Your Job Title _____   Non-Exempt: _____

Union: _____

Degree of Match _____   1 = Less than above description

2 = Very close/Matches description

3 = More than above description

Reports To (Title): _____

Job Title: Administrative Assistant

Duties: Provides professional administrative support services to a Director and other staff members as necessary. Works independently to organize work for accuracy, efficiency and attention to detail. Proficient in word processing and spreadsheet software. Minimum 50 WPM typing. High school diploma or equivalent.

Geographic Location	# of Incumbents in Position	Minimum	Salary Ranges Midpoint	Maximum	Average Salary

Your Job Title _____   Non-Exempt: _____

Union: _____

Degree of Match _____   1 = Less than above description

2 = Very close/Matches description

3 = More than above description

Reports To (Title): _____

Job Title: Customer Service Representative

Duties: Receives customer questions and concerns via telephone, correspondence, and fax. Professionally and accurately provides information, innovative solutions, product information, and general help to customers with consistency and attention to detail. Ability to operate P.C. for word processing. High school diploma or equivalent.

Geographic Location	# of Incumbents in Position	Minimum	Salary Ranges Midpoint	Maximum	Average Salary

Your Job Title _____   Non-Exempt: _____

Union: _____

Degree of Match _____   1 = Less than above description

2 = Very close/Matches description

3 = More than above description

Reports To (Title): _____

Job Title: Human Resources Generalist

Duties: Coordinates and performs a variety of human resources activities related to recruitment, hiring, orientation, employee relations, compensation and policy administration. Provides general H.R. support to management and employees that focuses on attracting, retaining, and motivating the best qualified work force. Minimum 4 years job specific experience and a bachelor's degree.

Geographic Location	# of Incumbents in Position	Minimum	Salary Ranges Midpoint	Maximum	Average Salary

Your Job Title _____   Non-Exempt: _____

Union: _____

Degree of Match _____   1 = Less than above description

2 = Very close/Matches description

3 = More than above description

Reports To (Title): _____

Job Title: Staff Accountant

Duties: Responsible for all fixed asset accounting: fixed asset additions, disposals, and transfers into the fixed asset system (FAS) and reconciles the related transactions to the general ledger. Prepares adjusting journal entries for fixed asset transactions and prepares and distributes the financial management package. Minimum 2 years job-related experience. Bachelors degree in accouting or business administration or equivalent related experience.

Geographic Location	# of Incumbents in Position	Minimum	Salary Ranges Midpoint	Maximum	Average Salary

Your Job Title _____   Non-Exempt: _____

Union: _____

Degree of Match _____   1 = Less than above description

2 = Very close/Matches description

3 = More than above description

Reports To (Title): _____

Job Title: Technical Support Specialist I

Duties: Provides quality technical services to users of products and contributes to the collective resources and knowledge of the technical support department. Answers user questions and solves user problems via telephone and written responses; researches and documents problems, tracks users communications; handles special projects. A.A.S. or B.S. degree or equivalent experience.

Geographic Location	# of Incumbents in Position	Minimum	Salary Ranges Midpoint	Maximum	Average Salary

Your Job Title _____   Non-Exempt: _____

Union: _____

Degree of Match _____   1 = Less than above description

2 = Very close/Matches description

3 = More than above description

Reports To (Title): _____

EMPLOYEE FOCUS GROUP QUESTIONNAIRE

Script: Thank you for joining us today for our focus group discussion on employee recognition. The company is investigating various methods of motivating employees, and you have been selected to participate. Your input will be valuable to us.

This session is just to get some information. If there are changes, they may take some time to develop, so don't expect immediate results. You were selected as a cross section to represent a diversity of employees. What you say will be confidential as to the specific person who made the recommendation, but I will be taking notes to make sure all your ideas are recorded.

I'd appreciate your input on the first questions.

1. What do you believe motivates employees?
2. How is our current program working?
3. Specifically discuss each benefit.
4. What type of recognition should the company be using?

5. What recognition programs have you heard about or had in the past that has worked for you?

6. Is there anything else you would suggest?

7. Any other comments you want to add?

APPENDIX THREE

MANAGEMENT INCENTIVE DESIGN QUESTIONNAIRE

1. How do you measure each goal of the plan?
2. Who will be in the plan?
3. What is the size of award for the participants?
4. How often will the plan pay out to the participants?
5. What are the threshold numbers?
6. Do employees need to be employed to receive payout?
7. What is the definition of salary?

8. Does everyone receive the same incentive?

9. When does the payout occur?

10. Who is responsible for the calculations and communications?

11. Who measures performance?

12. Will you pilot the plan?

13. Does the plan pay out all monies due or is there a hold back provision?

14. What is the life of the plan?

APPENDIX FOUR

EMPLOYEE INCENTIVE DESIGN QUESTIONNAIRE

1. What is your job? Tell us about your duties, length of service and responsibilities.

   _____

   _____

2. What should be expected of a successful practitioner of your job?

   _____

   _____

3. What specific behaviors do you want from other team members?

   _____

   _____

4. What does the company do?

   _____

   _____

5. What does your team contribute to the company?

   _____

   _____

6. Who do you think should be included in your team?

   _____

   _____

7. What is the strategic advantage of your product, service and/ or company?

   _____

   _____

8. What are the team goals for this year?

   _____

   _____

9. How are the team output's measured?

   _____

   _____

10. Do you think the team measurement is fair? Why? Why not?

    _____

    _____

11. Do you think the team measurement is accurate?

    _____

    _____

12. What do you think should be measured for accurate evaluation of team output?

    _____

    _____

13. Who supports your team? Should we get their input?

    _____

    _____

14. How did you get rewarded last year?

    _____

    _____

15. Do you have any suggestions for bonus programs for your team?

    _____

    _____

16. How effective is the communication on your team?

    _____

    _____

17. How could we improve efficiency on your team?

_____

_____

18. Do you feel team members have sufficient information to be effective? How could it improve?

_____

_____

19. Do you feel that you can make a difference in team total results? Why? Why not?

_____

_____

20. Are your team members empowered to make change?

_____

_____

21. Is there training that could help improve team output?

_____

_____

22. Any other comments or suggestions?

_____

_____

APPENDIX FIVE

SALES INCENTIVE QUESTIONNAIRE (PART ONE)

1. What is the strategic advantage of the company?

   _____

   _____

2. How do sales influence the strategic advantage?

   _____

   _____

3. What are the measurable results of the sales force? What are the sales objectives?

   _____

   _____

4. Who else is involved in sales and to what extent?

   _____

   _____

5. How has the sales force been compensated in the past? What is the ratio of base to incentive now?

   _____

   _____

6. What do the competitors pay? How do you know?

   _____

   _____

7. How the the sales personnel want to be incentivized? What do they want to measure?

   _____

   _____

8. Are the measurements credible? Is the competitors system accurate?

   _____

   _____

9. How sophisticated is the sales force with computers?

    _____

    _____

10. What is the sales climate?

    _____

    _____

11. What key factors affect the sales force both positively and negatively?

    _____

    _____

12. How clear have goals been in the past?

    _____

    _____

13. How much input do sales personnel have in selling quotas or goals?

    _____

    _____

14. How is marketing supporting sales?

    _____

    _____

15. Should a quota be set for a total dollar amount or should quotas be set or major product lines?

    _____

    _____

16. How often is there a long-cycle, large dollar sale?

    _____

    _____

17. How often does a sales person open a new account? What is the history.

   _____

   _____

18. How much sales activity is in new accounts and how much is in existing business ordering?

   _____

   _____

19. What is the long range growth of a territory?

   _____

   _____

20. What is the long range growth goals of the company?

   _____

   _____

21. What is the career potential for a sales person?

   _____

   _____

22. How are the sales personnel trained and supported?

   _____

   _____

23. In percentages what is the percentage over quota that can be achieved by an outstanding salesperson?

   _____

   _____

24. What percentage under quota could an average salesperson expect in a very bad year?

   _____

   _____

25. What other information would be relevant to know?

_____

_____

26. Are there tools for the sales personnel? What are they, who pays for them, and are there tools that would improve efficiency that they don't have?

_____

_____

27. How much time is selling vs. other activities? What are the other activities?

_____

_____

28. Does the sales job require special technical know-how?

_____

_____

29. What non-sales functions do the sales personnel perform? Who does training of new sales personnel? How long does the follow-up after the sales is made take?

_____

_____

30. Do salespeople function independently or as a team? If team, to what extent?

_____

_____

APPENDIX SIX

SALES INCENTIVE QUESTIONNAIRE (PART TWO)

1. Tell me about your job and what is generally expected of a successful salesperson?

    _____

    _____

2. What is the strategic advantage of the company?

    _____

    _____

3. What are the goals for this year?

    _____

    _____

4. How are sales goals measured at this time?

    _____

    _____

5. Do you think the measurement is fair? Why? Why not?

    _____

    _____

6. Do you think the measurement tools of the company are accurate? Why? Why not?

    _____

    _____

7. What do you think should be measured for effective rewards?

    _____

    _____

8. How much time do you spend not selling?

    _____

    _____

9. Who supports the direct sales effort?

    _____

    _____

10. Who should be on the "sales team"?

    _____

    _____

11. Do you have direct knowledge of any other sales incentive plan that has been successful?

    _____

    _____

12. What is the role of marketing, customer service, advertising or installation in the sales process?

    _____

    _____

13. Is there a non-sales function that requires time to be successful on the sales team?

    _____

    _____

14. If you were going to design a new sales incentive what would it look like?

    _____

    _____

15. How should sales splits be handled?

    _____

    _____

16. How should returns be accounted for within the plan?

    _____

    _____

17. Is there anything the company can change to improve the sales team's efficiency?

    _____

    _____

18. Is there any training that could improve results?

    _____

    _____

19. Do you have a suggestion how best to communicate a new sales team incentive?

    _____

    _____

20. Any other ideas or comments?

    _____

    _____

APPENDIX SEVEN

QUESTIONNAIRE FOR INCENTIVE PLAN ANALYSIS

1. Briefly describe your own incentive plan.

2. Did the plan work?

3. What worked well?

4. What didn't work?

5. What is the company's strategic advantage?

6. How do you influence the strategic direction of the company?

7. What are your three top business priorities this year?

8. For each business priority, define three performance measures.
   How should the success of the total organization be considered in an incentive plan for profit center management?

9. How should the success of the specialty areas enter into profit center manager's?

10. What is a reasonable office operating profit expectancy?

APPENDIX EIGHT

POSITION QUESTIONNAIRE

Job Title: _____

Reports To: (title) _____

Department: _____

Basic Functions: _____

DESCRIBE PRIMARY ROUTINE JOB DUTIES (start with most important):

A. _____

B. _____

C. _____

D. _____

E. _____

DESCRIBE THE DISTRIBUTION OF TIME SPENT ON PRIMARY JOB DUTIES:

A. _____ ____ %

B. _____ ____ %

C. _____ ____ %

D. _____ ____ %

E. _____ ____ %

(Attach additional pages if necessary)

Weekly Duties: _____

_____

Monthly Duties: _____

_____

Yearly Duties: _____

_____

Positions Supervised: _____

Difficulties Encounted On This Job: _____

_____

_____

Background Needed To Do The Job: _____

_____

_____

Comments And/or Recommendations: _____

_____

_____

_____

_____

Completed By _____ Title: _____ Date: _____

Supervisor's Approval: _____

APPENDIX NINE

JOB DESCRIPTION QUESTIONNAIRE

EXEMPT

_____   _____
Job Title   *Supervisor's Title*

_____   _____
Division   *Department*

1. **GENERAL PURPOSE OF JOB:** Briefly describe the job's primary purpose or contribution to the department or organization.

   _____

   _____

   _____

   _____

   _____

   _____

   _____

2. **DUTIES AND RESPONSIBILITIES:** List the job's essential or most important functions and responsibilities. Include all important aspects of the job - whether performed daily, weekly, monthly, annually; and any that occur at irregular intervals. (List on the next page.)

3. **SUPERVISORY RESPONSIBILITIES:**

   Are there subordinate supervisors reporting to this job? (check one)

   Yes [ ]   No [ ]

   If yes, how many? _____

   What are the names of the departments or units managed by the subordinate supervisor.

   _____

   _____

2. DUTIES AND RESPONSIBILITIES:

a. _____

b. _____

c. _____

d. _____

e. _____

f. _____

g. _____

h. _____

i. _____

j. _____

k. _____

l. _____

m. _____

n. _____

o. _____

How many employees in total report to the subordinate supervisor? _____

Are there other non-supervisory employees who report directly to this job? _____ How many? _____

4. EQUIPMENT USED:

List specific equipment, tools or computer software used in this position.

_____

_____

5. QUALIFICATION REQUIREMENTS:

5a. What sort and how much experience, education, and/or training is truly necessary to perform these functions?

_____

_____

_____

5b. In the areas of mathematics, language, and reasoning, what basic knowledge, skills, and abilities are required?

_____

_____

_____

5c. Are other knowledge and skills required, such as bilingual ability, familiarity with special terminology or the ability to type or take shorthand and speed required.

_____

_____

_____

5d. Are special licenses or certificates required?

_____

_____

_____

6. PHYSICAL DEMANDS:

6a. How much on-the-job time is spent in the following physical activities? Show the amount of time by checking the appropriate boxes below.

- AMOUNT OF TIME -

	none	up to 1/3	1/3 to 2/3	2/3 more
Stand				
Walk				
Sit				
Use hands to finger handle or feel				
Reach with hands and arms				
Climbs or balance				
Stoop, kneel crouch or crawl				
Talk or hear				
Taste or smell				

6b. Does this job require that weight be lifted or force be exerted? If so, how much and how often. Check the appropriate boxes below.

- AMOUNT OF TIME -

	none	up to 1/3	1/3 to 2/3	2/3 more
Up to 10 pounds				
Up to 25 pounds				
Up to 50 pounds				
Up to 100 pounds				
More than 100 pounds				

6c. Does this job have any special vision requirements? Check all that apply.

_____ Close Vision (clear vision at 20 inches or less)

_____ Distance Vision (clear vision at 20 feet or more)

_____ Color Vision (ability to identify and distinguish colors)

_____ Peripheral Vision (ability to observe an area that can be seen up and down or to the left and right while eyes are fixed on a given point)

_____ Depth Perception (three-dimensional vision, ability to judge distances and spatial relationships)

_____ Ability to Adjust Focus (ability to adjust the eye to bring an object into sharp focus)

_____ No Special Vision Requirements

6d. Make notes on the specific job duties that require the physical demands selected above.

_____

_____

7. WORK ENVIRONMENT:

7a. How much exposure to the following environmental conditions does this job require? Show the amount of time by checking the appropriate boxes below.

- AMOUNT OF TIME -

	none	up to 1/3	1/3 to 2/3	2/3 more
Wet humid conditions (non-weather)				
Work near moving mechanical parts				
Work in high precarious places				
Fumes or airborne particles				
Toxic or caustic chemicals				
Outdoor weather condition				
Extreme cold (non-weather)				
Extreme heat (non-weather)				
Risk of electrical shock				
Work with explosives				
Risk of radiation				
Vibration				

7b. How much noise is typical for the work environment of this job? Check the appropriate level below.

_____ Very Quiet (Examples: forest trail, isolation booth for hearing test)

_____ Quiet (Examples: library, private office)

_____ Moderate Noise (Examples: business office with typewriters and/or computer printers, light traffic)

_____ Loud Noise (Examples: metal can manufacturing department, large earth-moving equipment)

_____ Very Loud Noise (Examples: jack hammer work; front row at rock concert)

7c. Make notes on the specific job duties that are affected by the environmental conditions selected above

_____

_____

_____

8. **COMMENTS:** Include any other information that will aid in the preparation of an accurate description of this job.

_____

_____

9. **QUESTIONNAIRE PREPARED BY:**

_____   _____
Name   _Date_

_____
Title

Basis for knowledge of job: ____   hold job now: ____   supervise job: ___
other, explain: _____

For easy evaluation of job descriptions, refer to data input sheets for the title and description of each position.

DATA INPUT SHEET

Job Title: Vendor Relations - Account Representative

Duties: Maintain information about vendors, services, cost rates and master contracts of international television transmission. Liaison to vendor. Maintain documents and vendor records. Develop new sources. Handle discrepancy in invoices and services.

Geographic Location	# of Incumbents in Position	Minimum	Salary Ranges Midpoint	Maximum	Average Salary

Your Job Title _____   Non-Exempt: _____

Union: _____

Degree of Match _____   1 = Less than above description

2 = Very close/Matches description

3 = More than above description

Reports To (Title): _____

Increases based on ( ) Tenure   ( ) Performance   ( ) Both   ( ) Other _____

Shift Differentials   ( )Yes   ( ) No   How Often: _____

Comp Time Off? _____   How much: _____

APPENDIX TEN

POSITION EVALUATION GUIDE

This chart refers to the evaluation outlines that appear on the following pages. Use this chart as the master sheet for evaluating all positions.

Position Title:_____

POSITION EVALUATION FACTORS	DEGREES/POINTS				
	1st	**2nd**	**3rd**	**4th**	**5th**
A. Skill	20	40	60	80	100
B. Education	20	40	60	80	100
C. Previous Experience	20	40	60	80	100
D. Responsibility	20	40	60	80	100
E. Impact/Result	20	40	60	80	100
F. Communication Skills	20	40	60	80	100
G. Leadership/ Coach	20	40	60	80	100
H. Supervision	10/20	10/40	20/60	20/8	30/100
I. Customer Impact	20	40	60	80	100

Total: _____

A. SKILL

This factor measures the knowledge the employee must possess to do acceptable work, plus the skills and judgment needed to apply such knowledge in order to achieve effective results.

DEGREE	LEVELS	POINTS
1	Knowledge of simple, routine tasks. Skill to operate simple equipment and follow simple procedures. Requires no previous training or experience.	20
2	Knowledge of basic procedures and operations. Skill and judgment to apply procedures, or to operate equipment requiring a moderate degree of previous training or experience.	40
3	Knowledge of standardized but moderately complex procedures and operations, requiring training and experience. Skill to apply procedures, or operate varied equipment for purposes of performing standard operations.	60
4	Knowledge of procedure in a special or technical field to perform various or complex assignments. Requires considerable training and experience. Skill to apply complex procedures requiring judgment, to use and adjust varied equipment or processes for purposes of performing standard, special and diagnostic operations.	80
5	Knowledge of an extensive body of procedures or operations, requiring special skills developed from special training and extensive experience. Independent judgment is an important element of positions at this level	100

B. EDUCATION

This factor measures the position's educational requirement. It evaluates how much formal training in a traditional, educational or trade school is necessary to perform the job effectively.

DEGREE	LEVELS	POINTS
1	No formal education of any type necessary for this work. Basic English, math or craft skill needed.	20
2	A high school degree or equivalent trade school education is needed.	40
3	Two years of advanced study beyond high school and a degree or formalized technical training such as computer or secretarial school.	60
4	University degree required. Educational proficiency at the 4-year level.	80
5	Advanced formal degree or technical training beyond the college level. *EXAMPLE: CPA, Law degree.*	100

C. PREVIOUS EXPERIENCE

This factor measures the position requirements which are based on previous experience. It evaluates the amount and the type of experience necessary in order to perform in the position at a satisfactory level.

DEGREE	LEVELS	POINTS
1	Very little experience required. The experience required would be of a general nature such as previous office experience or part-time experience during high school.	20
2	This position requires 0-6 months exact experience in the field or area directly applicable to the job being performed.	40
3	This position requires 1-2 years specific experience in the exact position or a position very similar in nature.	60
4	2-5 years experience in a position of similar responsibility and duties. Possibly at various levels of responsibility prior to advancing into a more senior area.	80
5	6-10 years exact experience in the position or a position of similar responsibility and duties. The incumbent may have moved through several subordinate positions to ultimately attain the position involved.	100

D. RESPONSIBILITY

Responsibility involves the extent of the position's impact on customer satisfaction, welfare of residents, costs and assets. Degree of supervision received and decision-making responsibilities are also considered.

DEGREE	LEVELS	POINTS
1	Minimal impact upon customer satisfaction, product, costs and assets. Work is performed under immediate supervision and/or in accordance with procedures. Slight leeway for decision-making.	20
2	Moderate impact on customer satisfaction, product, costs and assets. Work is performed under immediate supervision with advice and assistance usually available. Matters dealt with are usually controlled by established procedures.	40
3	Direct but supervised, impact on customer satisfaction, product, costs and assets. Work is done under supervision, but advice and assistance are not always readily available. Matters dealt with are governed by procedures or policies that are established in general terms, but with some latitude for interpretation. Decisions and actions on difficult problems are subject to prior approval.	60
4	Significant impact on customer satisfaction, product, costs and assets. Work is done under general supervision in accordance with general procedures or policies, but with latitude for the exercise of independent judgment. Decisions and actions are subject to prior approval in unusual cases.	80
5	Major direct impact on customer satisfaction, product, costs and assets. Work is done in accordance with general policies and objectives, and with considerable latitude in the exercise of independent judgment. Decisions and actions are subject to review only where major issues are involved.	100

E. IMPACT/RESULTS

This factor measures positions direct impact of obtaining strategic results of the company. Evaluate the contribution this job makes to meeting goals and success of the company.

DEGREE	LEVELS	POINTS
1	Generally limited impact. Consequences are not serious.	20
2	Moderate impact. Results of this job could cause loss to the company. May impact monthly results.	40
3	Major impact. Results of this job have an effect on total business results for several months.	60
4	Could result in a major economic loss that's not recoverable. Significant contributor to annual or 3-5 years success of company.	80
5	Critical to the long term welfare of the company.	100

F. COMMUNICATION SKILLS

This factor evaluates the amount of interaction, interpersonal skills and degree of written and oral communication skills necessary to perform the job.

DEGREE	LEVELS	POINTS
1	Generally very little interaction in a one on one basis.	20
2	Positions requiring average or ordinary interaction with others while performing job duties. May also interface with others frequently about routine information.	40
3	Work requiring regular interaction in a one on one basis which frequently requires a good degree of interpersonal and communication skills. Answers a variety of inquires.	60
4	Major function of job responsibilities requires constant interaction at a complex communication level. Negotiating skills as well as diplomacy and timeliness required.	80
5	Heavy emphasis on interaction in a one on one basis with the addition of a sense of urgency and the ability to make independent decisions. Communication of a complex and technical nature. Excellent communication skills required both written and verbal.	100

G. LEADERSHIP/COACH

This factor measures the degree to which the incumbent is required to coach, train, facilitate group process and get work done through other people.

DEGREE	LEVELS	POINTS
1	Light leadership on work teams required but isolated and simple.	20
2	Leadership required on a part-time basis. Required to teach and coach others. May show leadership initiative outside work group.	40
3	Spends a great deal of time heading, coaching and counseling others. Leadership is routine and not complex.	60
4	Require a professional level of competence as a leader. Coaches and trains in complex assignments. Supervises a variety of activity.	80
5	Leadership role is key to organization. Directs others, coaches advises and sets leadership standards.	100

H. SUPERVISION OF OTHERS

This factor measures the degree to which the incumbent requires planning, organizing, directing or supervising the work of others.

In rating positions on this factor, it is intended to consider the number, variety and skill levels of employees under the control of the position, whether the position directly supervises or indirectly supervises through a subordinate supervisor.

POINTS

(Select the column that most accurately reflects responsibility.)

Degree	Number of employees under regular control	**A** Supervision of a limited variety of activities of ordinary complexity. Usually a "working supervisor"	**B** Supervision of a variety of activity or activities of complex nature
1	1	10	20
2	2	10	40
3	3-5	20	60
4	6-10	20	80
5	11-25	30	100

I. CUSTOMER IMPACT

This factor evaluates the amount of customer interaction, delivery of customer needs and degree of satisfaction to the customer.

DEGREE	LEVELS	POINTS
1	Generally very little customer interaction on a one on one basis. Little impact on customer satisfaction.	20
2	Positions requiring average or ordinary interaction with customers while performing job duties. May also satisfy needs of customers in a routine manner.	40
3	Work requiring regular customer interaction and satisfaction. Requires a good degree of customer knowledge and knowledge of customer expectations.	60
4	Major function of job responsibilities requires constant customer interface or satisfaction at a complex level. Negotiating skills as well as diplomacy and timeliness required.	80
5	Heavy emphasis on customer interaction and satisfaction with the addition of a sense of urgency and the ability to make independent decisions. May evaluate long-term delivery of customer needs. Requires broad understanding of markets and competitors.	100

APPENDIX ELEVEN

CUSTOMER SURVEY

Customer_____ Phone#_____ Contact_____

1. Do you know who you spoke with?

2. What was your overall feeling at the end of the conversation?
     Very satisfied   Satistisfied   Dissatisfied   Uncertain

3. How would you rate our service?

BASICS

4. Convenient hours and easily accessible when you call?
     1   2   3   4   5   6   7   8   9   10

5. Do you receive a call back from a team member the same day after you leave a
     voice mail message? If no, what percentage?
     10   20   30   40   50   60   70   80   90   100

6. Clear understanding of your request?
     1   2   3   4   5   6   7   8   9   10

7. Helpful in responsing to your requests?
     1   2   3   4   5   6   7   8   9   10

8. Timely and accurate follow through on your requests?
     1   2   3   4   5   6   7   8   9   10

JOB KNOWLEDGE

9. Knowledgeable answers to all of your requests?
     1   2   3   4   5   6   7   8   9   10

BEYOND THE BASICS

10. Positive representative of our company?

    1   2   3   4   5   6   7   8   9   10

11. Discussed other programs, services and products?

    1   2   3   4   5   6   7   8   9   10

12. Compared to other suppliers?

    1   2   3   4   5   6   7   8   9   10

13. Tell us about the supplier who offers you the best service. _____

_____

_____

_____

_____

14. What one word would you use to describe XYZ's service? _____

_____

_____

_____

_____

15. What can we do to give YOU better service? _____

_____

_____

_____

_____

APPENDIX TWELVE

STATEMENT OF OBJECTIVES

FOR:_____ **DATE:** _____

DESIRED RESULTS	PLANNED ACTION (Steps)	DATA Projected Actual	COST Projected Actual	REVIEW OF PROGRESS

APPROVED:_____

COMMENTS: _____

_____

_____

APPENDIX THIRTEEN

INCENTIVE COMPENSATION EFFECTIVENESS RATING

Name:_____ Date: _____

KEY AREAS	EFFECTIVENESS RATING
1. Volume/Quantity	0 1 2 3 4 5
2. Teamwork survey	0 1 2 3 4 5
3. Performance Improvement Plan	0 1 2 3 4 5
4. Special Project/Committee Participation Commitment to Positive Change	0 1 2 3 4 5

TOTAL POINTS _____

EFFECTIVENESS RATINGS ARE BETWEEN 0-5 AND WILL BE EVALUATED BY THE SUPERV SOR BASED ON THE FOLLOWING:

- Size of book and number of clients serviced.
- Results of the *Teamwork Survey*.
- Successful completion of the Performance Incentive Plan.
- Special project involvement or committee participation or commitment to initiating positive change.

TEAMWORK SURVEY

Please indicate your personal perception of each team member by indicating:

6 = Always   5 = Often   3 = Sometimes   1 = Rarely   0 = Never

The findings will be confidential except that your own results will be shared with you.	Name:	Name:	Name:	Name:	Name:	Name:	Name:	Name:
1. Works effectively with others.								
2. Accepts assignments willingly.								
3. Friendly, cheerful disposition.								
4. Participates in group projects.								
5. Willingly trains others.								
6. A problem solver.								
7. Enthusiastically motivates others.								
8. Follows up/follows through.								
9. Demonstrates an awareness to cost effectiveness/streamlining.								
10. Patiently listens.								
11. Readily assists others whenever necessary.								
12. Accepts criticism positively and without defensiveness.								
13. Demonstrates effective use of computer systems.								
14. Demonstrates professionalism under stress.								
15. Supports group decisions.								
16. Demonstrates pride in Mulligan & Murtis.								
17. Accepts and adapts to change well.								
18. Identifies problems and offers solutions rather than complaining.								
19. Treats others with respect.								
20. Works without destracting group effort.								

Thank you for participating.

Jorgensen, Inc., (818) 957-8838, Copyright, © 1996

APPENDIX FIFTEEN

INCENTIVE PLAN GOAL WORKSHEET

Use this worksheet multiple times—for each goal identified as part of the incentive plan.

GOAL: (Explain in detail)

HOW WILL IT ENHANCE COMPANY GOALS?

GENERAL OUTLINE OF HOW IT WILL BE ACCOMPLISHED:

PROS AND CONS:

WHAT IS MEASUREMENT?

WHAT IS COST AND TIMETABLE?

Participant:_____   Supervisor:_____

APPENDIX SIXTEEN

SAMPLE COMPENSATION PLAN OUTLINE

I. COMPENSATION POLICY

The objective of the total compensation package is to pay above the market when individual performance, team and company performance goals are achieved. The Company will compensate all of its staff based on the individual's job performance level, type of position, internal equity, and market salary basis. Salaries will be at or near the market based on similar size companies, duties and skill levels. Additional compensation will be variable based on business, team or individual performance.

The Company is an equal opportunity employer and this policy is administered and based on job performance and job responsibilities only.

II. RESPONSIBILITY

1. Total policy responsibility rests with the President and is executed through the Compensation Committee.

2. The Compensation Committee is made up of 5 voting members. They are the President, Executive Vice President, General Manager of Company XYZ, Vice President Sales, and the Vice President Controller. A quorum consists of the President and two other voting members.

3. The Compensation Committee meets as needed to evaluate and approve performance reviews and salary increases. The Committee approves exceptions to the Policy, reviews the salary structure, adjusts the salary ranges, approves new positions, and must approve all changes to the compensation program.

4. Department Supervisors and Managers are responsible for the day-to-day administration of the policy within budget limitations. They are responsible for submitting proposed increases within the guidelines of the policy.

5. Department Managers and Supervisors are responsible for:

    - Conducting individual performance appraisals.

    - Recommending salary and promotional increases.

    - Reviewing job descriptions periodically to ensure accuracy, and recommending salary level changes when the duties of a position change substantially.

    - Communicating salary policy to new and existing employees.

III. COMMUNICATION

A salary program is only effective when all Supervisors and employees understand how salary decisions are made.

1. All employees will be informed by their Supervisors of their salary level, range and the date of their next review.

2. All Managers will know the salary levels and salary ranges of employees for whom they have salary decision responsibility.

3. New hires will receive a job description, their review schedule and their salary level at the time of hire.

IV. POSITION DESCRIPTIONS

1. Written descriptions for each position are included in this Compensation Program.

2. When the functions and/or duties of a position change, or a new job description is written, the job will be re-evaluated by the Compensation Committee. New position descriptions will be completed by the employee performing the job, if possible.

3. The Compensation Committee will assign salary ranges to new positions based upon the responsibilities of the job.

4. All new positions must have a position description approved by the Compensation Committee prior to transferring or hire decision.

V. SALARY STRUCTURE

1. The salary structure is designed to provide a range of pay that is competitive with market pay levels and is equitable in relation to pay opportunity for positions of comparable responsibility within the Company.

2. The salary range is the single most useful guide to determining appropriate salary levels and hiring rates.

   - The range represents the pay level for a grouping of jobs whose evaluations are similar, based on universal job factors selected by the Company. They are attached.

   - The minimum salary represents a rate of pay for an incumbent who has the minimum qualifications for the position. This applies to both promotion and hiring salaries. Normally, salaries will not be paid below the minimum, although exceptional circumstances may justify doing so, i.e., someone with high potential to learn position assigned.

   - The mid-point represents a rate of pay for fully satisfactory performance in a given position.

- Employees with consistent outstanding performance over a period of time will be eligible for salaries in excess of the mid-point for their position level.

- Maximum salaries represent the rate of pay for a fully-seasoned practitioner. No employee may make more than the maximum for the grade.

VI. HIRING SALARIES

1. GENERAL

- Normally, a new employee will be hired between the minimum and mid-point of the appropriate salary level, depending on qualifications and experience. Salary offers over the mid-point require the approval of the Compensation Committee.

- All new hires will be eligible for reviews but prorated increase consideration effective July 1st each year.

2. REPLACEMENT POSITIONS

The Compensation Committee member responsible for area approves any hire salary lower than the mid-point. Hire salaries should be consistent with existing salaries for the same or similar work within the unit and directly commensurate with current pay levels of the hire.

3. NEW POSITIONS

For a newly created position, a position description will be completed by the Supervisor and submitted to the Compensation Committee. The President must approve all new positions.

VII. PERFORMANCE REVIEWS

1. PURPOSE

Each staff member's performance is evaluated informally by his/her Supervisor on a continuing basis. A written performance appraisal is prepared at least once each year. A formal, written review must be done for any increase in salary. However, a review may be done without any salary change.

The purpose of the review is to:

- Document the employee's performance according to reasonable expectations and standards for the position.

- Determine how the employee may improve work performance.

- Evaluate career potential and development.

- Achieve a closer working relationship between the employee and Supervisor.

2. TIMING

Written Performance Appraisals are conducted as follows:

NEW HIRES: 90 days after hire.

ALL EMPLOYEES: At least once a year during month of June.

- Although all employees participate in performance reviews, consideration for salary increase is optional based on performance.

- A Supervisor or an employee may request a formal appraisal, at any time, if there is a misunderstanding or question about performance.

3. FORMS

Reviews are prepared on appraisal forms. The review is prepared by the Supervisor who submits it to a Committee Member for approval before a review is conducted. Once approved it is given in a meeting to the employee. The completed appraisal form is signed by the employee and the Supervisor and/or Manager, and then given to Payroll Administration for inclusion in the employee's file.

VII. SALARY INCREASES

Salary increases are not automatic. They are granted on the basis of individual merit, team and company performance and market conditions. Although all staff salaries are reviewed yearly, increase consideration will be a decision of the Supervisor based on performance. Not all employees will receive increases.

1. TIMING

Salary review will occur in June for July implementation.

2. APPROVALS

All Levels:

- Once the performance review is complete, the increases that are within approved budget and salary guidelines require the approval of the Compensation Committee.

3. SALARY INCREASE GUIDELINES

- The Salary Increase Guidelines will be determined each year in relation to the budget. Increases should be related to the employee's performance. Consideration should also be given to the position of the employee's current salary in the salary range, the employee's potential for promotion, and competitive market factors.

- The Salary Increase Guidelines are an important factor in helping Supervisors and Managers make salary decisions within their budgets.

The guidelines for Fiscal 1997 are as follows:

<u>PROPOSED GUIDELINES FOR 1997</u>

Performance Rating

	Not Achieving	Meets Expectations	Exceeds Expectations	Outstanding Performance
Below Mid-Point	0-3%	3-4%	4-5%	5-6%
At Mid-Point	0	2-3%	3-4%	4-5%
Above Mid-Point	0	1-2% lump sum	2-3% lump sum	3-4% lump sum

IX. <u>BONUS</u>

The Company has developed individual, team, and Company wide bonuses to supplement monthly salaries. Bonuses are paid for exceeding job duties and contributing to the success of Company XYZ's. Bonuses are not entitlements and must be earned by meeting measured results. The Company reserves the right to forego bonuses if Company financials are not met.

The bonus plan is updated each year based on company goals. All employees participate. Supervisors will be announcing goals, timetables and awards for their teams.

X. <u>PROMOTIONS AND PROMOTIONAL INCREASES</u>

1. <u>DEFINITION</u>

A promotion is defined as movement from a position in one salary level to a position in a higher salary level, or reclassification of a position to a higher salary level due to a change in the scope of responsibility of that position.

2. APPROVALS

When a promotion is made, the employee will be considered for a salary increase; such increase is not automatic, they are granted on the basis of merit, company performance, and market condition.

- Promotions, except factory hourly, require the approval of the Compensation Committee.

- Promotion to exempt status is reserved for those employees who function in a managerial, professional or administrative role, and whose work directly influences the success of the Company.

3. TIMING

An increase is effective following the written performance evaluation and promotional approval.

4. INCREASE AMOUNT

Employees who are promoted will be evaluated by their Manager in the framework of the new grade. The percent of increase will be decided by the Manager to allow flexibility in the new grade. Promotional increases will generally be between 3% - 15%.

XI. TRANSFERS

A transfer is defined as movement from one position to another in the same salary level. Employees who transfer will not be considered for a salary increase, but will retain the same increase cycle they had in their former position. Such employees, however, may be considered for review if the position has greater responsibility than the previous position held.

XII. WITHHOLDING/RESCHEDULING SALARY INCREASE

In some cases, a decrease in grade might be the best movement for an employee. When this occurs, the Supervisor or Manager must indicate when the employee will next be reviewed.

XIII. BUDGET DEVELOPMENT

1. Each year, a budget, expressed as a percent of salary range standards, will be provided to each Manager. Throughout the year, salary decisions will be made in accordance with the salary policy and within the budget.

2. To determine the annual budget, the Controller will obtain information from area and financial institution surveys on past salary trends and expected salary growth for the coming year. Based on this information and consideration of the Company's

economics, a budget will be prepared for the consideration by the Committee. The Committee will recommend a budget for the President's review. Final approval of the budget is obtained from the President.

XIV. KEEPING THE PROGRAM CURRENT

The Compensation Program is responsive to a constantly changing environment. To ensure the greatest flexibility, combined with the shortest response time feasible, the following steps will be taken:

1. POSITION DESCRIPTIONS

   - Position descriptions are reviewed jointly by the incumbents and the appropriate Supervisor or Manager, each year.

   - Position descriptions are automatically subject to review each time the position is to be filled.

   - The Committee will monitor the maintenance of position descriptions, and may require new position descriptions if maintenance procedures have been inadequate.

2. SALARY STRUCTURE

   - The Salary Structure will be reviewed annually by the Committee to ensure that it continues to be competitive and effective in meeting the needs for which it was developed.

   - The Salary Structure may be adjusted according to the amount of change in market pay levels and company performance that has occurred during the year.

3. POSITION RANKING

   - The importance and value of positions will change over time, due to organizational changes, changes in scope and function of positions, and changes in competitive pay levels.

   - The Compensation Committee will review the placement of positions in salary levels relative to survey benchmark data each year as part of the review and updating of the salary program. Any significant changes in competitive pay levels for benchmark positions will be submitted to the appropriate Manager for consideration.

   - A Manager can request a re-evaluation of a position at any time. Such request is submitted to the Committee.

   - Re-ranking of positions requires the approval of the Committee.

   - The Compensation Committee will maintain a current itemization of position titles, salary levels, and ranges as part of the policy.

APPENDIX SEVENTEEN

SAMPLE PROFIT CENTER MANAGER BONUS PLAN

1. Purpose:

   The purpose of the Plan is to provide additional incentive to the Profit Center Managers to meet individual goals and company operating plan objectives.

2. Standard Bonus:

   The standard bonus amount is $15,000 to $45,000 based on office revenues for achievement of objectives. The operating profit objective is 12% margin without interest income.

Office Revenue	$ 0 - 2.5 million = $15,000 Bonus
Office Revenue	$2.5 - 5 million = $22,500 Bonus
Office Revenue	$5 - 7.5 million = $30,000 Bonus
Office Revenue	$7.5 - 10 million = $37,500 Bonus
Office Revenue	Over 10 million = $45,000 Bonus

   The standard amount will vary depending upon how well the manager meets the objective.

3. Calculation of Bonus:

   The award will be governed by the Profit Centers' total operating profits and by individual performance relative to MBO goals. The standard bonus for the manager's position is divided 70% based on pre-agreed upon MBO targets; and 30% of the bonus is based on operating profit to your office.

   A. 70% based on Profit Center operating profits

   B. 30% based on preset MBO criteria. The company must make their budgeted operating profit of 3% in 19__ as set at the beginning of the year for this MBO to be payable.

Below is an example of measurable, individual MBO goals:

— 50% revenue targets or total sales growth

— 25% ratio of staff costs to sales at 57% or less

— 25% new business exceeding 19____ goals

4. 70% Standard Amount Operating Profit Portion is Leveraged as follows:

> 20% + Profit = 240% of Standard Amount of Bonus
>
> 19% + Profit = 220% of Standard Amount of Bonus
>
> 17% + Profit = 200% of Standard Amount of Bonus
>
> 16% + Profit = 180% of Standard Amount of Bonus
>
> 15% + Profit = 160% of Standard Amount of Bonus
>
> 14% + Profit = 140% of Standard Amount of Bonus
>
> 13% + Profit = 120% of Standard Amount of Bonus
>
> 12% + Profit = 100% of Standard Amount of Bonus
>
> 11% + Profit = 75% of Standard Amount of Bonus
>
> 10% + Profit = 50% of Standard Amount of Bonus
>
> Below 10% Profit = 0% Standard Amount of Bonus

5. <u>30% MBO Portion:</u>

All MBO goals must be measurable, approved in writing, and submitted through the Regional to the Executive Committee for final approval. Once approved, they can not be changed without authorization.

The MBO portion of the bonus will only be funded if the company achieves its goal or forecast of 3% profit before tax and bonuses.

If the company makes it's profit goal, and all MBO goals are not achieved, a percentage equivalent to the results will be paid. For example, if a new business goal was 25% growth but only 8% was achieved, only 8/25th of that portion of the MBO was achieved.

Application of Formula to Fiscal 19____ and Future Years:

The plan parameters are for Fiscal 19__ only. The Plan parameters will be reviewed and will be modified for Fiscal 19__ based on change in overall financial goals.

6. Other Provisions:

   A. The tables above indicate various references for determining the bonus award that will be payable if particular levels of performance are reached. Intermediate awards will be determined by straight line interpolation between the pertinent references. All awards should be rounded to the nearest $100.

   B. Incentive awards are payable in lump sum early in the next year, immediately following the determination of profit performance and competition of year end audit.

   C. The eligibility of an employee who is discharged or resigns during the Plan year will be automatically canceled. Mangers must be employed to collect a bonus. Bonuses are prorated for new hires or transfers.

   D. The Plan will not be deemed to give any participant the right to be retained in the employment of the company.

   E. This Plan supersedes all previous short-term incentive compensation plans unless a written contract exists.

APPENDIX EIGHTEEN

SAMPLE SALES STAFF INCENTIVE PLAN

ACCOUNT REPRESENTATIVE INCENTIVE COMPENSATION PLAN:

PURPOSE:

The Account Representative Incentive Compensation Plan is designed to motivate outside sales personnel, create teamwork, and reward effective efforts in achieving the company sales objectives. Base salaries are intended to provide normal living requirements.The incentive payments are added to salary to provide additional remuneration for increased effort in terms of specific, measurable results.The plan is based on the successful attainment of territorial sales goals, effective management of a territory, and the success of the total sales effort based on profit and new account goals.

COMPENSATION PHILOSOPHY:

The compensation philosophy is to provide Account Representatives with a total compensation program that is the best within our marketplace. We believe our desire to be a leader in your industry requires a highly motivated and skilled Account Representative group.

To accomplish this, the company will pay base salaries, benefits, perquisites, and bonuses that enable Account Representatives to significantly increase cash compensation.

SALES GOALS:

- More profitable, higher margin ordering
- Increased order volume with existing accounts
- Sell new accounts
- Gain a larger share of the market

TOTAL COMPENSATION PROGRAM

Your total compensation program is made up of:
- Base Salary
- Bonuses
- Benefits
- Perquisites

Base salary is designed to provide you with a stable income and to reflect your individual experience in managing your territory and developing sales. The base salary provides for normal living requirements.

Your performance will be evaluated in writing annually around your anniversary date of hire.

- Orders and new business performance
- Customer service
- Problem management
- Communications
- Teamwork

Salary increases will be determined on the basis of performance and position in salary range. Salary ranges will be adjusted periodically to retain their competitiveness. Each account representative will be given a written performance review highlighting strengths, weaknesses, and appraisal of the past year's job performance.

BONUS INCENTIVE

The incentive compensation target for this plan is $2,500 per sales personnel monthly. This incentive will be paid for meeting sales profit goals and opening new accounts.

Fifty percent of the monthly maximum target of $2,500 will be based on territorial goals set by the Vice President of Sales and the Account Representative for the territory.

Fifty percent of the monthly maximum target will be based on total team sales goals.

Cooperation between Account Representatives is key to obtaining company-wide results.

An additional incentive of $500 will be paid on any new account opened after the second new account in a year. A "new account" has not ordered from our firm for the last five years.

How the Incentive Works

At the start of the plan, sales administration will develop individual territory business goals for each sales person. The goals will be based on previous territory sales, total company sales, economic trends, and discretionary sales goals. Returns will be subtracted from monthly revenue for profit as they are incurred.

Fifty Percent Individual Territory Profit

The individual monthly goals will be determined based on last year's orders and this year's anticipated growth.

Company thresholds must be met before individual payouts will occur. The actual profit per territory will be determined minus returns.

The actual profit divided by the expected incremental increase in profit will determine the 50 percent of the bonus each month. If sales personnel go over 100 percent of the goal this portion of the bonus will be proportionately increased. If an individual sales person makes more than their monthly profit, any amounts over maximum goal can be applied to any monthly actual profit below goal for that individual.

Fifty Percent Based on Company Profit Monthly

The companywide monthly goal payout ratios below will be used:

Threshold for any payout is $16,800 per month in profit before tax and bonus.

At a profit of $16,800 there will be no bonus

At a profit of $21,760 = bonus of $500

At a profit of $26,720 = bonus of $1,000

At a profit of $31,680 = bonus of $1,500

At a profit of $36,640 = bonus of $2,000

At a profit of $41,600 = bonus of $2,500

Bonuses will be pro-rated between profit levels.

Example Assumptions:

Profit is $32,00 companywide for a month. Territory profit goals were $8,500 and actual profit was $8,000.

Three new accounts have been opened in the territory.

Bonus Results

50% individual payment =	$721
8,000/ 8,500 =	94.12%
94.12% x $1,532	$1,441.88
50% total company payment =	$766
Profit of $32,000 = potential of $1,532 x .50% =	$766
$1,441.88 x .50% =	$720.94
New Account Bonus =	$500
Total Monthly Payout =	$1,987

BENEFITS

Our comprehensive and highly competitive benefits package adds as much as 34 percent to your pay and includes:

- Medical
- Dental
- Life Insurance
- Vacation and Holidays
- Disability Leaves
- LTD - STD
- Individual Benefit Accounts

The Company provides you with a competitive travel and expense budget to allow you to achieve your territory account order goals.

PROMOTIONS AND TRANSFERS

A participant who is transfered or promoted into a new position during the plan year will participate on a pro rate basis. If promoted from an Account Representative to a Senior Account Representative, a base salary increase may occur.

TERMINATION OF EMPLOYMENT

An indidual leaving the employment of the company for any reason will be entitled to all bonuses earned up to and including the date of termination.

DISABILITY, DEATH, OR RETIREMENT

If a participant is disabled by an accident or illness, and is diabled long enough to be placed on disability, his or her bonuses will be paid to the date of disability. No incentives shall be earned during the period on disability.

In the event of retirement or death, The company will pay all incentives due to the participant or the estate of the participant.

MISCELLANEOUS

The plan will not be deemed to give any participant the right to be retained in the employment of the company, nor will the plan interfere with the right of the company to discharge any participant at any time.

The plan, as set forth in this document, represents the guidelines the company presently intends to utilize determining what commissions, if any, will be paid.

PARTICIPATION

Outside account representatives are immdeiately eligible for participation in this plan.

EFFECTIVE DATE

This plan supersedes all previous incentive compensation, commission, or bonus plans. It became effective January 1,_____ subject to the company's rights as described below to amend, modify, or discontinue the plan at any time during the specified period— the plan will remain in effect until December 31,_____.

PLAN ADMINISTRATION

This plan is authorized and administered by the Vice President of Sales. Administration provides support for establishing and tracking sales goals and results.

The Vice President of Sales has the sole authority to interpret the plan and to make or nullify any rules and procedures as neccesary for proper plan administration. Any determination of the Vice President of Sales about the plan will be final and binding on all participants.

PLAN CHANGES OR DISCONTINUANCE

The company has developed this plan based on existing business; market and economic conditions; current services; and personnel assignments.

The company may add to amend, modify, or discontinue any of the terms or conditions of the plan at any time during the plan's specified period.

ACCOUNT REPRESENTATIVE INCENTIVE COMPENSATION PLAN

Effective January 1,_____ to December 31, _____

PARTICIPATION AGREEMENT

I understand the plan does not constitute a contract of employment with any participant or to be consideration for the employment of any participant; rather, I understand that the company and I have the right to terminate my employment for any reason at any time, and that this policy may be modified only in a written document signed by the President/Chief Executive Officer.

I have read and reviewed the Account Representative Compensation Plan including the Terms and Conditions, and understand their applicability.

Participant's Signature:_____   Date:_____

APPENDIX NINETEEN

SAMPLE "EMPLOYEE OF THE QUARTER" PROGRAM

Outstanding performance and dedicated service are qualities that are valued and appreciated by the company and its management. It is the exceptional service and extra effort of our employees that contribute and are responsible for the success of our company.

To officially recognize those employees in the company who perform their responsibilities in a highly exemplary manner, who go the extra mile in the performance of their duties, and who otherwise perform above and beyond the call of duty, the SUPERSTARS PROGRAM has been implemented.

Each quarter the manager of each branch and department has the opportunity to nominate employees who they believe exemplify the Superstar. The Executive Committee then selects employees from the nominations to be saluted for their notable performance.

Employees selected as Superstars receive a personal letter from our President, a commemorative plaque and an award selected by the Executive Committee.

Quarter _____

EMPLOYEE OF THE QUARTER EVALUATION FORM

Name _____   Branch _____

Needs Improvement	Satisfactory	Good	Very Good	Outstanding	Points

1. Good Attendance Record (Outstanding rating only for no absences in Quarter)

   0   2   5   7   10   _____

2. Promptness (Arriving on time; breaks and lunches according to schedule with consideration for others)

   0   2   5   7   10   _____

3. Neatness, Accuracy, and/or Balancing (Time taken to balance; adequate detail on balance sheet; neat and accurate typing; little or no proofing necessary on typing and other work; attention to detail. Tellers with cash differences of more than $100 in one occurrence or $10 in three occurrences are ineligible. Consideration should be made on how many times there were differences that were located by proof with a maximum of five occurrences over $10.)

   0   2   5   7   10   _____

4. Job Knowledge and Technical Competence (Familiarity with job duties; experience and comprehension of job field)

   0   2   5   7   10   _____

5. Productivity (How consistently is work done; accomplishes tasks without wasting time; utilizes time to best potential)

   0   2   5   7   10   _____

6. Interest, Initiative and Willingness to Learn (Interested in learning new areas; willing to help others when own work is completed)

   0   2   5   7   10   _____

7. Adherence to Bank Procedures and Policy (Follows limits and guidelines; observes security procedures; aware and utilizes standard operating procedures)

   0   2   5   7   10   _____

8. Attitude (Positive attitude; pride in organization; will go out of the way to help others)

   0   2   5   7   10   _____

9. Professional Appearance and Attitude (Adherence to dress code; clean; neat appropriate clothing; good choice in language; personal cleanliness)

   0   2   5   7   10   _____

10. FOR EMPLOYEES WITH CUSTOMER CONTACT:
    Good Relations with Fellow Workers (Goes out of the way to cooperate with others; works well with those on same or higher levels, maintains harmonious relations with co-workers; alert to needs of co-workers and supervisors)

   0   2   5   7   10   _____

TOTAL POINTS (100 POINTS POSSIBLE): _____

_____   _____
Manager   Operations Officer

_____
Administrative Committee

APPENDIX TWENTY

SAMPLE SERVICE AWARD PLAN

Dedication and longevity of service are the foundation of every successful business and we are especially fortunate in having many highly skilled and motivated people. As our way of saying "THANK YOU", employees will receive service awards in recognition of their continuous service and commitment to this company.

The following anniversary dates will determine your award eligibility:

Length of Service	Award
3 Years	A Service Award Tac Pin
	Letter of Congratulations from President
5 Years	A Service Award Tac Pin with 1 Diamond
	Lunch for the Recipient
	Service Award Certificate
	Letter of Congratulations from President
10 Years	A Service Award Tac Pin with 2 Diamonds
	Dinner for the Recipient Along with a Guest
	Service Award Certificate
	Letter of Congratulations from President
15 Years	A Service Award Tac Pin with 3 Diamonds
	Lunch with an Executive
	Service Award Certificate
	Letter of Congratulations from President
	A Special Presentation at the Corporate Office by President
	Expense Paid Trip to Corporate Headquaters, Plus Travel Allowance.

APPENDIX TWENTY-ONE

SAMPLE EMPLOYEE PURCHASE PLAN
Inter Office Memo

Date: February 23, 1996

To: Salaried Employees

From:

Re: Employee PC Purchase Program

To assist employees in the purchase of personal computers, _____ Manufacturing has approved a new _____assisted employee purchase program for personal computers. The Company feels that the program will help increase the employees knowledge and use of personal computers and thereby make the employees more productive at their jobs.

The following steps must be followed to qualify for this program:

1. The employee select the vendor (s) computer system desired (including hardware, software included with the system, and cabling).

2. The employee will be responsible for placing their order with the selected vendor(s). The employee must receive, from each vendor, a copy of an acknowledgment, or invoice documenting the following:

   ➤ itemized pricing (breakdown of all hardware, software, etc.),

   ➤ delivery cost applicable,

   ➤ sales tax,

   ➤ terms, and

   ➤ approximate delivery date and "ship" to address.

3. The employee will submit the acknowledgment or invoice to the MIS Manager to review. Upon approval, the list is forwarded to the Human Resource Manager.

4. Based on the approved list (step 3), the employee must sign a Promissory Note (copy attached) with the Human Resource Manager stating terms of payment (not to exceed 24 months). Absent default, no interest will be charged. The Human Resource Manager will make 3 copies of the promissory note to be given to:

   ➤ The Payroll Specialist

   ➤ The Accounts Payable Supervisor, or

➤ Employee

The Human Resource Manager will put the original promissory note in the employee's personnel file.

5. The Payroll Specialist will set up a payroll deduction based on the signed promissory note.

6. In addition to the copy of the promissory note (step 4), the Human Resource Manager will send a check request to the Accounts Payable Supervisor requesting a check payable to the employee.

7. Accounts payable will process and deliver the check to the employee.

8. Within fourteen (14) days after receiving the payroll advance, the employee will provide the Human Resource Manager with a copy of the paid invoice(s) as proof the system was delivered and the invoice paid. This copy will be filed with the original promissory note in the employee's personnel file.

9. If the amount of the payroll advance exceeds the total purchase price of the approved items (step 3), the difference must be repaid to _____ at the time the invoice copies are given to the Human Resource Manager.

10. Failure to provide invoice copies within the fourteen day period will result in an accelerated repayment schedule. This schedule will consist of 6 equal semi-monthly payroll deductions (each deduction equaling 1/6 of the payroll advance plus interest). Deductions will bear interest at the highest rate permitted by law.

If you have any questions, please contact me. I believe this is an excellent opportunity for you to purchase a personal computer for your home.

ADDITIONAL INFORMATION/RESTRICTIONS:

Employees must have worked at the company ___months to be eligible for this program.

Because of the potential large number of employees using this program, questions to MIS personnel should be restricted to non-working hours.

MIS will not provide hardware and/or software support to systems purchased for home use. Make and model of the computer system is entirely at the employee's discretion.

Items covered include the basic computer hardware, printer, accessories, software, shipping charges and sales tax. For employees who already own a personal computer, the purchase of a PC mother board and memory will also be permitted under this program.

The employee is responsible for current state and local sales tax and/or use tax where applicable.

According to normal accounting procedures, check requests received by Tuesday will be processed and checks distributed on Friday. Requests for hand checks will not be accepted.

An employee may purchase only one system every three years. Maximum expenditure is $2,500 for any one system. The employee is responsible for any amount over the $2,500 limit at the time the vendor invoice is paid.

After the initial promissory note has been signed and the payroll advance has been given, the employee may not request additional advances under this program until the original advance has been paid in full. For example, if the initial request is for $2,000, the employee cannot request an additional $500 until the initial $2,000 has been repaid and the 3 year waiting period has expired.

An employee is responsible for making semi-monthly payments as agreed to in the promissory note , even if the employee is in an inactive employment status. Upon termination of employee's employment for any reason, any unpaid balance will be due immediately per terms specified in the promissory note.

The computer system is intended for the employee's personal use, not for outside business ventures or resale to others.

The Company requires strict compliance with all copyright laws and software license agreements. Pirating or installation of Company software could be considered cause for disciplinary actions or discharge.

The Company reserves the right to modify or discontinue this program at its discretion.

PROMISSORY NOTE

EMPLOYEE NAME:_____

$:_____   DATE:_____

FOR VALUE RECEIVED, the undersigned (hereafter the "Employee") promises to pay _____ (hereinafter the "Employer"), the sum of $_____ in equal semi monthly payroll deductions of $_____ beginning on _____ until the payroll advance is paid in full.

Failure to comply with the terms and conditions of the Employee Purchase Plan will result in an accelerated repayment schedule. This schedule consists of 6 equal semi-monthly payroll deductions each deduction equaling 1/6 of the payroll advance plus interest). Under this schedule, the payroll advance will bear interest at the highest rate permitted by law until fully repaid.

In the event of a termination of the Employee's employment, any balance due hereunder shall be immediately due and payable and, to the extent permitted by law, The Employee authorizes deduction of the same from any monies due the Employee from the Employer at or after the time of such termination. So long as payments are made in accordance with the terms of this Note, it shall not bear interest; provided, however, that upon default in the payment of any sum due hereunder, any unpaid balance of principal shall thereafter bear interest at the highest rate permitted by law.

In the event that this Note is placed in the hands of an attorney for collection, reasonable attorney fees and costs of suit shall be added to the amount due hereunder.

I have received, read, fully understand, and will comply with the terms and conditions of the "Employee Purchase Program" and this "Promissory Note".

EMPLOYEE:_____ DATE:_____

WITNESS:_____ DATE:_____

Distribution: Personnel File (original)

               Accounts Payable

               Payroll

               Employee

APPENDIX TWENTY-TWO

EDUCATIONAL REIMBURSEMENT PROGRAM

The company has designed an educational reimbursement program to provide financial assistance for employees to take academically related courses.

Reimbursement will be provided if the education is undertaken for at least one of the following reasons:

- Maintain or improve competency in the current job.

- Provide related knowledge in order to advance to a higher level position within the field. Such positions must exist within the company, although they need not be open at the time course work is commenced.

- Provide the training/knowledge needed to progress on an approved career path in a logical and realistic manner.

- Provide special training/knowledge which is in the best interest of the company.

- Meet the company's express condition that the education is required for the employee's retention of present salary, status or employment.

Eligibility:

To participate in the program, the employee must be a regular full-time employee with at least satisfactory completion of the new employee introductory period. The employee's performance prior to the start of the course may be satisfactory.

Prior to the start of each course, applications for participation in the educational assistance program must be approved by the employee's immediate supervisor, second level manager, and Human Resources.

Reimbursement:

- Prior approval is mandatory.

- The reimbursement will be 100% of the required registration, tuition, lab fees, parking, baby-sitting and book allowance of $50 per course up to a maximum of $2,000 per calendar year, when all other conditions are met. Any expenses incurred that are not covered by this policy will be paid entirely by the employee.

- Courses must be taken at an accredited college or university, technical or business school. Correspondence courses are required to complete a degree.

- Non-academic courses as art, history or physical education are not eligible for reimbursement regardless of whether or not those courses are required to complete a degree.

- The employee must pass the course with a grade of "C" or better.

- Audit classes and courses not completed for grades are ineligible for reimbursement.

- The employee must be on active status at the time reimbursement is paid.

- Employees who receive educational benefits from other sources such as G.I. Bill, a scholarship fund, etc., will be reimbursed only for moneys that are not covered by these sources.

To take advantage of this program, you should discuss your educational goals with your supervisor and submit an Educational Reimbursement Request form to the Human Resources Department prior to the start of class.

APPENDIX TWENTY-THREE

SAMPLE SAFETY PLAN

SAFE TEAMS

SAFE TEAMS is a bingo game played by all the employees on a daily basis.

The SAFE TEAMS pot starts at $50.00.

Everyday a new word is drawn.

If no loss time accidents or reported injury/illness the previous day, $15.00 will be added to the pot every day.

If all orders the previous day were shipped on time, $10.00 will be added to the pot everyday.

The average amount of time to win at bingo is approximately 21 days.

If an employee has an accident that requires first aid off the premises, the pot goes to $0, and that game continues. If the employee is not back to work within 4 hours, that employee is not eligible for the rest of the game, or the next game.

If an employee is absent, they can not mark the work of the day that they were out, unless it was preapproved vacation with at least 2 weeks notice.

APPENDIX TWENTY-FOUR

SAMPLE OUTSTANDING PERFORMANCE NOTICE

The company values each of its employees, managers and staff members. Our ongonig endeavor is to provide superior service with the highest levels of ethical and professional conduct in a compassionate manner.

I would appreciate it if you would recognize any member of the company family for extending service excellence by completing the card below. This will allow us to recognize those valuable employees who provide the extra measure of service.

Sincerely,

President & Chief Executive Officer

- -

APPLAUSE

Today's date _____

The following individual(s) deserve special recognition for extending an extra measure of service:

Name:_____ Dept._____

Name:_____ Dept._____

(Comments/details)

_____

_____

_____

_____

_____

Thank you for your comments.

Signature:_____

I am a (check one)   ____ Customer   ____Vendor

                         ____ Employee   ____ Other_____

(Please give this card to an employee or send it through the U.S. mail.)

APPENDIX TWENTY-FIVE

BONUS PAYOUT FORM

Congratulations. Because of your quality work and the company's financial achievement during this period, you have qualified for a bonus under the company's incentive plan. Please compare your bonus to the kind and amount described on this form. If you have any questions, please ask your supervisor or the appropriate human resources staff member. From all of us, thank you for your work and dedication.

PARTICIPANT: _____

SALARY: _____

BONUS GRADE: _____

BONUS AMOUNT: _____

TOTAL: _____

APPENDIX TWENTY-SIX

UNIVERSAL STUDIOS HOLLYWOOD
COMPENSATION RESEARCH QUESTIONNAIRE

1. Describe how employees earn raises at Universal Studios Hollywood today. Exempt and non-union exempt.

2. Explain how exempt employees are evaluated. What is the process?

3. Explain how non-exempt employees are evaluated. What is the process?

4. Do you personally think the process is fair?

5. Do you think others perceive the pay process as fair?

6. What have the historical raises been?

7. How do you know that you are performing at a satisfactory level? Your subordinates?

8. If you could set up the pay process differently, what would you like to see happen?

9. What is your perception of the market as compared to Universal Studios Hollywood in the following areas:

   Perception of salary?
          benefits?
          incentive?

10. How are employees incentivised? Exempt, non-exempt?

11. What is the evaluation process for bonuses?

12. How would you change the bonus system?

13. Is there a particular form completed that is used in the evaluation process? If yes, what would you like changed?

14. What is the compensation philosophy of Universal Studios Hollywood?

15. What do you think it should be?

APPENDIX TWENTY-SEVEN

NYLON MOLDING CORPORATION
GOALS AND BONUS PROGRAM

<u>Philosophy</u>

Nylon Molding Corporation wants to reward its key managers with a cash bonus incentive based on their individual performance and contribution to company growth.

Beginning in 19____, a Goals and Bonus Program will be used to evaluate performance for a management bonus. The Program will be based on objective criterion that can be measured to evaluate contribution and performance of the managers in the plan. The Program payouts will be based on company performance and completion of preagreed goals set each year by the participants. This program has been developed to attract and retain top managers as well as reward and recognize meaningful contribution to the company.

The Goals and Bonus Program will also aid in developing better understanding and coordination at the management level by encouraging managers to work together for the best interests of the company. By setting specific measurable goals, the participants will target their efforts directly to the company's overall financial goals and growth objectives.

<u>Eligibility</u>

Eligibility is restricted to those key supervisors and managers who, through their position and performance, contribute substantially to the growth and profitability of the company.

The President shall have the sole responsibility of selecting participants for this plan.

How the Plan Works

At the start of the plan year, the selected participants will develop individual business goals that are significant and measurable. These goals must be beyond the daily operating responsibilites of the participants and involve areas of performance for which they are alone responsible.

After reviewing the goals with their superior, the Supervisor and the participant agree on the annual objectives in writing. They must also agree on a specific measurement criterion, i.e., budget, time frame, etc.

Quarterly the participant will report in writing his or her progress on each goal to their immediate supervisor. The supervisor will verbally review the objectives with the participant and evaluate the progress date.

All reports will then be submitted to the President for review.

At the end of the year, the final report on goal completion, costs, timing, and any other measurable criterion will be reported in writing for evaluation by the president.

Based on evaluation of completion and performance of agreed upon goals, the particpant will receive cash bonus. The award level for participants will be as follows:

Level I -   Supervisor Between 0 and 10%

Level II -   Administrative Managers Between 0 and 15%

Level III - Managers Between 0 and 20%

Financial Performance of Company

Payment of the bonus shall be leveraged according to how well the overall sales goals of the company are met. Sales volume based on 19_____ shipped goods. Based on sales volume, participants may earn up to 150% of their maximum level of bonus. The financial performance will influence the bonus levels in the multiples below.

Sales Volume	Leveraged Multiplier
6.25 million	50%
6.50 million	75%
6.75 million	100%
6.85 million	110%
6.95 million	120%
7.05 million	130%
7.15 million	140%
7.25 million	150%

Basis for Determining Rewards

Awards are determined annually after the end of the plan year, based on annual financial and individual goal performance results. Awards are based on a percentage of annual salary.

A minimum financial threshold exists of 6.25 million in sales for 19____ before any payout under this plan is made.

The awards are paid out immediately following the closing and auditing of the company's financial records for the Award Year.

<u>Amount of Award</u>

Assuming that the minimum financial performance standards are met and the threshold achieved, the awards will be determined or calculated, based on:

1. The incumbent must perform his/her current job duties in a satisfactory manner and one of the evaluation goals in order to obtain operating results in day-to-day responsibilties.

2. The participant will set up four goals beyond his/her daily job performance, the extent to which actual individual performance matched goals will be part of the evaluation process.

3. The extent to which actual financial performance matched goals.

4. Partial participation will be pro rated for death, retirement or a new employee entering during an award year.

5. The bonus amount will depend on how the participant completes his or her goals and how he/she has achieved fulfillment of job responsibiliies during an award year.

6. Outstanding Achievement receives maximum for level leveraged by the financial goal percentage.

7. Met all objectives in a competent manner between 80 percent and 100 percent.

8. Met most but not all objectives between 50 percent and 80 percent.

9. Individuals not meeting most of their objectives will earn between 0% and fifty percent of leveraged level.

All bonus awards will be subject to federal, state or local tax law and required amounts will be withheld.

The Company shall not be liable for the debts, contracts, or engagements of any participant or his or her beneficiaries. The rights to cash payments under this plan may not be taken in execution by attachment or garnishment or by any other legal proceedings while in the hands of the company. No participant or beneficiary has the right to assign, pledge or hypothecate any benefits or payments under this plan.

Termination

Managers must be on the payroll December 31 to receive any award. There will be no pro rating of potential awards if termination occurs other than those stated above, and participating in this plan does not in any way mean that bonus will be paid or that employment is assured.

Administration

The President shall administer the plan. The President retains the right to modify the plan.

The President shall approve all qualitative and financial measurements of the participants and approve final awards as recommended by supervisors.

Amedments or Termination of Plan

The plan may be amended or terminated at any time by the President.

Effective Date

The plan becomes effective January 1, 19_____ .

APPENDIX TWENTY-EIGHT

PLAN ANNOUNCEMENT

Memorandum

To: All Sullivan & Curtis Employees

From: Jan Smith

Date: December 11, 1995

Re: 1996 Compensation Program

As many of you heard today in our General Meeting, Sullivan & Curtis has added a new dimension to our 1996 Compensation Program. We will institute a profit sharing program for all employees when the company exceeds 7.5% profitability. Sullivan & Curtis will return 25% of the profits over 7.5% to the employees by mid-December in the form of a check. Anyone employed as of the payout date will be eligible to participate.

In addition to Profit Sharing, if we achieve 7.5% profitability by June 1, 1996, Sullivan & Curtis will award employees by instituting an every other half-day Friday vacation day beginning June 1 to September 1. The half days must be taken on Friday so that we can staff appropriately during this time.

The profitability goal will be posted in the lunch rooms and will be updated monthly showing our year-to-date progress.

We believe this new profit sharing component supports our company goal of building a more unified sales and service team. Through new business sales, client retention, workflow efficiency and expense control we can achieve our 7.5% profitability goal.

In addition to the new profit sharing program, we have lifted the salary freeze as of January 1, 1996. Sullivan & Curtis has researched and participated in a Compensation Benefits Program Survey to determine the competitiveness of our compensation program. We are pleased to report that in most cases employees are earning at market, and in many cases above market, salaries. With this in mind, we confirm that although the salary freeze has been lifted, your individual salary may or may not be increased.

Our bonus program will continue to be based on overall profitability and individual performance.

As a team, we have achieved many of our goals for 1995 and we appreciate the hard work, dedication and support you have shown this year. We look forward to the challenges we face in 1996 and know that through your efforts we can achieve higher results.

JS:jl

```
┌─────────────────────────────────────────────┐
│              PADRE* BONUS                     │
│            RECOMMENDATION                     │
│                                               │
│  Date: _____        CRITERIA       │
│                              Above & Beyond   │
│                                               │
│  From: _____        ____Results    │
│                                               │
│  To:_____        ____ Attitude  │
│     Bonus Recipient's Direct Supervisor       │
│                                               │
│  I recommend _____  │
│                                               │
│  for a cash bonus of $_____ based on:       │
│                                               │
│  _____  │
│                                               │
│  _____  │
│                                               │
│  _____  │
│                                               │
│  _____  │
│                                               │
│  _____  │
│                                               │
│  _____  │
│                                               │
│  _____  │
│                                               │
│  _____  │
│                                               │
│  _____  │
│                                               │
│  APPROVED: _____  APPROVED_____  │
│               Supervisor       Manager of Supervisor │
│                                               │
│  *PADRE = Producing a desired result efficiently. │
└─────────────────────────────────────────────┘
```

COMPENSATION ENHANCEMENTS:
Company Wide Bonus Plan:
It is the intention of this company to maintain an annual bonus plan available for all Associates as company profits permit.

The plan may be changed from year to year and based on current business conditions.

"PADRE" Bonuses:

PADRE stands for "Producing a desired result efficiently." PADRES are a more immediate type of reward available in the following manner:

PADRE Recommendation

Any Associate can write up a PADRE Recommendation for any other Associate based on their perception of "above and beyond results" produced. The Recommendation cannot exceed $100 and must be approved by the two Direct Supervisors of the person recommended.

APPENDIX THIRTY

SAMPLE PERFORMANCE REVIEW

This review is to be used as a dialogue to help you and your manager to better understand the expectations and requirements of the position. It is also for you to have an opportunity to be recognized for your contributions to the company. The review process is and interactive one, and we want you to participate in setting goals and helping us to better understand the work flow from your point of view. The review is designed to help you strengthen your areas that need to improve and to highlight and recognize those areas where you excel.

- RATINGS -

E-   **EXCELLENT:** Your work was outstanding in all areas. You're the kind of person who will keep the organization growing and successful. We recognize and appreciate your exemplary contributions. You are beyond your requirements.

EE-   **EXCEEDS EXPECTATION:** Your work has been consistently above average in many areas. While you have a few areas to work on, we appreciate your commitment and contribution.

ME-   **MEETS EXPECTATION:** Your work met the standards in most areas and you are fulfilling the basic requirements of your posistion. Continue your efforts and we'll work together to help you capture more of your potential.

ID-   **IMPROVEMENT DESIRED:** Your work is not up to the performance standards. While you performed acceptably in some areas, your performance was below standard in too many critical ones. You must raise your evaluation to "Meets Expectation" or above, within 90 days to continue your employment with the organization.

IE-   **IMPROVEMENT ESSENTIAL:** Your work is far below the performance standards in the critical aspects of your job. You will be permitted to stay in your current position for a 60-day probation. If, in this time, you raise your evaluation to a "Meets Expectation" or above, you will be allowed to remain with the organization. If you do not raise your evaluation, your employment will be terminated.

PERFORMANCE REVIEW

Name _____ Position _____ Date _____

QUALITY OF WORK   RATING: _____

Are you meeting the preset, qualitative performance standards of your position? How accurate, thorough and useful is your work? Are your projects completed with no "loose ends"? Are you taking your unit/department to higher quality levels?

_____

_____

_____

QUANTITY OF WORK   RATING: _____

How productive are you? Are you meeting the preset, quantitative performance standards for your position? How do you compare to others who have done or are doing your job? Do you consistenly meet or beat your deadlines?

_____

_____

_____

EFFICIENCY/COST CONTROL   RATING: _____

Do you look for, find and act to reduce inefficiency in the company? How well do you minimize or eliminate unnecessary procedures and time wasters? Are you an effective negotiator?

_____

_____

_____

CRITICAL THINKING/DECISION MAKING   RATING: _____

Do you use a common sense approach to handling situations? Do you think globally instead of falling prey to tunnel vision? Do you make objective, unbiased decisions based on facts? Do you keep an open mind? Are your decisions timely?

_____

_____

_____

PLANNING/ORGANIZATION   RATING: _____

Do you prioritize and plan your work effectively? How organized are you? Are your files, records and key documents in order, and easily accessible to others? Are you surprised by problems, or do you anticipate and solve them in advance? How good is your attention to detail?

_____

_____

_____

RESPONSIVENESS/TIMELINESS   RATING: _____

How quickly do you turn around documents which require a response? Do you respond within two hours to other voice-mail/screen-mail questions? Do you return phone calls promptly?

_____

_____

_____

INITIATIVE   RATING: _____

How often do you experiment to improve current systems? Do you take action without having to be asked? Do you offer solutions/options when you present problems?

_____

_____

_____

ADAPTING TO AND IMPLEMENTING CHANGE   RATING: _____

Are you open to new ideas and ways to do things? Are you able to "thrive on chaos" and, at the same time, minimize it? Do you adapt to change effectively?

_____

_____

_____

EMOTIONAL CONTROL/ENERGY LEVEL   RATING: _____

How well do you handle crises and emotional upset? Are your moods generally stable and upbeat, or are you prone to "flying off the handle"? Can you sustain a high energy level as required by your job?

_____

_____

_____

TRAINING/CONTINUOUS LEARNING   RATING: _____

Do you strive to learn more? Do you make it a point to participate in at least one training event per quater? Are you open to learning different operational areas, even though they may have no immediate relevance to your position?

_____

_____

_____

ATTENDANCE/PROMPTNESS   RATING: _____

What is your attendance record? Do you arrive and start on time? Are you prompt in reporting tardiness or absence? Do you attend meetings and appointments as scheduled?

_____

_____

_____

PERSONAL IMAGE/WORK AREA   RATING: _____

Do you dress and groom appropriately? How neat is your work area?

_____

_____

_____

INTERPERSONAL RELATIONSHIPS   RATING: _____

Do you get along with your fellow employees? How well do you work as a team member? How well do you inform your supervisor of your progress and possible problems? How cooperative and supportive are you?

_____

_____

_____

CONFLICT RESOLUTION   RATING: _____

Do your resolve conflicts directly, quickly and completely? Are you able to discuss unpleasant issues with courtesy and tact? How well do you give and take criticism?

_____

_____

_____

CUSTOMER SERVICE   RATING: _____

Are you known as a service giver to both internal customers (other departments and your colleagues), and external customers (those who buy our services and products)? How about carriers and the community at large?

_____
_____
_____

PROJECT WOLD IDENTITY   RATING: _____

Do you take charge and initiate actions towards accomplishing the organization's goals? To what degree do you "buy into" — and support — the organization's values? How well do you coach and develop others?

_____
_____
_____

COMMUNICATION   RATING: _____

Is your writing clear, concise and well organized? Do you communicate accurately, verbally and on paper? Is your grammar and usage correct? Are your documents proofread carefully? How well do you come across one-to-one or in a meeting?

_____
_____
_____

LISTENING   RATING: _____

Are you interested in what other people have to say? Do you show it? How well do people open up to you? When appropriate, do you check to make sure you understand properly?

_____
_____
_____

INFORMING   RATING: _____

How well do you let people in on decisions or changes? Do you inform people on a timely basis? Are you an accurate judge of who needs to know what?

_____
_____
_____

OVERALL RATING

After careful review of the performance factors above, you have earned the following overall rating for this appraisal period: _____. Below is the explanation and meaning of your rating:

Comments: _____

_____

_____

_____

_____

_____

Reviewer's Signature: _____ Date: _____

Your Comments: _____

_____

_____

_____

_____

_____

Your Signature*: _____ Date: _____

*NOTE: Your signature does not necessarily indicate agreement with the appraisal, only that it has been discussed with you. You are obligated to acknowledge the appraisal if your supervisor has discussed it with you.

PERFORMANCE IMPROVEMENT PLAN

I. To support the organization's objectives my individual goals are:

    1. _____

    2. _____

    3. _____

II. To improve my effectiveness I will:

    1. _____

    2. _____

    3. _____

III. To increase my responsibility, become more valuable to the company and increase job satisfaction, I will:

    1. _____

    2. _____

    3. _____

THE ABOVE ACTIONS/OBJECTIVES HAVE BEEN DISCUSSED AND AGREED TO:

Your Signature: _____ *Date:* _____

Reviewer's Signature: _____ *Date:* _____

APPENDIX THIRTY-ONE

SAMPLE EMPLOYEE SUGGESTION POLICY

Human Resources Policies and Procedures Manual

710

EXEC MGMT GP   **IDEAS/SUGGESTIONS**   1 of 1

Policy:

The Hospital encourages ideas that improve services or programs, reduce expenses, or increase revenues, as follows.

Procedure:

1. The Idea Forum

    Ideas intended to improve services or programs may be submitted to the Human Resources Department on forms available in the cafeteria. Ideas are reviewed by Administration and by the department director who would be responsible for implementation. If implemented, the employee submitting the idea will be eligible for a $25 cash award. For additional requirements see Form 710.1

2. Cost Containment Proposal

    Proposals intended to reduce Hospital expense or increase revenue may be submitted on forms available in the Human Resources Department. Proposals are reviewed by administration and by the department director who would be responsible for implementation. If implemented, the employee submitting the proposal will be eligible for an award of 10% of any measurable expense reduction or revenue increase resulting during the first year of implementation up to a maximum of $10,000. For additional requirements see Form 710.2

PAY FOR RESULTS

RECOMMENDED READING LIST

ACA News. American Compensation Association, July/August 1995

Blasi, J.R., Employee Ownership. Ballinger, 1988

Blinder, A. S., Paying for Productivity. Brookings, 1990

Colletti, Fiss, Designing Incentive Plans for Customer Teams. American Compensation Association, 1995

Collins, Lazier, Beyond Entrepreneurship. Prentice Hall, 1992

Jorgensen, Zimmerman, Personnel Issues & Answers. Parker & Son Publications, Inc. Carlsbad, CA

The Impact Of Incentives And Bonuses On The Bottom Line: A CEO Perspective. Meek & Associates

HRMagazine, Society For Human Resource Management, April 1996

Lawler, E. E., Pay and Organizational Effectiveness: A Psychological View. McGraw-Hill, 1971

Lawler, E. E., Motivation in Work Organizations. Brooks/Cole, 1973

Lawler, E. E., High-Involvement Management: Participative Strategies for Improving Organizational Performance. Jossey-Bass, 1986b

Lincoln, J. F., Incentive Management. Lincoln Electric Co., 1951

Mackay, Harvey, Swim With The Sharks Without Being Eaten Alive. William Morrow & Co., Inc., 1988

Nalbantian, H., Incentives. Cooperation. and Risk Sharing. Rowman and Littlefield, 1987

Nelson, Bob, 1001 Ways to Reward Employees. Workman Publishing, New York 1994

Overton, Steele, Designing Management Incentive Plans. American Compensation Association, 1992

Peters, T., Thriving on Chaos. Knopf, 1987

Peters, T. J., and Waterman, R. M., In Search of Excellence. Harper & Row, 1982

Sales Compensation: A Changing Environment (Survey Findings). Hewitt Associates, 1993

Schuster, Zingheim, The New Pay. Lexington Books, 1992

Stack, Jack, The Great Game of Business. Currency Doubleday, 1992

Wallace, Marc, Rewards and Renewal. The American Compensation Association, 1986

Whyte, W. F. (ed.), Money and Motivation An Analysis of Incentives in Industry. Harper & Row, 1955

Wilson, Thomas, Innovative Reward Systems for the Changing Workplace. McGraw Hill, 1994

SOURCE LIST

American Compensation Association
   Salary Budget Survey
   (602) 951-9191

U.S. Department of Labor, Bureau of Labor Statistices
   Occupational Compensation Survey
   (415) 975-4350

Society for Human Resource Management (SHRM)
   (800) 283-SHRM

Professionals in Human Resources Association (PIHRA)
   (213) 622-7472

Business and Legal Reports
   Survey of Exempt Compensation
   Survey of Non-exempt Compensation
   (203) 245-7448

William M. Mercer
   California Benchmark Compensation and Benefit Trends Survey
   (415) 393-5659

Wyatt Data Services
   Various ECS Salary Surveys
   (201) 843-1177

Ernst & Young, LLP
   Executive Compensation: The Middle Market Survey
   (216) 737-1880

INDEX